Army, Navy and Census of the U. S. of America

STATISTICAL POCKET MANUAL

Army, Navy and Census of the U. S. of America

STATISTICAL POCKET MANUAL

ISBN/EAN: 9783741124983

Manufactured in Europe, USA, Canada, Australia, Japa

Cover: Foto ©ninafisch / pixelio.de

Manufactured and distributed by brebook publishing software (www.brebook.com)

Army, Navy and Census of the U. S. of America

STATISTICAL POCKET MANUAL

STATISTICAL POCKET MANUAL,

OF THE

ARMY, NAVY, AND CENSUS

OF

The United States of America.

TOGETHER WITH

STATISTICS OF ALL FOREIGN NATIONS.

The people need FACTS and FIGURES, instead of theories and opinions. *Multum in parvo.*

COMPLETE IN ONE VOLUME.

14th Edition, Revised and Enlarged.

BOSTON:
D. P. BUTLER, PUBLISHER,
142 Washington Street.

FLAGS OF ALL COMMERCIAL NATIONS

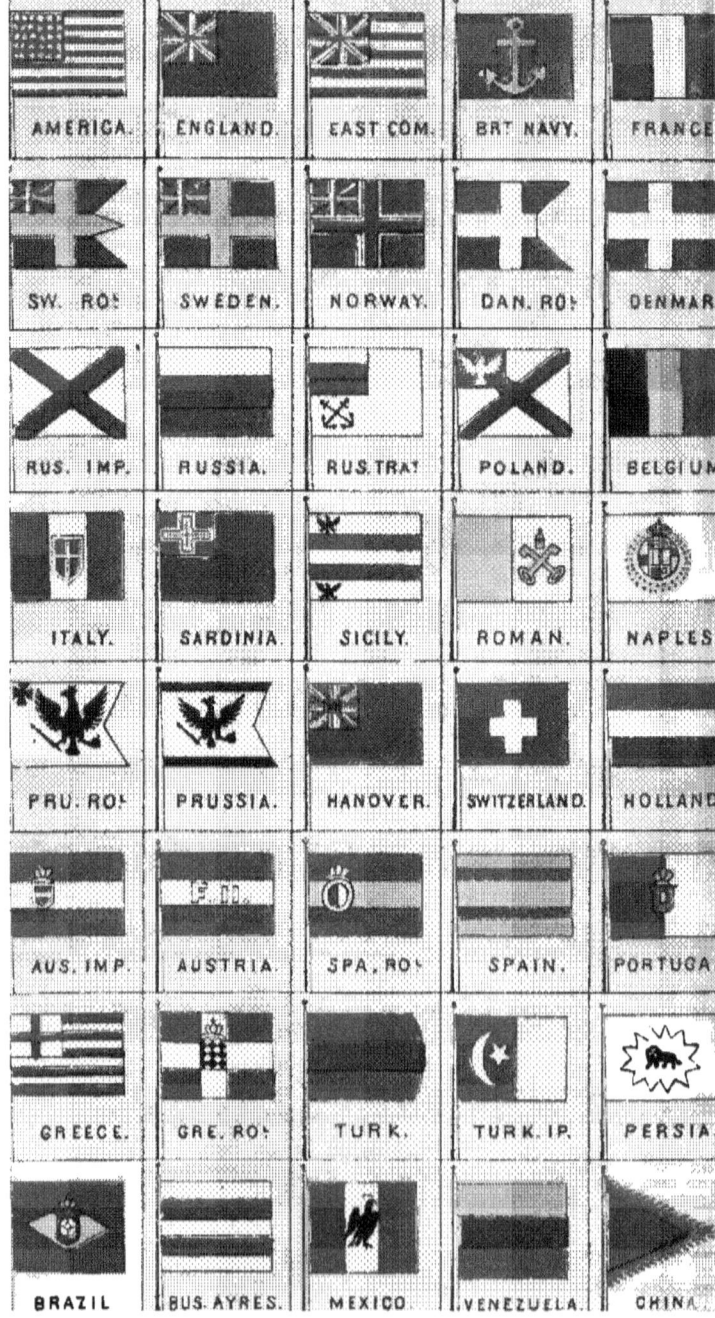

STATISTICAL

POCKET MANUAL.

PART I.

Pay of Army Officers, per month.

RANK AND CLASSIFICATION OF OFFICERS

LIEUTENANT GENERAL.

Monthly pay	$270	00
40 Rations	360	00
6 Horses	50	00
4 Servants	98	00
Total monthly pay	$778	00

AIDE-DE-CAMP, AND MILITARY SECRETARY TO LIEUTENANT GENERAL, EACH.

Monthly pay	$80	00
5 Rations	45	00
3 Horses	24	00
2 Servants	49	00
Total monthly pay	$198	00

MAJOR GENERAL.

Monthly pay	$220	00
15 Rations	135	00
3 Horses	24	00
4 Servants	98	00
Total monthly pay	$477	00

SENIOR AIDE-DE-CAMP TO GENERAL-IN-CHIEF.

Monthly pay	$80 00
4 Rations	36 00
3 Horses	24 00
2 Servants	49 00
Total monthly pay	$189 00

AIDE-DE-CAMP.
(In addition to pay, &c., of Lieutenant.)

Monthly pay	$24 00
1 Horse	8 00
Total monthly pay	$32 00

BRIGADIER GENERAL.

Monthly pay	$124 00
12 Rations	108 00
3 Horses	24 00
3 Servants	73 50
Total monthly pay	$329 50

AIDE-DE-CAMP.
(In addition to pay, &c., of Lieutenant.*)

Monthly pay	$20 00
3 Rations	
1 Horse	8 00
Total monthly pay	$19 00

ADJUTANT GENERAL'S DEPARTMENT.

ADJUTANT GENERAL—COLONEL.

Monthly pay	$110 00
6 Rations	54 00
3 Horses	24 00
2 Servants	49 00
Total monthly pay	$237 00

*Entitled to only three rations per day as Lieutenants.

ASSISTANT ADJUTANT-GENERAL—LIEUT.-COLONEL.

Monthly pay	$95 00
6 Rations	45 00
3 Horses	24 00
2 Servants	49 00
Total monthly pay	$213 00

ASSISTANT ADJUTANT-GENERAL—MAJOR.

Monthly pay	$80 00
4 Rations	36 00
3 Horses	24 00
2 Servants	49 00
Total monthly pay	$189 00

ASSISTANT ADJUTANT-GENERAL—CAPTAIN.

Monthly pay	$70 00
4 Rations	36 00
1 Horse	8 00
1 Servant	24 50
Total monthly pay	$138 50

JUDGE-ADVOCATE—MAJOR.

Monthly pay	$80 00
4 Rations	36 00
3 Horses	24 00
2 Servants	49 00
Total monthly pay	$189 00

INSPECTOR GENERAL'S DEPARTMENT.

INSPECTOR GENERAL—COLONEL.

Monthly pay	$110 00
6 Rations	54 00
3 Horses	24 00
2 Servants	49 00
Total monthly pay	$237 00

SIGNAL DEPARTMENT.

SIGNAL OFFICER—MAJOR.

Monthly pay...	$80 00
4 Rations	36 00
3 Horses	24 00
2 Servants	49 00
Total monthly pay	**$189 00**

QUARTERMASTER'S DEPARTMENT.

QUARTERMASTER-GENERAL—BRIGADIER-GENERAL.

Monthly pay	$124 00
12 Rations	108 00
3 Horses	24 00
3 Servants	73 50
Total monthly pay	**$329 50**

ASSISTANT QUARTERMASTER-GENERAL—COLONEL.

Monthly pay	$110 00
6 Rations	54 00
3 Horses	24 00
2 Servants	49 00
Total monthly pay	**$237 00**

DEPUTY QUARTERMASTER-GENERAL—LIEUT.-COLONEL.

Monthly pay	$95 00
5 Rations	45 00
3 Horses	24 00
2 Servants	49 00
Total monthly pay	**$213 00**

QUARTERMASTER—MAJOR.

Monthly pay	$80 00
4 Rations	36 00
3 Horses	24 00
2 Servants	49 00
Total monthly pay	**$189 00**

ASSISTANT QUARTERMASTER—CAPTAIN.

Monthly pay	$70 00
4 Rations	36 00
1 Horse	8 00
1 Servant	24 50
Total monthly pay	$138 50

SUBSISTENCE DEPARTMENT.

COMMISSARY-GENERAL OF SUBSISTENCE—COLONEL.

Monthly pay	$110 00
6 Rations	54 00
3 Horses	24 00
2 Servants	49 00
Total monthly pay	$237 00

ASSISTANT COM.-GEN. OF SUBSISTENCE—LIEUT.-COL.

Monthly pay	$95 00
5 Rations	45 00
3 Horses	24 00
2 Servants	49 00
Total monthly pay	$213 00

COMMISSARY OF SUBSISTENCE—MAJOR.

Monthly pay	$80 00
4 Rations	36 00
3 Horses	24 00
2 Servants	49 00
Total monthly pay	$189 00

COMMISSARY OF SUBSISTENCE—CAPTAIN.

Monthly pay	$70 00
4 Rations	36 00
1 Horse	8 00
1 Servant	24 50
Total monthly pay	$138 50

ASSISTANT COMMISSARY OF SUBSISTENCE.
(In addition to pay, &c., of Lieutenant.*)

Monthly pay.... .... $20 00
3 Rations..... ....

      Total monthly pay............ $11 00

MEDICAL DEPARTMENT.

SURGEON GENERAL.
Total monthly pay........................ $228 33

SURGEONS OF TEN YEARS' SERVICE.
Monthly pay................................ $80 00
8 Rations................................... 72 00
3 Horses.................................... 24 00
2 Servants.................................. 49 00

      Total monthly pay............ $225 00

SURGEONS OF LESS THAN TEN YEARS' SERVICE.
Monthly pay................................ $80 00
4 Rations................................... 36 00
3 Horses.................................... 24 00
2 Servants.................................. 49 00

      Total monthly pay............ $189 00

ASSISTANT SURGEONS OF TEN YEARS' SERVICE.
Monthly pay................................ $70 00
8 Rations................................... 72 00
1 Horse..................................... 8 00
1 Servant................................... 24 50

      Total monthly pay............ $174 50

†Entitled to only three rations per day as Lieutenant.

ASSISTANT SURGEONS OF FIVE YEARS' SERVICE.

Monthly pay	$70 00
4 Rations	36 00
1 Horse	8 00
1 Servant	24 50
Total monthly pay	$138 50

ASSISTANT SURGEONS OF LESS THAN FIVE YEARS' SERVICE.

Monthly pay	$53 33
4 Rations	36 00
1 Horse	8 00
1 Servant	24 50
Total monthly pay	$121 83

PAY DEPARTMENT.

PAYMASTER-GENERAL.

Total monthly pay	$228 83

DEPUTY PAYMASTER-GENERAL.

Monthly pay	$95 00
5 Rations	45 00
3 Horses	24 00
2 Servants	49 00
Total monthly pay	$213 00

PAYMASTER.

Monthly pay	$80 00
4 Rations	36 00
3 Horses	24 00
2 Servants	49 00
Total monthly pay	$189 00

OFFICERS OF THE CORPS OF ENGINEERS, CORPS OF TOPOGRAPHICAL ENGINEERS, AND ORDNANCE DEPARTMENT.

COLONEL.
Monthly pay	$110 00
6 Rations	54 00
3 Horses	24 00
2 Servants	49 00
Total monthly pay	$237 00

LIEUTENANT-COLONEL.
Monthly pay	$95 00
5 Rations	45 00
3 Horses	24 00
2 Servants	49 00
Total monthly pay	$213 00

MAJOR.
Monthly pay	$80 00
4 Rations	36 00
3 Horses	24 00
2 Servants	49 00
Total monthly pay	$189 00

CAPTAIN.
Monthly pay	$70 00
4 Rations	36 00
1 Horse	8 00
1 Servant	24 50
Total monthly pay	$138 50

FIRST LIEUTENANT.
Monthly pay	$53 33
4 Rations	36 00
1 Horse	8 00
1 Servant	24 50
Total monthly pay	$121 83

SECOND LIEUTENANT.

Monthly pay	$53 33
4 Rations	36 00
1 Horse	8 00
1 Servant	24 50
Total monthly pay	**$121 83**

BREVET SECOND LIEUTENANT.

Monthly pay	$53 33
4 Rations	36 00
1 Horse	8 00
1 Servant	24 50
Total monthly pay	**$121 83**

OFFICERS MOUNTED DRAGOONS, CAVALRY, RIFLEMEN, AND LIGHT ARTILLERY.

COLONEL.

Monthly pay	$110 00
6 Rations	54 00
3 Horses	24 00
2 Servants	49 00
Total monthly pay	**$237 00**

LIEUTENANT-COLONEL.

Monthly pay	$95 00
5 Rations	45 00
3 Horses	24 00
2 Servants	49 00
Total monthly pay	**$213 00**

MAJOR.

Monthly pay	$80 00
4 Rations	36 00
3 Horses	24 00
2 Servants	49 00
Total monthly pay	**$189 00**

CAPTAIN.

Monthly pay	$ 70 00
4 Rations	36 00
2 Horses	16 00
1 Servant	24 50
Total monthly pay	$146 50

FIRST LIEUTENANT.

Monthly pay	$ 53 33
4 Rations	36 00
2 Horses	16 00
1 Servant	24 50
Total monthly pay	$129 83

SECOND LIEUTENANT.

Monthly pay	$ 53 33
4 Rations	36 00
2 Horses	16 00
1 Servant	24 50
Total monthly pay	$129 83

BREVET SECOND LIEUTENANT.

Monthly pay	$ 53 33
4 Rations	36 00
2 Horses	16 00
1 Servant	24 50
Total monthly pay	$129 83

ADJUTANT REG'L QUARTERMASTER.

Monthly pay, in addition to pay of Lieutenant..$ 10 00

OFFICERS OF ARTILLERY AND INFANTRY.
COLONEL.

Monthly pay	$ 95 00
6 Rations	54 00
3 Horses	24 00
2 Servants	49 00
Total monthly pay	$222 00

LIEUTENANT-COLONEL.

Monthly pay	$ 80 00
5 Rations	45 00
3 Horses	24 00
2 Servants	49 00
Total monthly pay	**$198 00**

MAJOR.

Monthly pay	$ 70 00
4 Rations	36 00
3 Horses	24 00
2 Servants	49 00
Total monthly pay	**$179 00**

CAPTAIN.

Monthly pay	$ 60 00
4 Rations	36 00
1 Servant	24 50
Total monthly pay	**$120 50**

FIRST LIEUTENANT.

Monthly pay	$ 50 00
4 Rations	36 00
1 Servant	24 50
Total monthly pay	**$110 50**

SECOND LIEUTENANT.

Monthly pay	$ 45 00
4 Rations	36 00
1 Servant	24 50
Total monthly pay	**$105 50**

BREVET SECOND LIEUTENANT.

Monthly pay	$ 45 00
4 Rations	36 00
1 Servant	24 50
Total monthly pay	**$105 50**

ADJUTANT.

Monthly pay, in addition to pay, &c., of Lieut.. $ 10 00
1 Horse... 8 00

Total monthly pay...........$ 18 00

REG'L QUARTERMASTER.

Monthly pay, in addition to pay, &c., of Lieut.. $ 10 00
2 horses... 16 00

Total monthly pay...........$ 26 00

The officer in command of a company is allowed $10 per month for the responsibility of clothing, arms, and accoutrements.

Every commissioned officer below the rank of a Brigadier-General is entitled to one additional ration a day for every five years' service.

Paymaster's clerks, $700 per annum, and 75 cents per day when actually on duty.

Chaplains in army, $40 to $60 per month and four rations a day.

Chaplains in Volunteers, same as Captain of Cavalry.

MONTHLY PAY OF NON-COMMISSIONED OFFICERS, PRIVATES, &c.

CAVALRY.

Sergeant-Major................................	$21 00
Quartermaster-Sergeant......................	21 00
Chief Bugler...................................	21 00
First Sergeant.................................	20 00
Sergeant.......................................	17 00
Corporal.......................................	14 00
Bugler..	13 00
Farrier and Blacksmith.......................	15 00
Private...	13 00

STATISTICAL POCKET MANUAL. 15

ORDNANCE.

Master-Armorer, Master Carriage-Maker, or Master Blacksmith.	$34 00
Armorer, Carriage-Maker, or Blacksmith	20 00
Artificer	17 00
Laborer	13 00

ARTILLERY AND INFANTRY.

Sergeant-Major	$21 00
Quartermaster Sergeant	17 00
First Sergeant	20 00
Sergeant	17 00
Corporal	13 00
Artificer, artillery	15 00
Private	13 00
Principal Musician	21 00
Musician	12 00

SAPPERS, MINERS, AND PONTONIERS.

Sergeant	$34 00
Corporal	20 00
Private, first class	17 00
Private, second class	13 00
Musician	12 00

Medical Cadets	30 00
Hospital Steward, first class	22 00
" " second class	20 00
Matron	6 00

Female Nurses, 40 cents per day and 1 ration.

"Two dollars per month is to be retained from the pay of each private soldier until the expiration of his term of enlistment, and 12½ cents per month from all enlisted men, for the support of the "Soldier's Home." All enlisted men are entitled to $2 per month additional for re-enlisting, and $1 per month for each subsequent period of five year's service, provided they re-enlist within one month after the expiration of their term.

Volunteers and militia, when called into service of the United States, are entitled to the same pay, allowances, &c., as regulars."

RANK OF ARMY OFFICERS.

1. —Lieutenant-General.
2. —Major-General.
3. —Brigadier-General.
4. —Colonel.
5. —Lieutenant-Colonel.
6. —Major.
7. —Captain.
8. —First Lieutenant.
9. —Second Lieutenant.
10. —Cadet.
11. —Sergeant-Major.
12. —Quartermaster-Sergeant of a Regiment.
13. —Ordnance Sergeant and Hospital Steward.
14. —First Sergeant.
15. —Sergeant.
16. —Corporal.

"Officers serving *by commission* from any state of the Union take rank next after officers of like grade *by commission* from the United States."

"Brevet rank takes effect only in the following cases: 1st, by special assignment of the President in command composed of *different corps;* 2d, on courts-martial or *detachments* composed of different corps. Troops are on *detachment*, only when sent out *temporarily* to perform a *special* service."

COMMAND OF ARMY OFFICERS ACCORDING TO RANK.

1. —For a Captain at least a company.
2. — " Major " 2 "
3. — " Lieutenant-Colonel at least 4 companies.
4. — " Colonel at least 1 regiment or 10 "
5. — " Brigadier-General 2 " " 20 "
6. — " Major-General 4 " " 40 "
7. — " Lieutenant-General 8 " " 80 "

SALUTES.

President of the United States,............21 guns.
Vice-President   "   " 17   "
Heads of the great Executive Departments of
   the National Government,............ 15   "
General commanding the Army,..............15   "
Governor of a State or Territory,...........15   "
Major-General,........ 13   "
Brigadier-General......................,....11   "
Foreign Ships-of-War, ... gun for gun.
Officers of the Navy, according to relative rank.
Foreign Officers, as guests, "   "   "
Envoys and Ministers—United States and
   foreign powers.. ....13 guns.

FUNERAL ESCORTS.

GENERAL commanding-in-chief,—one regiment of infantry, one squadron of cavalry, and six pieces of artillery.

MAJOR-GENERAL—One regiment of infantry, one squadron of cavalry, and four pieces of artillery.

BRIGADIER-GENERAL—One regiment of infantry, one company of cavalry, and two pieces of artillery.

COLONEL—One regiment.

LIEUTENANT-COLONEL—Six companies.

MAJOR—Four companies.

CAPTAIN—One company

SUBALTERN—Half a company.

NON-COMMISSIONED STAFF OFFICER—Sixteen rank and file.

SERGEANT—Fourteen rank and file.

CORPORAL—Twelve rank and file.

PRIVATE—Eight rank and file, commanded by a CORPORAL.

Funeral escorts are commanded by an officer of the same rank with the deceased; or, if none such be present, by one of the next inferior grade.

BADGES OF RANK.

EPAULETTES.

Major-General Commanding the Army—Gold, with three silver embroidered stars.

Other Major-Generals—Gold, two stars, instead of three.

Brigadier-General—Gold, one star.

Colonel—Gold, silver embroidered eagle instead of a star.

Lieutenant Colonel—Silver embroidered leaf, instead of the eagle.

Major—Same as Colonel, omitting the eagle.

Captain—Two silver embroidered bars instead of the eagle.

First Lieutenant—One silver embroidered bar.

Second Lieutenant—Same as First Lieutenant, omitting the bar.

Brevet Second Lieutenant—Same as Second Lieutenant.

All officers of military rank wear an epaulette on each shoulder. The epaulette may be dispensed with when not on duty and on certain duties of parade.

SHOULDER STRAPS.

Major-General commanding the Army—Dark blue cloth; border, of gold embroidery; three silver embroidered stars of five rays.

Other Major-Generals—Two stars instead of three.

Brigadier-General—One star instead of two.

Colonel—A silver embroidered spread eagle—cloth of the straps as follows: for the *General Staff and Staff Corps*—Dark blue; *Artillery*—Scarlet; *Infantry*—Light or sky blue; *Cavalry*—Yellow.

Lieutenant Colonel—Silver embroidered leaf at each end, instead of the eagle.

Major—Gold embroidered leaf at each end

Captain—Two gold embroidered bars.

First Lieutenant—One gold embroidered bar.

Second Lieutenant—The same as for a Colonel, omitting the eagle.

Brevet Second Lieutenant—The same as for a Second Lieutenant.
Medical Cadet—A strip of gold lace in the middle of a strap of green cloth.
The shoulder straps to be worn whenever the epaulette is not.

CHEVRONS.

The rank of non-commissioned officers is marked by chevrons upon both sleeves of the uniform coat and overcoat, above the elbow, of silk or worsted binding, as follows:

Sergeant-Major—Three bars and one arc, in silk.
Quartermaster Sergeant—Three bars and a tie, in silk.
Ordnance Sergeant—Three bars and a star, in silk.
Hospital Steward—A half chevron, of emerald green cloth embroidered with yellow silk.
First Sergeant—Three bars and a lozenge, in worsted.
Sergeant—Three bars, in worsted.
Corporal—Two bars, in worsted.
Pioneer—Two crossed hatchets of cloth, same color and material as the edging of the collar, in the place indicated for a chevron.

OVERCOAT.

For Commissioned Officers.

A "cloak coat" of dark blue cloth, extending down the leg from six to eight inches below the knee.
To indicate rank, a knot of flat black silk braid, as follows:

General—Of five braids, double knot.
Colonel— " " single "
Lieutenant Colonel—Four braids, single knot.
Major—Three braids, single knot.
Captain—Two braids, single knot.
First Lieutenant—One braid, single knot.
Second Lieutenant—A plain sleeve without knot or ornament.
Brevet Second Lieutenant—Same as Second Lieutenant.

ROOMS AND FUEL FOR OFFICERS AND MEN.

Major-General—Five rooms as quarters, and one as kitchen; and six cords of oak wood per year.

Brigadier-General or Colonel—Four rooms as quarters, one room as kitchen and five cords oak wood.

Lieutenant-Colonel or Major—Three rooms, as quarters, and one as kitchen; and four and one half cords of oak wood.

Captain or Chaplain—Two rooms as quarters; one as kitchen; and three and three quarter cords of oak wood.

Lieutenant—One room as quarters, one as kitchen; and two and one half cords of hard wood.

Military Store-Keeper—One room as quarters and one as kitchen.

The General commanding the army has three rooms as offices and three cords of oak wood.

The commanding officer of a Division or Department, an assistant or Deputy Quartermaster General—two rooms as offices and two cords of oak wood.

Coal, at the rate 1500 lbs. anthracite, or 30 bushels bituminous, to the cord; may be furnished instead of oak wood; or two cords of pine in lieu of one of oak.

ALLOWANCE OF CAMP AND GARRISON EQUIPAGE.

A *General*, three tents, in the field, one axe and one hatchet.

Field or Staff Officers. above the rank of Captain, two tents, one axe, one hatchet.

Other Staff Officers or Captains, one tent, one axe, one hatchet.

Subalterns of a Company, every two, one tent, one axe, one hatchet.

To every 15 foot and 13 mounted men, one tent, two spades, two axes, two pickaxes, two hatchets, two camp-kettles, and five mess-pans.

Bedsacks are provided for troops in garrison, and iron pots may be furnished to them instead of camp-kettles.

In barracks, each man, servant, and company woman, is allowed twelve pounds of straw per month, for bedding. For the sick allowance and change of straw regulated by the Surgeon.

ARMY TRANSPORTATION.

When troops are moved, or officers travel with escorts or stores, the means of transport is provided for the whole command.

The baggage to be transported is limited to camp and garrison equipage, and officers' baggage. Officers baggage shall not exceed as follows:

General Officers, in the field, 125 lbs; changing stations, 1000 lbs.

Field Officers, in the field, 100 lbs.; changing stations, 800 lbs.

Captains, in the field, 80 lbs.; changing stations, 700 lbs.

Subalterns, in the field, 80 lbs.; changing stations, 600 lbs.

These amounts may be reduced *pro rata* by the commanding officer when necessary, or increased by the Quartermaster-General in special cases.

THE RATION.

The quantity of each part of the ration is as follows: 12 ounces of pork or bacon, or 1 pound 4 ounces of fresh or salt beef, 1 pound 2 ounces of bread or flour, or 12 ounces of hard bread, or 1 pound 4 ounces of corn meal; 64-100 of a gill of beans, 1 6-100 of an ounce of rice, or 1 5-100 of an ounce of desicated potatoes, 1 6-100 of an ounce of coffee, or 24-100 of an ounce of tea; 2 4-100 ounces of sugar, 32-100 of a gill of vinegar, 16-100 of an ounce of sperm candles, 64-100 of an ounce of soap, 16-100 of a gill of salt, 1 ounce of mixed vegetables.

"During the rebellion in the Southern States, the ration is to be increased as follows:—Twenty-two ounces of bread or flour, or one pound of hard bread, instead of the present issue; fresh beef shall be issued as often as the commanding officer of any detachment or regiment shall require it, when practicable, in place of salt meat; beans and rice shall be issued in the same ration in the proportion now provided by the regulation, and one pound of potatoes per man shall be issued at least three times a week, if practicable; and when those articles cannot be issued in those proportions, an equivalent in value shall be issued in some other proper food, and a ration of tea may be substituted for a ration of coffee upon the requisition of the proper officer."

When a soldier is detached on duty, and it is impracticable to carry his subsistence with him, or when stationed in a city with no opportunity of messing, the ration is commuted at 75 cents per day.

ALLOWANCE OF CLOTHING.

A soldier is allowed the uniform clothing in the following statement, or articles thereof of equal value. When a balance is due him at the end of the year, it is added to his allowance for the next.

Cap, complete—2 the first year, 1 the second, 2 the third, 1 the fourth, 1 the fifth—total, 7 in five years.
Hat, with trimmings complete—one each year.
Fatigue Forage Cap—one each year
Pompon—1 the first, and 1 the third year.
Eagle and Ring—1 the first, and one the third year.
Cover—one each year.
Coat—2 the first, 1 the second, 2 the third, 1 the fourth, and 2 the fifth—total, 8 for 5 years.
Trowsers—3 the first, 2 the second, 3 the third, 2 the fourth, and 3 the fifth—total, 13 in 5 years.
Flannel Shirt—3 each year—total, 15.
Flannel Drawers—1 the first, and 1 the third year—total, 2 for 5 years.
*Bootees—4 pair each year—total, 20 in 5 years.
Stockings—4 pair each year—total, 20 in 5 years.
Leather Stock—1 the first and 1 the third—total, 2 in 5 years.
Great-coat—1 the first year.

*Mounted men may receive *one* pair of "boots" and *two* pairs of "bootees," instead of *four* pairs of bootees.

Stable-frock, for mounted men—1 the first, 1 the third—total, 2 in 5 years.
Fatigue Overalls, for Engineers and Ordnance—1 each year—total, 5 in 5 years.
Blanket—1 the first and 1 the third year—total, 2 in 5 years.

Forts, Castles, Batteries and Arsenals,

OF THE UNITED STATES.

FORTS.

Adams, Rhode Island—Newport harbor, east side of the entrance, on Brenton's Point.
Calhoun, Virginia—Hampton Roads of the Chesapeake, at the Rip Raps.
Carroll, Maryland—Baltimore harbor, at Soller's Point Flats.
Caswell, North Carolina—On Oak Island, mouth of Cape Fear River.
Clinch, Georgia—On Amelia Island, mouth of St. Mary's River.
Columbus, New York—On Governor's Island, harbor of New York.
Constitution, New Hampshire—Portsmouth Harbor.
Delaware, Delaware—Pea Patch Island, Delaware River.
Gaines, Alabama—Mobile Bay, on Dauphin Island.
George, Upper Canada—British, opposite Fort Niagara.
Gibson, New York—On Ellis Island, New York harbor.
Hamilton, New York—Harbor of New York, left of "The Narrows," near Fort Lafayette.
Independence, Massachusetts—On Castle Island, south side of inner harbor of Boston.
Jackson, Georgia—West bank of Savannah River.
Jackson, Louisiana—Right bank of the Mississippi River, 70 miles below New Orleans.
Jefferson, Florida—At the Garden Key, Tortugas.
Johnson, North Carolina—At Smithville, right bank of Cape Fear River, 28 miles from Wilmington.

LaFayette, New York—Harbor of New York, left of "The Narrows."
Livingston, Louisiana—On Grand-terre Island, in Barataria Bay.
McClary, Maine—Portsmouth harbor.
McHenry, Maryland—Baltimore harbor.
Mackinack, Michigan—On the Island of Michilimackinack.
Macomb, Louisiana—Outlet of Lake Pontchartrain.
Macon, North Carolina—Beaufort Harbor.
Madison, Maryland—At Annapolis.
McRae, Florida—Pensacola harbor.
Mifflin, Pennsylvania—On Mud Island, seven miles below Philadelphia.
Monroe, Virginia—On Old Point Comfort, Hampton Roads.
Montgomery, New York—At Rouse's Point.
Morgan, Alabama—At Mobile Point.
Moultrie, South Carolina—Charleston harbor.
Nelson, Virginia—Norfolk harbor.
Niagara, New York—Right bank of Niagara River.
Ontario, New York—Right bank of the river.
Pickens, Florida—On Santa Rosa Island, Pensacola Harbor.
Pike, Louisiana—At the Rigolets, an outlet of Lake Pontchartrain.
Porter, New York—Redout near Buffalo harbor, at Black Rock.
Phœnix, Massachusetts—Fairhaven, opposite Palmer's Island.
Preble, Maine—On Spring Point, Portland harbor.
Pulaski, Georgia—On Cockspur Island, mouth of Savannah river.
Richmond, New York—On Staten Island, at "The Narrows."
St. Philip, Louisiana—70 miles below New Orleans.
Scammel, Maine—On House Island, Portland harbor.
Schuyler, New York—At Throg's Neck, on Long Island Sound.
Severn, Maryland—At Annapolis.
Sullivan, Maine—At Eastport.
Sumpter, South Carolina—Charleston harbor.

Taber, Massachusetts—Clark's Point, NewBedford harbor.
Taylor, Florida—At Key West.
Tompkins, New York—On Staten Island.
Trumbull, Connecticut—At New London.
Warren, Massachusetts—Boston harbor.
Washington, Maryland—On the Potomac River, 15 miles below Washington city.
Wayne, Michigan—On the Detroit Straits, 3 miles below Detroit.
Winthrop, Massachusetts—Boston harbor, on Governor's Island.
Wolcott, Rhode Island—On Goat Island, Newport harbor.
Wood, New York—On Bedloe's Island, New York harbor.

CASTLES.

Clinton, New York—Off the Battery, New York City.
Pinckney, South Carolina—Charleston harbor.
Williams, New York—Governor's Island.

BATTERIES.

Hudson, New York—On Staten Island.
Morton, New York—On Staten Island.
West Head, Massachusetts—Boston harbor.

ARSENALS.

Arsenal.	State or Territory.
Kennebec	Maine.
Watertown	Massachusetts.
Watervleit	New York.
New York	New York.
Alleghany	Pennsylvania.
Frankfort	Pennsylvania.
Pikesville	Maryland.
Washington	District of Columbia.
Fort Munroe	Virginia.
North Carolina	North Carolina.
Charleston	South Carolina.
Mount Vernon	Alabama.
Baton Rouge	Lousiana.
Texas	Texas.
St. Louis	Missouri.
Benicia	California.

There is a National Armory at Springfield, Mass., Captain Dyer, U. S. Army, Superintendent, and one at Harper's Ferry, Va., Henry W. Clowe, Civil Superintendent. The Detroit Arsenal, at Dearbornville, Mich.; the Champlain Arsenal and Ordnance Depot at Vergennes, Vt.; the Rome, at Rome, N. Y.; the Augusta, at Augusta, Ga.; the Appalachicola, at Chattahooche, Fla.; the Little Rock Arsenal, Ark,, and the Santa Fe, at Santa Fe, New Mexico, are under charge of military storekeepers. The Bellona Arsenal is not used at present. An Ordnance Sergeant is at the post, in charge of the buildings and grounds.

Military Posts of the United States.

DEPARTMENT OF THE EAST.

Augusta Arsenal................... ......Georgia
Fort Mackinac....................... Michigan
Plattsburgh Barracks................. New York
Fort Independence.............. ..Massachusetts
West Point........................ New York
Fort Columbus........... .... "
Fort Hamilton....... .... "
Carlisle Barracks........ ....Pennsylvania
Fort Sumter... ....Charleston, S. C.
Newport Barracks................. ...Kentucky
Fort Monroe..... ....Virginia
Fort Moultrie... .... South Carolina
Barrancas Barracks..................... Florida
Key West Barracks................ .... "

DEPARTMENT OF THE WEST.

Fort Ripley........................ Minnesota
Fort Abercrombie..................... "
Fort Ridgely........ .... "
Fort Randall.................... ... Nebraska
Fort Laramie ....'.... "

Fort Kearney .... Nebraska
Fort Leavenworth ....Kansas
Fort Ripley.... .. .. "
Fort Wise .... "

DEPARTMENT OF TEXAS.

Fort Cobb... ....Wichita City
Fort Arbuckle...... ....Choctaw Nation
Fort Washita............ .... Chickasaw
Camp Cooper............... ....Texas
Fort Chadbourne........... .... "
Camp Colorado........ .... "
Camp Stockton..................... "
Fort Quitman..... .... "
Fort Mason .... "
Fort Lancaster....... .... "
Fort Davis. .... "
Camp Hudson...................... "
Camp Verde .... "
San Antonio Barracks..... .... "
Fort Clark. .... "
Fort Inge .... "
Fort Brown......................... "
Fort Duncan .... "
Fort McIntosh........ .... "
Ringgold Barracks...................... "

DEPARTMENT OF NEW MEXICO.

Fort Garland...... ....New Mexico
Fort Fauntleroy .... "
Fort Breckenridge................... "
Fort Union....................... "
Fort Defiance .... "
Fort Marcy... .... "
Albuquerque.... .... "
Fort Craig..................... ... "

Fort Stabton..........................New Mexico
Fort Filmore....................   "
Fort Bliss...........................Texas
Fort Buchanan..... ....New Mexico.

DEPARTMENT OF CALIFORNIA.

Fort Umpqua..........................Oregon
Fort Ter-waa........................California
Fort Gaston...........................   "
Fort Crook............................   "
Fort Humboldt.........................   "
Fort Bragg............................   "
Benicia Barracks......................   "
Presidia.............................San Francisco
Fort Mojave..........................New Mexico
Fort Tejoo...........................California
New San Diego.........................   "
Fort Yuma.............................   "
Fort Churchill................ Utah Territory

DEPARTMENT OF UTAH.

Fort Bridger...................Utah Territory
Camp Floyd.....................   "

DEPARTMENT OF OREGON.

Harvey Depot...Colville Valley, Washinton Territory
Camp Pickett...................San Juan Island
Fort Townsend. ....   "
Fort Chehalis.................   "
Fort Stellacoom...............   "
Fort Wella-Walla. ....   "
Fort Cascades................   "
 ort Vancouver ....   "
Fort Dalles ....Oregon
Fort Yamhill......... ....   "

Military Terms.

Adjutant communicates orders, forms the Regiments for drill, parade, etc., and acts as an assistant to the Lieut-Colonel. Adjutant-General's Department, Inspector-General's, Quartermaster-General's Commissary, Engineer, Ordnance, Pay, and Medical Department. *Army Corps*—A division of the army organized for a campaign—composed of Infantry, Cavalry and Artillery. The backbone of an army is the Infantry, which is sometimes divided into light and heavy Infantry. Four fifths of an army should be composed of Infantry. *Battalion*—A body of Infantry, or two or more Companies, under one command. A Regiment or a part of it, may be a Battalion. A Colonel may divide his Regiment into several parts, assigning separate commands to subordinate officers, and each part will be a Battalion. *Batteries*—When a number of Field-pieces of Artillery are arranged together they constitute a Battery. A Battery of Field Artillery is usually composed of six pieces. The cannon are six pound brass pieces, or twelve pound howitzers. *Brigade*—Two or more Regiments. *Brigadier-General*—Commander of a Brigade, entitled to one aid. The Columbiad or Paixham (pronounced payzan) is a large gun, designed principally for firing shells—it being far more accurate than the ordinary short mortar. Embrasure is the hole or opening through which guns are fired from fortifications. Loop-holes are openings in walls to fire musketry through.

We have now an army of upwards of 650,000 men. If we add to this the number of the discharged three months' volunteers, the aggregate force furnished to the government since April last, exceeds 750,000.

The Telegraph Lines along the Coast,

Proposed by Cyrus W. Field, and approved by General McClellan.

Assuming that there can be no question as to the great advantages to be derived by the War and Navy Departments, and, in fact, the whole government, from the establishment of direct telegraphic communication between the seat of government and the principal military and naval stations which the government may have on our Southern Atlantic and Gulf coast, I would most respectfully recommend.

Miles.

1. That the land line of telegraph be extended from its present terminus in Delaware, through Accomac and Northampton counties, in Virginia, to a point on the coast near Cape Charles.
2. That a submarine cable be laid from said point to Fortress Monroe 20¼
3. That Newport News and Fortress Monroe be connected by a submarine cable..................... 6¼

    Total to Fortress Monroe and Newport News.... 27

Thus, by the completion of this short land line, and the use of only 27 miles of submarine cable, direct communication would be established between Washington and Fortress Monroe and Newport News. Or, if there be any doubt about the government being able to maintain the land line through Accomac and Northampton counties in Virginia, a cable can be laid from Fortress Monroe and Newport News to Annapolis, or any other point desired, on the west coast of the Chesapeak Bay, near Washington.

4. That a cable be laid from Fortress Monroe to Fort Clark at Hatteras Inlet.......................... 152

    Total to Hatteras Inlet........................... 179
5. That Fort Clark at Hatteras Inlet, be connected with Fort Beauregard at Bay Point, Port Royal entrance 352

    Total to Port Royal............................. 531
6. That Fort Beauregard and Fort Walker at Hilton Head, be connected by a cable..................... 2¼

7. That the southern point of Hilton Head Island be connected with Tybee Island at the entrance to Savannah, Ga. (The opposite ends of Hilton Head Island can be connected by a short land line)....... 6

Total to Tybee Island.......................... 53 9¾
Or, instead of connecting the opposite ends of Hilton Head Island by a land line, a cable can be laid direct from the fort on Hilton Head to Tybee Island.

8. That a cable be laid from Tybee Island to Fernandina, Florida 97

Total to Fernandina........................... 636¾
From Fernandina across Florida to Cedar Keys there is a railroad and a good land line of telegraph in operation.

9. That a cable be laid from Cedar Keys to Fort Pickens 271

Total to Fort Pickens......................... 907¾
10. That a cable be laid from Fort Pickens to Ship Island... 102

Total to Ship Island.........................1,009¾

Should government desire it to be done at any time, branch lines to connect with the main line, can be laid—
From Ship Island to Galveston, Texas............432 miles.
From Cedar Keys to Key West....................329 "
From Key West to Tortugas...................... 72 "
or to any other points on the coast with which it may be desirable to have telegraphic communication.

A careful examination of the charts of the above proposed routes will show that nature has interposed no obstacle to the successful prosecution of this enterprise.

The cable throughout the route may, and should be, laid in deep water, beyond the reach of either accidental or intentional injury.

ROUTE ONE.

Miles.
Cape Charles to Fortress Monroe................... 20¼
Fortress Monroe to Newport News.................. 6¼
Fortress Monroe to Fort Clark, at Hatteras Inlet.... 152
Fort Clark, at Hatteras Inlet, to Fort Beauregard, at Bay Point, Port Royal entrance.................. 352
Fort Beauregard to Fort Walker, at Hilton Head.... 2¾
Southern point of Hilton Head Island to Tybee Island, entrance to Savannah, Ga 6
Tybee Island to Fernandina, Fla................... 97

From Fernandina across Florida to Cedar Keys, there is a railroad and a good land line of telegraph in operation.
From Cedar Keys to Fort Pickens................. 271
From Fort Pickens to Ship Island................. 102

Total 1,009¼
Branches.
Cedar Keys to Key West........................ 329
Key West to Tortugas.......................... 72

Total 401
Ship Island to Galveston...................... 432
           — 833

Total 1,842¼
ROUTE TWO.
Cape Charles to Fortress Monroe................ 20¼
Fortress Monroe to Newport News................ 6¼
Fortress Monroe to Fort Clark, at Hatteras Inlet.... 152
Fort Clark, at Hatteras Inlet, to Fort Beauregard, at Bay Point, Port Royal Entrance................ 352
Fort Beauregard to Fort Walker, at Hilton Head.... 2¾
Southern point of Hilton Head Island, to Tybee Island, entrance to Savannah, Ga....................... 6
Tybee Island to Fernandina, Fla................. 97

Total 636¼
Fernandina to Key West........................ 528
Key West to Tortugas.......................... 72
Tortugas to Fort Pickens....................... 475
Fort Pickens to Ship Island..................... 102

Total 1,813¼
Branches.
Ship Island to Galveston...................... 432

Total 2,245¼
The cable can be landed at any other point on the coast that may be desired.

EXPERIMENTS WITH ARMOR.

An experiment is to be made upon a suit of steel armor, imported as a sample of armor to be worn by officers. It has been subjected to very severe tests, and is capable of resisting even a Minnie ball, at an ordinary distance.

The Army Appropriation Bill.

The bill reported from the Committee of Ways and Means, making appropriations for the support of the army, provides for the support of the army for the year ending the 30th of June, 1863, as follows:—

For expenses of recruiting, transportation of recruits, and compensation to citizen surgeons for medical attendance,	$180,000 00
For purchase of books of tactics and instructions for volunteers,	50,000 00
For pay of the army,	8,905,318 00
For commutation of officers' subsistence,	1,574,186 50
For commutation of forage for officers' horses,	283,414 00
For payments to discharged soldiers for clothing not drawn,	150,000 00
For payments in lieu of clothing for officers' servants,	71,630 00
For pay of volunteers under acts of 22d and 25th of July, 1861,	147,283,282 00
For subsistence in kind for regulars and volunteers,	58,429,170 80
For the regular supplies of the Quartermaster's Department,	30,800,000 00
For the incidental expenses of Quartermaster's Department	16,000,000 00
For the purchase of cavalry and artillery horses,	3,913,680 00
For mileage or the allowance made to officers of the army for the transportation of themselves and their baggage, when travelling on duty, without troops, escorts or supplies,	1,000,000 00
For hire or commutation of quarters for officers on military duty, hire of quarters for troops, of storehouses for the safe keeping of military stores, of grounds for summer cantonments, for the construction of temporary huts, hospitals and stables, and for repairing public buildings at established posts,	3,500,000 00
For heating and cooking stoves,	75,000 00
For gun-boats on the Western rivers,	1,000,000 00
For contingencies of the army,	400,000 00
For clothing for the army, camp and garrison equipage, and for expenses of offices and arsenals,	30,630,717 91
For the Medical and Hospital Department,	3,500,000 00
For contingent expenses of the Adjutant General's Department, at Department Headquarters	200,000 00
For compensation of the Clerk and Messenger in the office of the Commanding General	200,000 00

For contingent expenses of the office of the Commanding General,........................ 300 00
For supplies, transportation and care of prisoners of war,.................................. 1,124,576 00
For amount of fortifications,................ 1,620,500 00
For the current expenses of the ordnance service, 732,600 00
For ordnance, ordnance stores and supplies, including horse equipments for all mounted troops,................................... 7,380,000 00
For the manufacture of arms at the National Armory,.................................. 1,800,000 00
For repairs and improvements and new machinery at the National Armory at Springfield, Mass.,.................................... 150,000 00
For the purchase of gunpowder and lead,...... 1,100,000 00
For additions to and extension of shop-room, machinery, tools and fixtures at arsenals,.... 500,000 00
For survey of military defences,............ 100,000 00
For purchase and repair of instruments,...... 10,000 00
For printing charts of lake surveys,......... 10,000 00
For continuing the survey of the Northern and North-western lakes, including Lake Superior 105,000 00
For pay of two and three years' volunteers,....50,000,000 00
For payments to discharged soldiers for clothing not drawn,........................... 50,000 00
For subsistence in kind for two and three years' volunteers,........................... 26,768,902 00
For transportation of the army and its supplies, 14,000,881 00
For the purchase of dragoon and artillery horses,..................................... 1,661,040 00
For clothing, camp and garrison equipage,....12,173,546 77
For the medical and hospital department,..... 1,000,000 00
For amount required to refund to the States expenses incurred on account of volunteers called into the field,........................15,000,000 00

Total,........................$442,833,744 98

HEAVY ORDNANCE ORDERED.

The Ordnance Department has issued orders to the three largest cannon foundries in the country — the Fort Pitt in Pittsburgh, the West Point, and Alger's in Boston — to manufacture to their utmost capacity, 10-inch columbiads, for the next twelve months. Their present make would, in that time, yield eighteen hundred guns. Contracts for immense quantities of small ordnance, rams, and shot and shell, have been made.

IRON CLAD STEAMERS,

FOR RIVER, HARBOR, AND COAST DEFENSE.

These vessels, with the exception of those for the Mississippi river and its tributaries, will be propelled by screws; those for the Mississippi river and tributaries may be propelled by paddle wheels. The hulls will be either wholly of iron (which would be preferred) or of iron and wood combined, as the projectors may consider most suitable for the object proposed, but their sides and decks must be protected with an iron armature sufficient to resist the heaviest shot and shells.

The vessels for the Mississippi river and its tributaries are not to draw more than six feet water when fully equipped and armed, at which draft they are to be able to maintain a permanent speed of nine knots per hour in still water, and carry sufficient coal in the bunkers for six days steaming at that speed. Their armament will consist of not less than six eleven-inch guns.

The vessels for harbor defense are not to draw more than twelve feet water when fully equipped and armed, at which draft they are to be able to maintain a permanent speed of ten knots per hour in smooth water, and carry sufficient coal in the bunkers for seven days steaming at that speed. Their armament will consist of not less than from two to four eleven-inch guns.

The vessels for coast defense are not to draw more than twenty feet water when fully equipped and armed, at which draft they are to be able to maintain a permanent speed of fifteen knots per hour at sea, and carry sufficient coal in the bunkers for twelve days steaming at that speed. Their armament will consist of one or two fifteen or twenty-inch guns.

The guns of the vessels for harbor and coast defense are to train to all points of the compass without change in the vessels position.

The Fortification Appropriation Bill.

The Fortification Bill which passed the House makes the following appropriations for the year ending June 30, 1862:—

For fortifications on the Northern frontier, including fortifications at Oswego, Niagara, Buffalo, Detroit and Mackinaw,	$750,000
For Fort Montgomery, at the outlet of Lake Champlain, N. Y.	50,000
For Fort Knox, Penobscot River, Me.	50,000
For Fort on Hog Island Ledge, Portland harbor, Me.	50,000
For Fort Winthrop and the exterior batteries at Boston harbor, Mass.	50,000
For Fort at New Bedford harbor, Mass.	50,000
For Fort Adams, Newport, Rhode Island	50,000
For Fort Schuyler, East river, New York,	25,000
For Fort at Willett's Point, opposite Fort Schuyler, N. Y.	50,000

For Fort Richmond, Staten Island, New York...... 25,000
For Fort on the site of Fort Tompkins, Staten Island New York.... 50,000
For the commencement of the casemate at the battery on Staten Island, New York.................. 100,000
For a new battery at Fort Hamilton, at the Narrows, New York 100,000
Fort Mifflin, near Philadelphia, Pennsylvania...... 25,000
For a new fort opposite Fort Delaware, on the Delaware shore,..................................... 200,000
For Fort Monroe, Hampton Roads, Va............. 50,000
For Fort Taylor, Key West, Fla..................... 100,000
For Fort Jefferson, Garden Key, Fla.............. 100,000
For an additional Fort at the Tortugas, Fla........ 200,000
For a Fort at Ship Island, Coast of Mississippi..... 100,000
For contingencies of fortifications,.................. 100,000
For bridges, trains and equipage................... 250,000

The following appropriations are for the year ending June 30, 1863:—

For Fort Montgomery, at the outlet of Lake Champlain, New York 100,000
For Fort Knox, at the narrows of Penobscot river, Maine,... 100,000
For the Fort on Hog Island Ledge, Portland harbor, Maine, ... 100,000
For Fort Warren, Boston harbor,.................... 75,000
For Fort Winthrop Boston harbor,................. 50,000
For Fort at New Bedford harbor,................... 100,000
For Fort at Willet's Point, opposite Fort Schuyler, New York....................................... 200,000
For Fort on the site of Fort Tompkins, Staten Island, New York,....................................... 200,000
For Fort at Sandy Hook, New Jersey............... 300,000
Fort Delaware, on Delaware river................... 60,000
Fort Carroll, Baltimore harbor, ... 200,000
Fort Calhoun, Hampton Roads,..................... 200,000
For Fort Taylor, Key West, Florida................. 200,000
For Fort Jefferson, Garden Key, Fla............... 200,000
Fort at Fort Point, San Francisco Bay, Cal.,....... 200,000
Fort at Alcatraz Island, San Francisco Bay, Cal.... 150,000
For Contingencies of fortifications, including field works... 500,000
For bridge trains and equipage for armies in the field.. 250,000
For tool and seige trains for armies in the field,.... 250,000

Total $5,960,000

DEFENSES OF BOSTON HARBOR.

The plan of defences for Boston harbor, when completed, will make it a perfect Sebastopol. It embraces a fort to be built on Nantasket Head, Fort Warren, a Fort off Long Island, Fort Independence, Fort Winthrop, and a Fort at Jeffries' Point, South Boston.

HEAVY GUNS RECEIVED.

The Navy Department is receiving thirty Dahlgreen guns of the heaviest calibre every week, which are immediately mounted on board the new gun-boats and other war vessels.

The House has passed the following bills:—Providing for the construction of twenty iron-clad steam gun-boats, which are to cost over half a million dollars each; a milion of dollars for gun-boats in the Western waters; one hundred and fifty thousand to complete the defences of Washington.

USES OF THE TELEGRAPH IN WAR.

Gen McClellan sat by the telegraph operator at his head-quarters; Gen Buell did the same at Louisville, and Gen Halleck at St. Louis; and the circuit being made complete between the three, they conversed uninterruptedly for hours on the pending battle at Fort Donelson, and made all the orders and dispositions of forces to perfect the victory and pursue the broken enemy. The battle was ought, we may say, almost under the eye of Gen. McClellan. So remarkable an achievement has seldom adorned science.

PAY OF THE NAVY.

	Per annum
CAPTAINS, the senior flag officer	$4,500
" commanding squadrons	5,000
" all others on duty at sea	4,200
" on other duty	3,600
" on leave or waiting orders	3,000
COMMANDERS on duty at sea	
" 1st 5 yrs. after date of commiss'n	2,825
" 2d " " "	3,150
" on other duty,	
" 1st 5 yrs. after date of commiss'n	2,662
" 2d " " "	2,825
" all others	2,250
LIEUTENANTS, commanding at sea	2,550
" on duty at sea	1,500
" after 7 yrs. sea service in navy	1,700
" " 9 " "	1,900
" " 11 " "	2,100
" " 13 " "	2,250
" On other duty	1,500
" After 7 years' sea-service in the navy	1,600
" After 9 " " "	1,700
" After 11 " " "	1,800
" After 13 " " "	1,875
" on leave on waiting orders	1,200

LIEUTENANTS, after 7 yrs. sea service in navy 1,266
" " 9 " " 1,333
" " 11 " " 1,400
" " 13 " " 1,450
SURGEONS FLEET 3,300
SURGEONS on duty at sea,..............
" 1st 5 yrs. after date of commis'n... 2,200
" 2d " " " 2,400
" 3d " " " 2,600
" 4th " " " 2,800
" 20 years and upwards " 3,000
" on other duty... ....
" 1st 5 yrs. after date of commis'n... 2,000
" 2d " " " 2,200
" 3d " " " 2,400
" 4th " " " 2,600
" 20 years and upwards " 2,800
" on leave or waiting orders.. ......
" 1st 5 yrs. after date of commis'n... 1,600
" 2d " " " 1,800
" 3d " " " 1,900
" 4th " " " 2,100
" 20 years and upwards. 2,300
PASSED ASSISTANT SURGEONS................
" on duty at sea................... 1,500
" on other duty................... 1,400
" on leave or waiting orders......... 1,100
ASSISTANT SURGEONS on duty at sea. 1,250
" on other duty................... 1,050
" on leave or waiting orders.. 800
PAYMASTERS on duty at sea... ....
" 1st 5 yrs. after date of commis'n.... 2,000
" 2d " " " 2,400
" 3d " " " 2,600
" 4th " " " 2,900
" 20 years and upwards " 3,100

PAYMASTERS, on other duty,
" 1st 5 years after date of commis'n .. 1,800
" 2d   "   "   "   2,100
" 3d   "   "   "   2,400
" 4th   "   "   "   2,600
" 20 years and upwards   "   2,800
" on leave or waiting orders.........
" 1st 5 yrs. after date of commis'n. ... 1,400
" 2d   "   "   "   1,600
" 3d   "   "   "   1,800
" 4th   "   "   "   2,000
" 20 yrs. and upwards   "   2,250
CHAPLAINS same pay as Lieutenants..........
PROFESSORS of Mathematics, on duty......... 1,800
" on leave or waiting orders......... 960
MASTERS in the line of promotion......... ....
" on duty as such at sea............ 1,200
" on other duty................... 1,100
" on leave or waiting orders......... 825
PASSED MIDSHIPMEN, on duty as such at sea... 1,000
" on other duty.... 800
" leave or waiting orders........... 650
MIDSHIPMEN, at sea......... 550
" on other duty.. 500
" leave of absence or waiting........ 450
BOATSWAINS, ⎫ on duty at sea.... ....
GUNNERS,   ⎪ 1st three years sea service....
CARPENTERS, ⎬ after date of warrant. 1,000
SAILMAKERS, ⎭ 2d 3 yrs. after date of warrant 1,150
" 3d   "   "   "   1,250
" 4th   "   "   "   1,350
" 12 years and upward.... 1,450
" on other duty... ....
" 1st 3 yrs. sea service after date war. 800
" 2d   "   "   "   900
" 3d   "   "   "   1,000
" 4th   "   "   " 1.100

SAILMAKERS, 12 years and upwards aft. date war, 1,200
" on leave or waiting orders..........
" 1st 3 yrs. sea service, after date war.   600
SAILMAKERS, 2d three yrs. sea service, after date war 700
" 3d " " " .. 800
" 4th " " " .. 900
" 12 years and upwards............ 1,000
CHIEF ENGINEERS, on duty.... ....
" 1st 5 yrs. after date of commis'n.... 1,800
" 2d " " " 2,200
" 3d " " " 2,450
" 15 years " " 2,600
" On leave or waiting orders....... ...
" For 1st 5 yrs. after date of commis'n. 1,200
" For 2d " " " 1,300
" For 3d " " " 1,400
" After 15 years from " " 1,500
1ST ASSISTANT ENGINEERS, on duty... 1,250
" leave or waiting orders........... 900
2D ASSISTANT ENGINEERS, on duty.......... 1,000
" on leave or waiting orders 750
3D ASSISTANT ENGINEERS, on duty.......... 750
" on leave or waiting orders......... 600
NAVY AGENTS, commissions not to exceed... ...3,000
NAVY AGENTS at San Francisco.............4,000
TEMPORARY NAVY AGENTS..................
NAVAL STOREKEEPERS.....................
Officers of the navy on foreign stations......1,500
ENGINEERS IN CHIEF 3,000
NAVAL CONSTRUCTORS......... 2,600
" " when not on duty.... ...1,800
AGENTS for the inspection, &c, of hemp......1,000
" for the preservation of live-oak timber..1,000
SECRETARIES to commanders of squadrons when
commanding-in chief..................1,000
Not commanding-in-chief............ .:.. 900

CLERKS of navy yards—
  At navy yards Boston, New York, Norfolk
    and Pensacola.t.................. 1,200
  At navy yard Washington 1,440
  At navy yard Portsmouth, N. H., and Phila-
    delphia..... 900
FIRST CLERKS to commandants—
  At Boston, New York, Norfolk and Pensacola 1,200
  At Washington....... 1,400
  At navy yards Portsmouth, N. H., Philadel-
    phia and Mare Island 900
SECOND CLERKS to commandants—
  At Boston, New York, Norfolk and Pensacola 960
  At Washington..... 1,152
  At Philadelphia 750
  To commandants of squadrons..... 500
  To capt'ns of fleets and commanders of vessels 500
  To persons in ships-of-the-line............ 700
  To pursers in frigates,................. 500
    " smaller vessels than a frigate.... 400
    " at navy yards............... 500

YEOMAN—   Pay per month.
  In ships-of-the-line....... ....$45
  In frigates.. 40
  In sloops......... 30
  In smaller vessels.... 24
ARMORERS—
  In ships-of-the-line...................... 30
  In frigates........... 25
  In sloops. 20
MATES—Master's, (not warranted)............... 25
  Boatswain's..................... 25
  Gunner's....................,............. 25
  Carpenter's................................ 25
  Sailmaker's......,............. 20
  Armorer's....... 20

	Pay per month.
Master-at-arms	25
Ship's Corporals	20
Coxswains	24
Quartermasters	24
Quarter Gunners	20
Captains—	
Of forecastle	24
Of tops	20
Of afterguard	20
Of hold	20
Coopers	20
Painters	20
Stewards—	
Ship's	30
Officer's	20
Surgeon's	24
Cook's—	
Ship's	24
Officer's	20
Masters of the Band	20
Musicians—	
First class	15
Second class	12
Seamen	18
Ordinary Seamen	14
Landsmen	12
Boys	8, 9 & 10
Firemen—	
First class	30
Second class	25
Coal Heavers	18

Note.—One ration per day only is allowed to each Officer when attached to vessels for sea service, since the passage of the law of the 3d of March, 1835, regulating the pay of the Navy.

Table Showing the Pay and Emolument allowed to

GRADE.	PAY.		SERVANTS.	
	Monthly pay.	Annual pay.	Number of servants.	Annual pay and subsistence for service, at $22 50 per month.
COLONEL COMMANDANT	$95 00	$1,140 00	2	*$540 00
LIEUTENANT COLONEL—				
On leave	80 00	960 00	2	540 00
Commanding	80 00	960 00	2	540 00
MAJORS—				
On leave	70 00	840 00	2	540 00
Commanding	70 00	840 00	2	540 00
STAFF MAJORS—				
Adjutant and Inspector, Pay and Quartermaster	80 00	960 00	2	†564 00
STAFF CAPTAIN—				
Assistant Quartermaster	70 00	840 00	1	†282 00
CAPTAINS—				
At sea or on leave	60 00	720 00	1	270 00
Shore duty	60 00	720 00	1	270 00
FIRST LIEUTENANTS—				
At sea, leave, or shore duty	50 00	600 00	1	270 00
SECOND LIEUTENANTS—				
At sea, leave, or shore duty	45 00	540 00	1	270 00

* All commissioned officers in the Marine Corps are entitled to one additional ration for every five years' service.

† Pay and subsistence allowed for each servant, $23 50.

NOTE No. 1.—DOUBLE RATIONS are allowed to commissioned officers of the Marine Corps as follows: When commanding permanent posts; to officers commanding the guard on board of receiving ships at Boston, New York, and Norfolk; to the commanding officer of the guard of a squadron, when the number of marines in the squadron is not less than the guard of a frigate; and to the commanding officer of the guard of a ship of-the-line or frigate when acting singly on separate service.

the Several Grades of Officers of the Marine Corps.

RATIONS.		FORAGE.		TOTAL.	
Number of daily ration.	Annual amount of rations, at 30 cts. per ration.	Number of horses.	Annual amount, at $8 per month each horse.	Total pay and emolument.	
12	*$1,314 00	3	$288 00	$3,282 00	
5	*547 50	....	....	2,047 50	
10	*1,095 00	3	288 00	2,883 00	
4	*438 00	3	288 00	2,106 00	
8	*876 00	3	288 00	2,544 00	
4	*438 00	3	288 00	2,250 00	
4	*438 00	1	96 00	1,656 00	
4	*438 00	....	....	1,428 00	See notes 1 and 2.
4	*438 00	....	....	1,428 00	See notes 1 and 2.
4	*438 00	....	....	1,308 00	See notes 1 and 2.
4	*438 00	....	....	1,248 00	See notes 1 and 2.

NOTE No. 2.—CLOTHING RESPONSIBILITY. All commissioned officers of the Marine Corps, when not above the rank of captain, or below that of lieutenant, are entitled to an allowance of $10 per month for the care and responsibility of marine clothing, when commanding the marines of the squadron having the number of marines allowed to a frigate, of ships-of-the-line or frigates in commission, and at naval stations.

NOTE No. 3.—Where there are no public quarters furnished a commutation is allowed. Officers on shore duty are allowed a commutation for fuel.

VESSELS OF WAR,

OF

THE UNITED STATES NAVY.

Names.	Guns.	Tons.
Ships of the Line, 10.		
Pennsylvania*	120	3241
Columbus†	80	2480
Ohio	84	2757
N. Carolina	84	2633
Delaware	84	2633
Vermont	84	2633
New Orleans	84	2805
Alabama	84	2633
Virginia	84	2633
New York	84	2632
Frigates, 10.		
Constitution	50	1607
United States	50	1607
Potomac	50	1726
Brandywine	50	1726
Columbia	50	1726
Congress*	50	1867
Raritan	50	1726
St. Lawrence	50	1726
Santee	50	1726
Sabine	50	1726

Names.	Guns.	Tons.
Sloops of War, 21.		
Cumberland†	24	1725
Savannah	24	1726
Constellation	22	1452
Macedonian	22	1341
Portsmouth	22	1022
Plymouth	22	989
St. Mary's	22	958
Jamestown (rebel)	22	985
Germantown	22	939
Saratoga	20	882
John Adams	20	700
Vincennes	20	700
Vandalia	20	783
St. Louis	20	700
Cyane	20	792
Levant (lost)	20	792
Decatur	16	566
Marion	16	566
Dale	16	566
Preble	16	566

*Burnt.   †Sunk.

Guns.	Tons.	Names.	Guns.	Tons.
'gs, 3.		Mohawk	6	464
6	259	Sumpter	5	464
6	280	Wyandott	6	454
4	224	Pocahontas	5	694

Screw Tender, 1

AMERS.

		Anacostia		217
st Class 8.				

Side-Wheel, 1st Class, 3.

12	4580	Mississippi	10	1692
40	3400	Susquehanna	15	2450
40	3400	Powhattan	9	2415
:cbcl) 40	3220			
40	3200	*Side-Wheel, 2d Class 1.*		
40	3200			
50	3680	Saranac	6	1446
· St'r 6	4683	*Side-Wheel, 3d Class 3.*		
l Class. 6.		Fulton	5	698
		Michigan	1	582
13	1446	Saginaw	3	453
18	2360			
16	2158	*Side-Wheel Tenders, 2*		
14	2070	Water-Witch	1	378
14	1990	Pulaski		395
14	1929			

Store Vessels, 3.

l Class, 15.		Relief	2	468
s 9	765	Supply	2	547
k 2	382	Release	1	327
6	984	*Permanent Store and Receiving Ships.*		
3	816			
6	1016			
6	997	Independence		2257
6	1289	Alleghany		989
6	996	Princetown		900
3	801	Warren		691
8	549	Fredonia		800
5	464	Falmouth		730

VESSELS PURCHASED.

Name.	Class.	Tonnage.	paid.
Flag	Propeller	938	$90,000
Massachusetts	Propeller	1155	172,500
South Carolina	Propeller	1165	172,500
Thos. Freeborn	Sidewheel steamer	269	32,500
Resolute	Propeller	90	15,000
Reliance	Propeller	90	15,000
Roman	Ship	350	7,400
Wm. Badger	Ship	334	7,150
Penguin	Propeller	389	75,000
Albatross	Propeller	378	75,000
Yankee	Sidewheel steamer	328	19,000
Keystone State	Sidewheel steamer	1364	125,000
Chas. Phelps	Ship	362	7,000
Connecticut	Sidewheel steamer	2250	200,000
Rhode Island	Sidewheel steamer	1517	185,000
Pampero	Ship	1375	29,000
National Guard	Ship	1046	35,000
Nightingale	Ship	—	23,000
J. C. Kuhn	Ship	888	32,000
Chotank	Schooner	53	1,250
Louisiana	Steamer	235	35,000
Stars and Stripes	Propeller	407	55,000
Brazeliera	Bark	540	22,000
Satellite	Steamtug	150 }	36,000
Gen. W. G. Putnam	Steamtug	123 }	
Jas. Adgar	Sidewheel steamer	1142	85,000
Fear Not	Sailing ship	1012	40,000
Cambridge	Steamer	—	80,000
Valley City	Propeller	190	18,000
Augusta	Sidewheel	1310	96,000
Alabama	Steamer	1261	93,000
Roebuck	Bark	455	20,000
Midnight	Bark	387	19,000
E. B. Hale	Propeller	220	23,000
Florida (1st)	Steamship	1261	87,500
Fernandina	Bark	297	15,000
Lucky Star	Bark	—	—
Flash	Bark	—	—
Amanda	Bark	368	15,000

STATISTICAL POCKET MANUAL. 49

Name.	Class.	Tonnage.	Paid.
Wm. G. Anderson		600	
Zephyr	Bark	—	
Young Rover	Steam bark	—	$27,500
Gem of the Sea	Bark	371	15,000
Mercedita	Steamship	1070	*100,000
Arthur	Bark	554	20,000
Gemsbok	Ship	622	*—
Kingfisher	Clipper whaler	451	17,000
Quaker City	Sidewheel	1428	117,000
Restless	Bark	266	12,000
Mercury	Steamtug	183 }	36,000
O. M. Petit	Steamtug	130 }	
Jacob Bell	Steamtug	229	12,000
Ceres	Steamtug	150	12,100
Varuna	Propeller	1300	135,000
New boat at Norwich	Propeller	400	31,000
Rescue (N. Y.)	Steamtug	—	17,300
R. R. Cuyler	Propeller	2040 }	
Huntsville	Propeller	840 }	305,000
Montgomery	Propeller	840 }	
Underwriter	Sidewheel steamer	—	18,500
R. B. Forbes (burnt)	Tug	—	52,500
Baltimore	Sidewheel steamer	250	35,000
Powhattan (2d)	Sidewheel steamer	—	*—
Philadelphia	Sidewheel steamer	—	*—
Rescue (Phila.)	Steamtug	—	17,500
Ino	—	895	40,000
De Soto	Sidewheel steamer	1675 }	322,000
Bienville	Sidewheel steamer	1600 }	
Florida	Bark	297	14,000
New London	Propeller	240	30,000
Racer	Schooner	200	7,500
Sarah Bruin	Schooner	233	7,000
Shepard Knapp	Ship	838	36,872
C. P. Williams	Schooner	210	6,000
Sophronia	Schooner	217	8,000
O. H. Lee	Schooner	200	7,000
Morning Light	Ship	910	37,500
Pursuit	Bark	600	22,000
Island Belle	Steamtug	150	24,000

*Owners add $15,060 to cost in addition.

Name.	Class.	Tonnage.	Paid.
Courier, (new)	Ship	554	$20,000
Onward	Ship	874	27,000
Bohio	Brig	197	9,000
H. Andrews	Propeller	—	24,000
Isaac Smith (new)	Propeller	—	50,000
J. E. Lockwood	Steamtug	180	16,000
Arletta	Schooner	250	8,500
Dan Smith	Schooner	150	8,000
M. Vassar, Jr.	Schooner	216	7,500
Wm. Bacon	Schooner	183	6,000
John Griffith	Schooner	210	8,000
Para (new)	Schooner	260	10,500
Eastern City	Sidewheel steamer	750	50,000
Emerald	Ship	600	5,500
Gunboat	Iron clad	1000	—
Ethan Allen	Bark	600	—
*Daylight,	Propeller	650	55,000
*Dawn	Propeller	400	35,000
Potomska	Propeller	237	33,000
Wamsutta	Propeller	270	27,000
Monticello,	Propeller	650	†105 000
Mount Vernon,	"	650	
Mississippi,	Steamship,	2,000	200 000
Eagle,	"	1,550	185 000
Dawn,	Bark.	387	19,000
Wyandank,	Ferryboat,	400	19 000
Sea Foam,	Brig	251	10 000
H. Beals	Bark	196	10 000
Young America,	Steamtug	180	20 000
S. Stones	Ferry-boat	—	20 000
West World	Propeller	—	37 000
Uncas	"	190	10 000
Sachem	"	180	10 000
Seneca	"	180	10 000
Henry James	Schooner	260	11 000
A. C. Powell	Steamtug	90	5 000

*The total amount paid previous to their purchase for the charter of the Dawn, was $36,886.66; Daylight, $38,400. †Including charter money due.

Name.	Class.	Tonnage.	Paid.
Narragansett	"	100	$14 500
Orretta	Schooner	171	8 000
S. C. Jones	"	245	10 500
M. J. Carleton	"	178	7 200
Com. Perry	Ferryboat	512	38 000
E. Allen	"	512	38 000
Madgie	Propeller	210	13 000
T A. Ward	Schooner	284	11 500
A. Houghton	Bark	330	11 500
Norwich	Propeller	450	43 000
H. Brincker	"	109	13 000
Patroon	"	186	15 500
I. N. Seymour	Tug	140	18 000
Norfolk Packet	Schooner	349	12 000
P. Jackson	Ferryboat	700	60 000
Morse	"	512	40 000
Victoria	Propeller	260	25 000

In a few instances the price is not given, complete returns not having been made.

Names.	Class.	Guns.	Tons
Maratanzo	Steamer	9	900
Shawsheene	Gunboat	2	—
Georgia	Gunboat	4	—
S. J. Holly	Propeller	4	—
Flambeau	Gunboat	7	950
Active	Steamer	4	480
Wm. L. Marcy	Steamer	6	190
Shubrick	Steamer	3	250
Whitehall	Ferryboat	—	—
Westfield	Ferryboat	—	1000
Clifton	Ferryboat	—	1000
Saxon	Propeller	2	400
Horace Beals	—	4	—

VESSELS BUILT AND BUILDING.

Adirondack, (sloop of war)   On the Stocks.
Lackawana, (Frigate)   On the Stocks.

Steam Sloops.

Name.	Yard where Built.
Juniata	Philadelphia Navy Yard.
Tuscarora	Philadelphia Navy Yard.
Oneida	New York Navy Yard.
Adirondack	New York Navy Yard.
Wachusett	Boston Navy Yard.
Housatonic	Boston Navy Yard.
Kearsage	Portsmouth Navy Yard.
Ossipee	Portsmouth Navy Yard.
Mahaska,	" "
Sebago,	" "
Sonama, (building)	" "
Conemaigh, "	" "
Sacramento, "	" "

Gunboats.

Name.	Where built.	By whom.
Tahoma	Wilmington, Del.	W. & A. Thatcher.
Wissahickon	Philadelphia	John Lynn.
Scioto	Philadelphia	John Birely.
Itasca	Philadelphia	Hillman & Streaker.
Unadilla	New York	John Englis.
Ottawa	New York	J. A. Westervelt.
Pembina	New York	Thos. Stack.
Port Royal	New York	Thos. Stack.
Seneca	New York	Jeremiah Simonson.
Chippewa	New York	Webb & Bells.
Winona	New York	C. & R. Poillon.
Owasco	Mystic River, Ct.	Maxson, Fish & Co.
Kanawha	E. Haddam	E. G. & W. H. Goodspeed
Cayuga	Portland	Gildersleeve & Son.
Huron	Boston	Paul Curtis.
Chocura	Boston	Curtis & Tilden.
Sagamore	Boston	Messrs. Sampson.
Marblehead	Newburyport	G. W. Jackman, Jr.

Name.	Where built.	By whom.
Kennebec	Thomaston, Me.	G. W. Lawrence.
Aroostook	Kennebunk, Me.	A. W. Thompson.
Kineo	Portland, Me.	J. W. Dyer.
Katahdin	Bath, Me.	Larrabee & Allen.
Penobscot	Belfast, Me.	C. P. Carter & Co.
Pinola	Baltimore	J. J. Abrahams.

The steam sloops are of about 1,200 and 1,400 tons burthen.

The gunboats are of about 500 tons burthen, are of light draught, strongly built, and are calculated to carry one 150-pound rifled gun and four 32-pounders.

THE STONE FLEET.

We give below a full official list of the old vessels purchased by the Navy Department, and loaded with stone, for the purpose of blocking up the Southern ports:

Name.	Class.	Where purchased.	Cost.
Corea	Ship	New London	$2300
Tenedos	Bark	New London	1650
Lewis	Ship	New London	3250
Fortune	Bark	New London	3250
Robin Hood	Ship	Mystic	4000
Archer	Ship	New Bedford	6300
Cossack	Bark	New Bedford	2200
Amazon	Bark	Fairhaven	3675
T. Henrietta	Bark	New Bedford	4000
Garland	Bark	New Bedford	3150
Harvest	Bark	Fairhaven	4000
American	Bark	Edgartown	3370
Timor	Ship	Sag Harbor	2290
Meteor	Ship	Mystic	4000
Rebecca Sims	Ship	Fairhaven	4000
L. C. Richmond	Ship	New Bedford	4000
Courier	Ship	New Bedford	5000
M. Theresa	Ship	New Bedford	4000
Kensington	Ship	New Bedford	4000
Herald	Ship	New Bedford	4000
Potomac	Ship	Nantucket	3500
Peter Demil	Ship	New York	2600

Phœnix	Ship	New London	2600
Leonidas	Bark	New Bedford	3050
S. America	Bark	New Bedford	3600
Edward	Bark	New York	4000
Mechanic	Ship	Newport	4300
Messenger	Bark	Salem	2250
India	Ship	New Bedford	5500
Noble	Bark	Sag Harbor	4300
Valparaiso	Ship	New Bedford	5000
N. England	Ship	New London	5000
Dove	Bark	New London	2500
Newburyport	Ship	Boston	4500
William Lee	Ship	Newport	4200
Emerald	Ship	Sag Harbor	5500
Majestic	Bark	New Bedford	3150
Stephen Young	Brig	New Bedford	1600

The total amount paid for old ships for blockading purposes is $160,205, including 21 schooners bought in Baltimore and sunk in the North Carolina Inlets.

IRON-PLATED VESSELS OF WAR.

Five iron-plated ships or batteries are now in process of construction—one in New York by J. Ericsson, another at Philadelphia by Merrick & Son, and a third at New Haven by Bushnell & Co. The cost of these vessels will be $1,290,750.

It is interesting to observe that while we now have five iron-clad vessels in progress, the Secretary of the Navy includes in his estimate the cost of building a fleet of *twenty* of these invincible monsters. The specifications are ready, and the contracts will soon be given out.

On the 4th of March last, all the Government vessels available for service against the rebels were only four in number, carrying twenty-five guns. Our navy now consists of 264 vessels of all sizes, carrying 2557 guns, and having an aggregate tonnage of 218,016 tons. The number of seamen now employed is 22,000. Of 136 vessels purchased, 79 are propelled by steam; all the 52 constructed or nearly finished are steam vessels.

STATISTICAL POCKET MANUAL. 55

BRIEF SUMMARY
OF THE NAVAL FORCE OF THE UNITED STATES.

Number of vessels, total,.............................264
" of guns, " 2,557
" of seamen, " 22,000
Number effective steam vessels,.......................164
" guns,...1,055
" effective sailing vessels,.........................82
" guns,...837
" effective vessels of war, total,................246
" guns,...1,892

The above statement of *effective* naval force does not include the store-ships and transports of the regular navy, or those chartered by government, for the emergencies of war.

POPULATION
OF THE PRINCIPAL
Cities, Towns, and Villages,
IN THE UNITED STATES IN 1860.

MAINE.		VERMONT.	
Portland,	26,342	Burlington,	7,713
Bangor,	16,407	Rutland,	7,577
Biddeford,	9,349		
Bath,	8,076	**MASSACHUSETTS.**	
Augusta,	7,609	Boston,	177,481
Rockland,	7,816	Lowell,	36,827
Saco,	6,223	Cambridge,	26,060
Calais,	5,621	Roxbury,	25,137
Belfast,	5,520	Charlestown,	25,063
Westbrook,	5,113	Worcester,	24,960
		New Bedford,	22,300
NEW HAMPSHIRE.		Salem,	22,252
Manchester,	20,107	Lynn,	19,083
Concord,	10,896	Lawrence,	17,639
Nashua,	10,065	Taunton,	15,376
Portsmouth,	9,335	Springfield,	15,199
Dover,	8,502	Fall River,	14,027

MASSACHUSETTS.

Newburyport,	13,401
Chelsea,	13,395
Gloucester,	10,903
Haverhill,	9,995
Dorchester,	9,769
Milford,	9,132
Abington,	8,527
Newton,	8,382
Pittsfield,	8,045
Somerville,	8,025
Fitchburg,	7,805
Weymouth,	7,742
Marblehead,	7,646
Chicopee,	7,261
Adams,	6,924
Northampton,	6,788
Quincy,	6,778
Woburn,	6,778
N. Bridgewater,	6,584
So. Danvers,	6,549
Waltham,	6,397
Dedham,	6,330
West Roxbury,	6,310
Plymouth,	6,272
Beverly,	6,154
Attleboro',	6,066
Marlboro',	5,911
Malden,	5,865
Randolph,	5,760
Natick,	5,515
Blackstone,	5,453
Brookline,	5,164
Barnstable,	5,129
Danvers,	5,110
Westfield,	5,054
Holyoke,	4,996

RHODE ISLAND.

Providence,	50,665
Smithfield,	13,283
N. Providence,	11,818
Newport,	10,508
Warwick,	8,916
Cumberland,	8,339
Cranston,	7,500
Bristol,	5,271

CONNECTICUT.

New Haven,	39,269
Hartford,	29,152
Norwich,	14,047
Bridgeport,	13,299
New London,	10,115
Waterbury,	10,004
Stonington,	7,740
Norwalk,	7,582
Meriden,	7,426
Danbury,	7,234
Stamford,	7,185
Greenwich,	6,522
Derby,	5,444
New Britain,	5,212
Enfield,	4,937

NEW YORK.

New York,	813,668
Brooklyn,	266,664
Buffalo,	81,131
Albany,	62,368
Rochester,	48,243
Troy,	39,235
Syracuse,	28,199
Utica,	22,528
Oswego,	16,817
Kingston,	16,640
Newburg,	15,198
Poughkeepsie,	14,726
Newtown,	13,725
Hempstead,	12,375
Yonkers,	11,848

STATISTICAL POCKET MANUAL. 57

NEW YORK.		NEW YORK.	
Auburn,	10,986	Middletown,	6,243
Flushing,	10,139	Manlius,	6,028
Cortland,	10,075	Cerning,	6,003
Brookhaven,	9,923	Little Falls,	5,989
Schenectady,	9,579	Verona,	5,966
Fishkill,	9,546	Champlain,	5,857
Saugerties,	9,556	Southold,	5,833
Morrisania,	9,245	Lisbon,	5,640
Oyster Bay,	9,168	Hector,	5,623
Parishville,	9,033	Ellisburgh,	5,614
Greenbush,	8,929	Phelps,	5,586
Huntington,	8,925	East Chester,	5,582
West Troy,	8,820	Lansingburg,	5,577
Johnstown,	8,811	N. Hempsted,	5,419
Cohoes,	8,800	Haverstraw,	5,401
Elmira,	8,682	Galen,	5,340
Seneca,	8,448	Arcadia,	5,318
Binghampton,	8,326	Milton,	5,255
Volney,	8,045	Sullivan,	5,233
Lenox,	8,024	Deer Park,	5.186
Watertown,	7,572	Bath,	5,187
Ogdensburgh,	7,410	Onondaga,	5,123
Hudson,	7,252	Amherst,	5,098
Barre,	7,227	Lyons,	5,077
Queensburg,	7,146		
Canandagua,	7,075	**NEW JERSEY.**	
Orangetown,	7,060	Newark,	71,941
Ithaca,	6,843	Jersey City,	29,226
Castleton,	6,778	Patterson,	19,588
Potsdam,	6,737	Trenton,	17,221
Plattsburg,	6,680	Camden,	14,358
Niagara,	6,603	Elizabeth,	11,567
Walkill,	6,603	N. Brunswick,	11,255
Malone,	6,565	Hoboken,	9,652
Saratoga,	6,521	Orange,	8,877
Lockport,	13,523	Bergen,	7,429
Jamaica,	6,515	Hudson,	7,229
Canton,	6,379	Rahway,	7,180
Catskill,	6,275	Hackensack,	5,483
Rome,	6,246	Burlington,	5,174

PENNSYLVANIA.

Philadelphia,	565,531
Pittsburg,	49,220
Alleghany,	28,703
Reading,	23,162
Lancaster,	17,603
Harrisburg,	13,406
Pottsville,	9,444
Erie,	9,419
Scranton,	9,223
Easton,	8,944
York,	8,605
Allentown,	8,026
Danville,	6,385
Birmingham,	6,046
Carlisle,	5,664
Carbondale,	5,573
Hempfield,	5,450
Chambersburg,	5,257
Columbia,	5,007

DELAWARE.

Wilmington,	21,258

MARYLAND.

Baltimore,	212,419
Cumberland,	8,478
Frederick,	8,143
Frostburg,	6,286

DIST'CT OF COLUMBIA

Washington,	61,118
Georgetown,	8,733

NORTH CAROLINA.

Wilmington,	9,553
Newbern,	5,434

SOUTH CAROLINA.

Charleston,	51,210
Columbia,	8,083

VIRGINIA.

Richmond,	37,910
Petersburgh,	18,266
Norfolk,	14,609
Wheeling,	14,184
Staunton,	14,124
Waynesboro',	13,626
Alexandria,	11,226
Portsmouth,	9,487
Lynchburg,	6,853
Fredericksburg,	5,022

GEORGIA.

Savannah,	22,292
Augusta,	12,493
Columbus,	9,621
Atlanta,	9,554
Macon,	8,247

FLORIDA.

Pensacola,	3,680
Key West,	2,832
Jacksonville,	2,128

ALABAMA.

Mobile,	29,258
Montgomery,	9,889
Tuscaloosa,	3,989
Prattville,	3,200

MISSISSIPPI.

Natchez,	13,553
Vicksburg,	4,591
Columbus,	3,308

LOUISIANA.

New Orleans,	168,472
Algiers,	5,816
Baton Rouge,	5,428
Jefferson,	5,107

TEXAS.

San Antonio,	8,274
Galveston,	8,177
Houston,	5,000

ARKANSAS.

Little Rock,	3,827
Fort Smith,	1,529
Camden,	1,348

TENNESSEE.

Memphis,	22,625
Nashville,	16,987

KENTUCKY.

Louisville,	69,740
Covington,	16,471
Newport,	10,046
Lexington,	9,321

OHIO.

Cincinnati,	161,044
Cleaveland,	36,054
Dayton,	20,482
Columbus,	18,555
Toledo,	13,768
Zanesville,	9,229
Sandusky,	8,408
Chilicothe,	7,657
Hamilton,	7,223
Springfield,	7,202
Portsmouth,	6,268
Steubenville,	6,154

MICHIGAN.

Detroit,	45,619
Grand Rapids,	8,058
Adrian,	6,213
Kalamazoo,	6,070

MINNESOTA.

St. Paul,	10,401
St. Anthony,	3,258
Minneapolis,	2,564

INDIANA.

Indianapolis,	18,612
New Albany,	12,647
Evansville,	11,486
Fort Wayne,	10,388
Lafayette,	9,426
Terra Haute,	8,594
Madison,	8,133
Richmond,	6,603
La Porte,	5,128

ILLINOIS.

Chicago,	109,263
Peoria,	14,425
Quincy,	13,718
Galena,	8,196
Bloomington,	7,076
Springfield,	6,499
Alton,	6,333
Aurora,	6,011
Galesburg,	5,626
Rockford,	5,281
Rock Island,	5,136

OREGON.

Portland,	1,371

WISCONSIN.

Milwaukee,	45,254
Racine,	7,822
Janesville,	7,703
Madison,	6,611
Oshkosh,	6,086
Fond du Lac,	5,450
Watertown,	5,302

IOWA.

Dubuque,	13,012
Davenport,	11,266
Keokuk,	8,137
Burlington,	6,706
Muscatine,	5,324
Iowa City,	5,214

MISSOURI.		WASHINGTON TERR'Y	
St. Louis,	151,780	Pt. Townsend,	264
St. Joseph,	8,932	**UTAH TERRITORY.**	
Hannibal,	6,505	Great Salt Lake City,	8,218
Lexington,	4,115	Ogden,	1,464
Jefferson City,	2,500	**NEVADA TERRITORY.**	
KANSAS.		Virginia City,	2,345
Leavenworth,	7,429	Carson City,	708
Atchison,	2,616	**NEBRASKA TERR'Y.**	
Lawrence,	1,645	Nebraska City,	1,912
CALIFORNIA.		Omaha,	1,888
San Francisco,	56,805	**NEW MEXICO.**	
Sacramento,	13,788	Santa Fe,	4,635
COLORADO TERR'Y.		Messiila,	2,406
Denver,	4,749	**DACOTAH TERR'Y.**	
Golden City,	1,014	Pembina,	3,556

Population of the United States.

From the Census of 1860.

States.	Population.	States.	Population.
Alabama	964,296	Maine	628,276
Arkansas	435,427	Maryland	687,034
California	380,015	Massachusetts	1,231,065
Connecticut	460,151	Michigan	749,112
Delaware	112,218	Minnesota	162,022
Florida	140,439	Mississippi	791,395
Georgia	1,057,327	Missouri	1,173,317
Illinois	1,711,753	New Hampshire	326,072
Indiana	1,350,479	New Jersey	672,031
Iowa	674,948	New York	3,887,542
Kansas	107,110	North Carolina	992,667
Kentucky	1,155,713	Ohio	2,339,599
Louisiana	709,433	Oregon	52,464

State.	Population.	TERRITORIES, ETC.	
Pennsylvania	2,906,370	Colorado	34,197
Rhode Island	174,621	Dakotah	4,839
South Carolina	703,312	Nebraska	28,842
Tennessee	1,109,847	Nevada	6,857
Texas	601,039	New Mexico	93,541
Vermont	315,116	Utah	40,295
Virginia	1,596,083	Washington	11,578
Wisconsin	775,873	Dist. of Columbia	75,076
		Total,	31,429,891

SLAVE POPULATION
OF THE UNITED STATES,
From the Census of 1860.

STATES

Alabama	435,132	S Carolina	402,541
Arkansas	111,104	Tennessee	275,784
Delaware	1,798	Texas	180,388
Florida	61,753	Virginia	490,887
Georgia	462,230	TERRITORIES, ETC.	
Kentucky	225,490	Nebraska	10
Louisiana	332,520	New Mexico	24
Maryland	87,188	Utah	29
Mississippi	436,096	Dist. Columbia	3,181
Missouri	114,965		
N. Carolina	331,081	Total,	3,952,801

Population of African Descent

ON THIS CONTINENT.

United States	4,500,000
Brazil	4,150,000
Cuba	1,500,000
South and Central America	1,200,000
Hayti	2,000,000
British Possessions	800,000
French	250,000
Dutch, Danish and Mexican	200,000
Total	14,600,000

ROUTES AND DISTANCES,

BY RAILROAD AND WATER.

DISTANCES FROM BOSTON.

To	Miles		Miles
Halifax, N. S.,	387	Savannah, Ga.	900
Liverpool, Eng.,	2,884	Fort Pickens, Fla.	1,850
Southampton "	2,886	Mobile, Ala.,	1,925
Fortress Monroe, Va.,	575	New Orleans, La.,	2,000
Charleston, S. C.,	800		

DISTANCES FROM BOSTON, (by Railroad.)

To	Miles		Miles
Albany, N. Y.,	200	New York City	236
Augusta, Me.,	166	Philadelphia, Pa.,	324
Baltimore, Md.,	422	Portland, Me.,	104
Buffalo, N. Y.,	500	Quebec, C. E.,	423
Charleston, S. C.,	1,020	Richmond, Va.,	590
Chicago, Ill.,	1,014	Savannah, Ga.,	1,142
Cincinnati, Ohio,	934	St. Louis, Mo.,	1,204
Montreal, Ca.,	320	Washington, D. C.,	485

DISTANCES FROM ST. ANTHONY (Via Mississippi River.)

To	Miles.		Miles
St. Paul, Min.,	12	Cairo, Ill.,	910
Dubuque, Iowa,	312	Memphis, Tenn.,	1.152
Galena, Ill.,	333	Vicksburg, Miss.,	1,535
Rock Island, Ill.,	420	Natchez, Miss.,	1.550
Burlington, Ill.,	509	Baton Rogue, La.,	1.810
Hannibal, Ill.,	618	New Orleans, La.,	1.950
St. Louis, Mo.,	742		

DISTANCES FROM PITTSBURG. (Via Ohio River.)

To	Miles.		Miles
Wheeling, Va.,	100	Louisville, Ky.,	635
Portsmouth, Va.,	382	Cairo, Ill.,	1.012
Cincinnati, Ohio,	495		

DISTANCES FROM WASHINGTON, by Railroad.

To	Miles.		Miles
Aquia Creek, by Water,	55	Norfolk, Va. 230, by	
Thence by Railroad to		Water,	155
Richmond, Va.,	130	Wilmington, N C.,	430
Petersburg, Va.,	152	Augusta, Ga.,	550
Weldon, N. C.,	216	Charleston, S. C.,	600
Lynchburg, Va.,	118	Savannah, Ga.,	710
Montgomery, Ala.,	1.018	Chicago, Ill.,	862
New Orleans, La.,	1.200	Cincinnati, Ohio,	667
Baltimore, Md.,	38	Cleveland, Ohio,	508
Boston, Mass.,	458	St. Louis, Mo.,	938
Buffalo, N. Y.,	440	Toronto, C. E.,	620

DISTANCES FROM WASHINGTON, By Railroad.

To	Miles.		Miles
Alexandria (by water)	7	Beltsville,	11
Annapolis Junction,	20	Cumberland, Md.,	140
Annapolis,	30	Charlottesville, Va.,	118
Baltimore,	38	Ft'rss Monroe (via C. Bay,)	
Bladensburgh,	5		225

STATISTICAL POCKET MANUAL.

	Miles.		Miles.
Fredericksburgh, Va.,	70	New York,	226
Havre de Grace, (via C. Bay		" via Sea, C. Bay, and	
and An. R. R.)	85	Potomac River,	530
Harrisburgh, Pa.,	123	Philadelphia,	136
Harper's Ferry, (by Potomac R., 53,)	84	Petersburgh,	152
		Richmond,	130
Jessup's Cut,	23	Washington Junction,	29
Laurel,	16	Weldon, N. C.,	216
Lynchburgh,	177	Wilmington, N. C.,	378
Manassas Gap Junction	35	White Oak Bottom,	14
Mt. Clare Junction,	36	Winchester,	81
Mt. Vernon (by water or road,)	14		

DISTANCES FROM RICHMOND, VA.

To	Miles.		Miles
Baltimore,	168	Staunton, Va.,	116
Charlottesville, Va.,	79	Weldon, N C.,	82
Lynchburgh, Va.,	132	Washington City	130
Norfolk, Va.,	116	Yorktown,	91

DISTANCES FROM NEW YORK, (By Water.)

To	Miles.		Miles
Aspinwall, via Havana,	2.340	London, Eng.,	3.200
		Melbourne, Aus.,	12.900
San Francisco, Cal.,	5.249	Nangasaki, Japan,	9.750
Calcutta, via Cape Good Hope	17.478	St. Petersburg, Rus.,	4.400
		Vera Cruz, Mexico,	2.190
Via Panama,	13.350	San Francisco, by the overland Mail,	3.000
Havana, Cuba,	1.275		

DISTANCES FROM WASHINGTON, (By Railroad.)

To	Miles		Miles
Bladensburgh,	5	Annapolis Junction,	20
Point Branch,	8	Jessup's Cut,	23
Beltsville,	11	Washington Junction,	29
White Oak Bottom,	14	Mt. Clare Junction,	36
Laurel,	16	Baltimore,	38
Watson's Cut,	18	Havre de Grace,	74

STATISTICAL POCKET MANUAL. 65

DISTANCES FROM BALTIMORE (By Railroad.)

To	Miles.		Miles
Annapolis Junction,	17	Norfolk (via water)	175
Cockeysville,	15	New York,	188
Cumberland,	178	Philadelphia,	98
Ellicott's Mills,	15	Parkersburgh, Va., on	
Frederic, at Monocacy River,	58	Ohio R.,	383
		Richmond,	188
Havre de Grace, Md.,	36	Washington,	38
Hanover Junction,	43	Wheeling, Va., on Ohio	
Harper's Ferry, Va.,	81	R.,	379
Harrisburgh, Pa.,	85	Williamsport, Pa., on	
Monocacy, Md.,	85	Susq. R.,	178

DISTANCES FROM CAIRO, ILL., Mouth of the Ohio River, by Steamboat.

To	Miles.		Miles
St. Louis, Mo.,	172	Pittsburgh,	1013
Columbus, Ky.,	18	To the Mounds, by the	
Memphis,	242	Chicago Railroad,	8
New Orleans,	1.040	Villa Ridge,	10
Paducha, or Tenn. River	47	Pulaski,	16
Louisville,	376	Wetang,	24
Cincinnati,	516	Jonesboro',	32
Wheeling,	913	Chicago,	365

GOVERNORS OF STATES AND TERRITORIES,
FOR 1862.

Alabama.........	—— Shorter..................	Rebel
Arkansas.........	Henry M. Rector............	Rebel
California........	Leland Stanford............	Union
Connecticut......	Wm. A. Buckingham........	Union
Delaware.........	William Burton.............	Union
Florida...........	John Milton.................	Rebel
Georgia..........	Joseph E. Brown...........	Rebel
Illinois..........	Richard Yates..............	Union
Indiana..........	Oliver P. Morton*..........	Union
Iowa.............	Samuel J. Kirkwood........	Union
Kentucky........	Beriah Magoffin............	Union
	George W Johnson.........	Rebel

3

Kansas	Charles Robinson	Union
Louisiana	Thomas O. Moore	Rebel
Maine	Israel Washburne, Jr	Union
Maryland	Augustus W. Bradford	Union
Massachusetts	John A. Andrew	Union
Michigan	Austin Blair	Union
Mississippi	Jacob Thompson	Rebel
Missouri	Hamilton R. Gamble	Union
	Claiborne F. Jackson	Rebel
Minnesota	Alexander Ramsey	Union
New Hampshire	N. S. Berry	Union
New Jersey	Charles C. Olden	Union
New York	Edwin D. Morgan	Union
North Carolina	—— Clark†	Rebel
	Marble Nash Taylor	Union
Ohio	David Tod	Union
Oregon	John Whiteaker	Union
Pennsylvania	Andrew G. Curtin	Union
Rhode Island	William Sprague	Union
South Carolina	Francis W. Pickens	Rebel
Tennessee	Isham G. Harris	Rebel
Texas	Frank R. Lubbock	Rebel
Vermont	Frederick Holbrook	Union
Virginia	Francis H. Pierrepont	Union
	John Letcher	Rebel
Wisconsin	Louis P. Harvey	Union
Territories.		
Nebraska	Alvin Sanders	Union
Nevada	James W. Nye	Union
Washington	Wm. H. Wallace	Union
Colorado	Wm. Gilpin	Union
Utah	John W Dawson	Union
New Mexico	—— Connelly	Union
Dacotah	——	
Arizona	——	In rebellion

* Mr. Morton was elected Lieutenant Governor, but became acting Governor on the election of Hon. Henry L. Lane to the Senate of the United States.

† Mr. Clark was elected Lieutenant Governor, but succeeded to the Executive chair after the death of John W. Ellis.

THE ENGLISH NAVY.

STEAM VESSELS.

Screw Ships of the Line.

Three deckers,........ 6 | Horse-power,* total,..18,780
Two Deckers,..........30 | Tonnage,   " ..107,847
Number vessels, total,...36 | Guns,   " 3,374
* Horse-power of one three-decker not given.

Screw Coast Guard and Block Ships.

Number vessels, total,......9 | Tonnage, total,.... ..76,046
Horse-power,   " ...2,800 | Guns,   " 540

Screw Frigates.

Number vessels, total,.....19 | Tonnage, total,.......45,158
Horse-power,   " ..10,300 | Guns,   " 813

Screw Corvettes.

Number vessels, total,.....14 | Tonnage, total,.......19,453
Horse-power,   " ..4,950 | Guns,   " 293

Screw Sloops.

Number vessels, total,.....33 | Tonnage, total,.......23,136
Horse-power,   " ..5,774 | Guns,   " 349

Paddle-Wheel Frigates.

Number vessels, total,......9 | Tonnage, total........ 984
Horse-power,   " ..4,730 | Guns,   " 169

Paddle-Wheel Corvettes.

Number vessels, total,......7 | Tonnage, total,........8,656
Horse-power,   " ..3,197 | Guns,   " 42

Paddle-Wheel Sloops.

Number vessels, total,...61 | Tonnage,* total,......42,323
Horse-power,* " ..14,517 | Guns,   " 129
*Tonnage and Horse-power of one sloop not given.

Paddle-Wheel Tugs.

Number vessels, total,.....18 | Tonnage.* total,......3,226
Horse-power, " ..1,990 | Guns,* " 15
* Tonnage of five, and guns of twelve Tugs not given.

Screw Gun Vessels.

Number vessels, total,....21 | Tonnage, total,......14,491
Horse-power, " ..4,580 | Guns, " 93

Screw Mortar Ships.

Number vessels, total,......4 | Tonnage, total,........4,698
Horse-power, " 850 | Guns, " 48

Screw Floating Batteries.

Number vessels, total,...... 8 | Tonnage, total,........13,498
Horse-power, " 1,400 | Guns, " 120

Screw Transports.

Number vessels, total,......6 | Tonnage,* total,........3,744
Horse-power, " ..1,810 | Guns, " 68
*Of four vessels. tonnage not given.

Screw Store-ships.

Number vessels, total,......9 | Tonnage,* total,........7,150
Horse-power,* " ..2,240 | Guns,* " 4
* Not given, Horse-power, 1; Tonnage, 4; Guns, 7

Paddle-Wheel and Sailing Tenders.

Number vessels, total,......30 | Tonnage,* total,........2,228
Horse-power,* " 12,000 | Guns,* " 31
*Not given, Horse-power, 19; Guns, 20; Tonnage, 22.

Yachts.

Number vessels, total,......8 | Tonnage,* total,........4,327
Horse-power,* " ..1,458 | Guns,* " 5
* Not given, Horse-power, 3; Guns, 4; Tonnage, 3.

SAILING VESSELS.

Ships of the Line.*

Number vessels, total,....43 | Guns, total,..............3,763
* 4 ordered to be fitted with screws. Only 13 or 15 really effective.

Frigates.*

Number vessels, total,....57 | Guns, total,............2,618
*4 being fitted with screws. Only 14 or 16 effective

Corvettes and Sloops.*

Number vessels, total .....71 | Guns, total, ...1,168
*Only 30 effective.

Brigs.*

Number vessels, total,....7 | Guns, total,..............58
*Only one effective.

Brigantines and Schooners.

Number vessels, total,......5 | Guns, total,..............13

Cutters.

Number vessels, total,....3 | Guns,* total,..............6
* One, guns not given.

Surveying Vessels.

Number vessels, total,....8 | Guns, total,..............28
* Four, guns not given.

DEPOTS, STORE-SHIPS, &C.

Number vessels, total, ...23 | Guns, total,.............350
*Eleven, guns not given.

TRAINING AND GUNNERY SHIPS.

Number vessels, total,....3 | Guns, total,..............205

In addition to the above, there are 46 mortar vessels, (from 20 to 170 tons), and 150 mortar "floats." In many instances, the number of guns given, indicates the *capacity*, instead of the *actual armament*.

Gun-Boats.

Number vessels, total,....161 | Guns, from 2 to 4 each.
Most of the gun-boats are under 240 tons each.

VESSELS ON THE STOCKS,
(Building or converting.)

Ships of the Line, (Screw.)†

Number vessels, total,....12 | Guns, total,............1,225
Horse-power,*   "   ..7,800 |
* Of two ships not given.
Of the above, six ships of the line, and five frigates were to be launched in 1859.

Frigates, (Screw.)*

Number vessels, total,....7 | Guns, total,.............303
Horse-power,* " 3,800
* Of one frigate, not given.

Corvettes, &c., (Screw.)

Number vessels, total,....12 | Guns, total,.............206
Horse-power,* " ... 860
* Of seven of the above not given.

VESSELS ORDERED.

Number vessels, total,....4 | Guns, total,.............254
Horse-power,* " 1,600
*Of two not given.

These statistics are compiled from the official documents of 1859. Several Iron Clad Ships have been built or converted since that date, also a large number of Gun-Boats.

BRIEF SUMMARY OF THE PRESENT NAVAL FORCE OF ENGLAND.

Steam vessels of war, total,.............................432
" ships of the line,...............................53
" Frigates,..40
" sloops,..98
" gun-boats,......................................189
Sailing vessels of war, total,...........................128
" ships of the line,..............................10
" frigates,.......................................17
" vessels now building,..........................54
Other vessels available at short notice,................100
Grand total of effective Steam and Sailing Vessels,.....614
Number of guns, not far from.........................12,000
Sailors,..84,000
Captains,..326
Lieutenants,...1,700

England's Iron-clad Ships.

To furnish some idea of what the English are doing in the construction of iron batteries, we may add the following notice of her plated ships. The Warrior and Black Prince, iron screw propellors, both of the same size and capacity, are three hundred and eighty feet long, between perpendiculars, (four hundred and twenty feet over all), of fifty-eight feet beam, forty-one and a half feet depth from spar deck to keel, twenty-six feet draught of water, and six thousand one hundred and seventy-seven tuns burden, (builders' measurement;) with engines of one thousand two hundred and fifty horse-power. The plating extends two hundred and five feet of the length, and consists of four and one-half inch plates of solid iron, backed with two layers of teak timber, altogether eighteen inches thick. This extends nine feet below load water-line. Iron bulk-heads of the same strength as the sides, extend across the ship fore and aft of the protected portion, and within this space are six water-tight compartments. Inner bulk-heads also extend all around the protected portion of the hull, leaving passages three and a half feet wide, between them and the sides. The main-deck ports, fifteen and a half feet apart, are about eight and a half feet above water. Though nominally thirty-six gun ships, the armament consists of forty-eight guns, which, however, can be increased, and consist of sixty-eight pounders for the main deck, ten Armstrong seventy-pounders on the spar-deck, and two pivot one hundred pounders, one at each end. The speed of the Warrior has proved to exceed fourteen knots; and at sea she is reported to have behaved admirably in stormy weather. The Black Prince has obtained a higher speed than the Warrior.

The Achilles, now building, is of about the same dimensions, and is to be completely incased with armor. The Valiant, of the same character, is to be a thirty-two gun ship, of eight hundred horse power engines. Six others of the same class, of sixty guns each, are to be built, three already ordered. Beside these, a large number of wooden ships of about four thousand tuns each, are building, with the express purpose of being armor-plated. Their estimated cost is thirty-nine million dollars, and it is expected that they will be ready for sea by the end of the present year.

THE FRENCH NAVY.

STEAM VESSELS.

Screw Ships of the Line.

No. vessels, (total,),......9 | Guns,................850
Horse-power,..........8,300 |

Screw Frigates, (Fast.)

No. vessels, (total,)........6 | Guns,................320
Horse-power,..........4,650 |

Screw Corvettes, (Fast.)

No. vessels, (total,).......7 | Horse-power,..........2,720
Iron,......................1 | Guns,................. 70

Screw Avisos, or Despatch Boats, (Fast.)

No. vessels,   total,.....14 | Horse-power, total,....2,420
Iron,   "   ......7 | Guns,   " 32
Wood and iron,   "   ......1 |

Ships of the Line, with Auxiliary Screws.

No. vessels,   total,......24 | Guns, total,..........2,170
Horse-power,   "   ..12,740 |

Frigates, with Auxiliary Screws.

No. vessels,   total,........9 | Guns, total,............445
Horse-power,   "   ....1,920 |

Corvettes, with Auxiliary Screws.

No. vessels, total......... 2 | Horse-power, total,.....320
Iron,   '   ....2 | Guns,   " 8

Avisos, with Auxiliary Screws.

Number vessels, total,.......3 | Horse-power, total,......155
Iron,   "   .. ...2 | Guns,   " 8

Floating Batteries, with Screws.

Number vessels, total,......5 | Guns,   total,..........90
Horse-power,   "   ..1,125 |

Screw Gun Boats.

Number vessels, total,.....20 | Guns, total,..............64
Horse-power, " ..2,040 |

Screw Gun-Vessels.

Number vessels, total,......8 | Guns, total,............. 24
Horse-power, " ...200 |

Steam Transports, with Auxiliary Screws.

Number vessels, total,.. .19 | Horse-power, total,...2,830
Iron, " .....3 | Guns, " 74

Steam Frigates, (paddle.)

Number vessels, total,.. .19 | Guns, total,...............284
Horse power, " ...9,340 |

Steam Corvettes, (paddle.)

Number vessels, total,......9 | Horse-power, total,.....2,640
Iron, " .....3 | Guns, " 53

Avisos, (paddles.)

Number vessels, total,.....50 | Horse-power, total, ...8,480
Iron, " .. 18 | Guns, " 168

Steam Tenders, (paddle.)

Number vessels, total,.....14 | Horse-power, total,......620
Iron, " ......4 | Guns, " 28

Line-of-Battle-Ships.

Number vessels, total,.....14 | Guns, total,............1,140

Frigates, (sailing.)

Number vessels total,.....28 | Guns total,............1,382

Corvettes, (sailing.)

Number vessels, total,....15 | Guns, total,.............286

Brigs, (sailing.)

Number vessels, total,....33 | Guns, total,.............340

Gun-Brigs, (sailing.)

Number vessels, total,......6 | Guns, total,..............24

Schooners, Cutters and small craft, (sailing.)

Number vessels, total,.....36 Guns, total,...............84

Mortar Vessels, (sailing.)
Number vessels, total,......5 | Guns, total,...............10
Transports, (sailing.)
Number vessels, total,.....26 | Guns, total,...............58

MEN-OF-WAR, (STEAM) ON THE STOCKS.
Screw Line-of-Battle Ships, (Fast.)
Number vessels, total,......4 | Guns, total,.............360
Horse-power, "...3,400 |

Screw Frigates, (Fast.)
Number vessels, total,......5 | Guns total,..............202
Horse-power, " .. 4,400 |

Screw Corvettes, (Fast.)
Number vessels, total,......2 | Horse-power, total,......800

Screw Avisos, (Fast.)
Number vessels, total,......8 | Horse-power, total,. ..1,400
Wood and iron, " .....4 |

Frigates with Auxiliary Screws.
No. vessels, wood and iron, | Horse power, total,......750
total,.................3 |

Transports, with Auxiliary Screws, (on the stocks.)
Number vessels, * total,....7 | Horse-power, total,....1,490
Iron, " ....2 | Guns, " 28
*20 more ordered.

SAILING VESSELS ON THE STOCKS.
Frigates.
Number vessels, total,.....12 | Guns, total,..............574

Corvettes.
Number vessels, total,......3 | Guns, total,..............66

Brigs-
Number vessels, total,......2 | Guns, total,..............24

Compiled from Official Documents for 1859.

BRIEF SUMMARY OF THE PRESENT NAVAL FORCE OF
FRANCE.

Steam War Vessels, total 265
Sailing   "   "   " 180
Grand Total, (Efficient, Sail and Steam,) 445
Ships of the Line,...............................40
Frigates,..61
Number of Guns, total,,.......................8,422
    "   Sailors,...........................30,000
    "   Captains,............................257

THE FRENCH ARMY AND NAVY.

The following admirably written statement of the condition and efficiency of the French Army and Navy, has been kindly furnished us for publication. It was prepared in Paris, by a thoroughly competent and faithful hand.

All the cannon now used by the French are rifled. The equipment secures rapid movement over heavy grounds; and plenty of spare men, horses and material, make up for casualties, and preserve efficiency in action.

I am also informed that the Emperor does not occupy himself much with new arms, but gives much attention to new modes of doing things, new drills, new tactics, new evolutions, new corps organized for special work in the field, the siege, the trenches, the escalades; new ways of crossing rivers, ditches, marshes, climbing walls or houses and surmounting obstacles of all sorts,—much practice in manœuvring large bodies massed, much athletic practice with arms, with sticks and without either—a great deal of target firing with guns, rifles, and muskets, at various ranges and over variable grounds; rapid marches and new paces, square, short, quick — a return in some degree to the athletic drill and physical discipline of the Roman Legions. The central ideas being the development of athletic endurance, rapidity of movement, accuracy of firing, and by the division of labor, speciality of employment and perfection of evolutionary drill, to produce the highest combined effect, with a given force.

As to the movements in ship building, &c., I can give
you no information, for I can get none— but it is pretty
clear that the Emperor does not consider the number of
men as any guage of the strength of an army. Small
armies have generally done the greatest work. The Russian
army on its present footing is about 850,000; the
Austrian, 740,000; the Prussian, 720,000; the French,
626,000; the English pretend to muster 534,000, but
this includes 218,000 blacks in India, 18,000 colonists,
and 61,000 militia and yeomanry, 140,000 volunteers,
15,000 pensioners, and 12,000 constables.

There are no breech-loading guns in the army. The
Emperor, I am told, does not like them; has tried them;
thinks them too liable to blow out or get out of order,
and too expensive; had experience of the Armstrongs in
the China war, alongside his own, and, on the whole, prefers
the latter. The artillery arm of the French army,
(for field work) consists of 32 batteries of horse artillery,
(6 guns) 192 guns; ten batteries foot artillery, sixty
guns; six squadrons train pontoonier, and one hundred
batteries mounted artillery, six hundred guns; in all,
eight hundred and fifty-two guns, thirty-seven thousand
men, and about as many horses. The mounted artillery,
one hundred batteries, is the great arm; each gun in
marching order is as follows:—First, one gun, six horses
and three postilions, (no man on the caisson); second,
eight mounted gunners; third, one caisson, six horses,
and three postilions; fourth, eight mounted ammunition
men; fifth, three spare wheels—that is to say, the
fore wheels of a gun carriage, with gun caisson, and
spare wheel, (making three,) with two horses and one
postilion; sixth, six spare horses and three postilions.
The rack gun has sixteen mounted men, six postilions,
and four spare postilions, eight spare horses, three spare
wheels, and one spare gun caisson; in all, twenty-six
men and twenty-six horses. Six of these form a battery.

My own impression is, that all breech-loading cannon
fail in rapid work—they get hot—the parts expand unequally
and no longer fit—gas gets in, and the parts become
deranged or burst. I don't believe Armstrong's
"cups" for gas, will afford any remedy. Nevertheless,
rifled guns are a great improvement, on account of

length of range and accuracy — and elongated shot are better for some work, but they will not ricochet.

It is difficult to arrive at a fair comparison of the naval forces of England and France; but I make it that the French are superior in steam and inferior in sails, and that, if the two entire navies were ranged in line of battle, the forces would be so nearly equal that it would be difficult to say which would win; and I judge from a speech of Lord Ellenborough, at an agricultural meeting, that he arrives at a similar conclusion, as he says, "It is useless to deny that we cannot rely on it, that we have any superiority of naval force."

THE SPANISH NAVY.

SAILING VESSELS.

	Guns.		Guns.
2 ships of the line, each of	80	10 schooners,	1
4 frigates,	32 to 42	5 luggers,	1
4 corvettes,	16 to 30	10 transports,	2 to 4
9 brigs,	10 to 20		
1 brigantine,	6		45

STEAMERS

	Guns.	Horse-power.
3 frigates,	37 to 50	300
5 schooners,	2 to 80	130

8 Screw Steamers,		
3 frigates,	16	500
8 brigs,	6	350
18 schooners	2 to 5	100 to 300

20 Paddle Steamers.

37

Altogether, 82 vessels, carrying 887 guns, and with engines of the aggregate power of 8,160 horses.

Besides the above, there are building 2 steam frigates, 37 guns, 360 horse power; 2 schooners, 200 horse power; 4 schooners, 80 horse power.

COAST GUARD.

24 feluccas,............87 estamparias

(*Official documents*, 1850.

BRIEF SUMMARY OF THE PRESENT NAVAL FORCE OF SPAIN.

		Guns.
Ships of the line,	3	272
Frigates,	18	783
Corvettes,	5	95
Brigantines,	8	120
Schooners,	25	68
Schooners, second class,	8	12
Side-wheel steamers,	27	135
Feluccas, first class,	6	13
Feluccas, second class,	25	25
Gun boats,	17	17
Total,	142	1,812

		Horse power.	Tons.
Steam transports, propellers,	9	1,080	9,100
Sailing, do	19	—	14,577

Total afloat, ... 170
In construction—Ships, ... 1
   do.   Frigates, ... 10
   do.   Schooners, ... 18

Grand total. .... 199 vessels, and 1,812 guns.

THE RUSSIAN NAVY.

STEAMERS.

Screw ships of the line,	7	Vessels of various kinds,	41
Screw frigates,	11	Tender,	1
Screw corvettes,	12		
Screw lugger,	1	Total,	73

SAILING VESSELS.

Ships of the line,	12	Clippers,	3
Frigates,	7	Yachts,	4
Corvettes,	7	Transports,	15
Brigs,	7	Barques,	7
Schooners,	11		
Xebecs,	7	Total,	85
Luggers,	5		

Grand total, 158. In addition to the above, the Russians have a considerable number of row gun-boats and screw gun-vessels.—*Official documents*, 1859.

SWEDISH NAVY.

Ships of the Line.

2 Screw steamers (300 to 350 horse-power) 80 to 62 guns.
5 Sailing, 80 to 62 guns.
1 Building, 80 to 62 guns.

Frigates.

1 Screw steamer builing (400 horse-power) 60 to 22 guns.
5 Sailing, 60 to 32 guns.

Corvettes.

3 Steam (300 to 200 horse-power.)
5 Sailing, 24 to 18 guns.
1 Gun brig.
7 Schooners and instruction-brigs.

Gun-Boats.

2 Screw steamers.
6 Screw steamers building.
13 Sailing schooners, rigged.
76 Large class (to row.)
122 Smaller class (to row.)
8 Mortar vessels.
3 Armed steam vessels (140 to 60 horse-power.)
5 Unarmed steam vessels.
25 Small sailing vessels.
21 Transports.

DUTCH NAVY.

	Guns.
2 Ships of the lines, each of...............	84
3 Ditto......................................	74
7 First class frigates (3 of them screws)........	54–45
8 Second class frigates	38–36
1 Ditto, rasse.............................	23
10 Corvettes, (5 of them screws)............	19–12
7 Brigs....................................	18–12
13 Schooners...............................	10–4
10 Ditto, screw............................	8
14 Of various kinds, presenting together........	94

2 Transports .... —
2 Frigates ⎫
1 Corvette ⎬ Guard vessels. ⎫
2 Ditto, training vessels. ⎬ 11
1 Brig, coast-guard. ⎭
55 Gun-boats................................... 174
2 Screw ditto.................................. 4
1 Schooner, gun vessel........................ 8

NORWEGIAN NAVY,

Frigates.

	Horse-power.	Guns.
1 Steam (building)......	500	52
1 Ditto.................	150	41
1 Sailing...............	—	44
1 Ditto.................	—	40

Corvettes.

1 Steam.................	225	14
1 Ditto.................	80	20
1 Ditto.................	200	6
1 Sailing...............	—	16
1 Ditto.................	—	10

Brigs.

1 Sailing...............		4

Schooners.

1 Steamer...............	20	6
1 Sailing...............	—	6
2 Ditto.................	—	5
2 Ditto.................	—	2

Steamers.

1 Steamer...............	120	2
1 (for towing gun-boats)	80	2
2 Ditto.................	80	—

Steam Gun-Boats.

2 Steam Gun-boats.......	60	2

Row Gun-Boats.

78 Row Gun-boats........	—	2
43 Ditto................	—	1

DANISH NAVY.

Sailing Ships of Line	4	Brigs.	4
Total number of guns	324	Total number of guns	56
Sailing Frigates	6	Schooners	3
Total number of guns	290	Total number of guns	10
Screw Frigates	3	Cutter	1
Horse-power	1000	Guns	6
Total number of guns	128	Screw Gun-boats	3
Corvettes	4	Paddle Steam-ships	8
Total number of guns	72	Horse-power	1270
Screw Corvettes	3	Total number of guns	48
Horse-power	820	Mortar vessels	3
Total number of guns	44	Transport ships	20

NAVY OF THE TWO SICILIES.

Aggregate number of guns.

2 Ships of the line	170	
5 Frigates	264	
2 Corvettes	36	
5 Brigantines	100	
2 Schooners	28—	598

Steamers.

	Total horse-power.	Guns.
2 Frigates	900	24
12 Ditto	3600	72
4 Corvettes	960	24
4 Smaller vessels	800	16
1 Ditto	120	4
6 Ditto	270	24
3 Transports		—
10 Mortar vessels		10
10 Gun-boats		20
30 Ditto		40

98—Total vessels—with an aggregate of 6650 horse-power, and carrying.............. 832

Since this list was prepared, however, the number of smaller vessels has been increased, bringing the total to

AUSTRIAN NAVY.

Description.	Horse-power.	Guns.	Men.
1 Screw ship of the line....	800	91	900
3 Ditto frigates.............	300	93	1125
4 Sailing ditto.............	—	171	1618
2 Screw corvettes..........	230	44	520
5 Sailing ditto............	—	82	757
5 Brigs....................	—	72	527
3 Steamers................	300–350	18	423
10 Smaller ditto	40–180	35	608
3 Screw schooners........	50–90	14	67
4 Brigantine (Transports)..		26	220
12 Gun sloops..............		40	92
12 Pinnaces.................		36	324
4 Row gun-boats..........		8	312
11 Ditto yawls.............		11	160
2 Pontoons................		20	330
1 Prahm, 1 mortar boat....		12	120
43 Piroques for lagunes.....		43	90
7 Transports..............		0	430
135		852	8707

BELGIAN NAVY.

1 Brig.............................12 shell-guns.
1 Schooner........................12 cannonades.
5 Mail steamers.........................

PERUVIAN NAVY.

	Guns.
2 Frigates............................	79
2 Steamers...........................	11
1 Brigantine.........................	14
4 Small steamers.....................	*
1 Mail steamer.......................	
5 Pontoons	
Total 15 vessels, carrying............	104
1 Battalions of marines...............	458 men.
A corps of pilots.....................	428 "

PORTUGUESE NAVY.

1 Ship of the line............Guns	80
1 Frigate..............................	50
3 Corvettes of 18 guns................	54
2 Brigs of 18 guns...................	36
3 Ditto of 16 guns...................	48
1 Ditto..............................	14
11 Schooners, &c.....................	45
9 Transports.........................	9
6 Steamers...........................	26
37	362

2 On the stocks.

PRUSSIAN NAVY.

2 Sailing frigates............Guns	86
2 Steam ditto........................	21
1 Screw corvette.....................	28
1 Paddle ditto.......................	28
1 Sailing ditto......................	12
1 Steam yacht........................	0
1 Transport..........................	6
3 Schooners..........................	6
1 Steamer............................	0
36 Gun boats, 2 guns each............	72
6 Ditto yawls........................	6
55 vessels of all kinds carrying.....	265

CHILIAN NAVY.

1 Corvette...................Guns	18
1 Brig...............................	14
1 Ditto..............................	10
1 Schooner...........................	4
1 Steamer............................	20
5....................................	66

Personnel.—Two admirals, 16 captains, 14 lieutenants, 12 midshipmen. Total, 54.

GREEK NAVY.

2 Corvettes, 48 guns. 1 Steam Corvette, 6. 3 Brigs. 32. 8 Schooners (4 steamers) 38. 1 Cutter, 8. 1 Yacht, 1. 2 Cutters (dispatch vessels). 4 Gun-boats, 12. 4 Gun vessels, 4. Total, 26 vessels, 149 guns.

MEXICAN NAVY.

This navy comprises 9 small vessels, carrying an aggregate of 35 guns. The crews amount altogether to 300 men.

SARDINIAN NAVY.

6 Steam frigates, 4 Sailing ditto, 3 Steam Corvettes, 4 Sailing ditto, 3 Steam avisos, or dispatch vessels, 4 Brigantines, 3 Steam Transports, 1 Tug. Altogether 29 vessels and 436 guns.

TURKISH NAVY.

7 Line of battle-ships, 6 Frigates, 4 Corvettes, 7 Brigs, 2 Mail packets, 23 Transports. Total 49.

BRAZILIAN NAVY.

Sailing Vessels.—1 Frigate, 5 Corvettes, 2 Barques, 5 Brigs, 7 Brigantines, 4 Schooners, 2 Gun-boats. 26.
Steamers.—7 Screw 8 Paddle, 1770 horse-power. 15.
In the province of Matto Grosso there are 29 gun-boats. In the autumn of 1858 the government were building 3 frigates, 4 corvettes, and a steamer.

Marines.

Commissioned and non-commissioned officers	672
Privates	2663
Total	3345

REBEL FORCES IN THE FIELD.

The recent Messages of the rebel Governors, and other official documents put forth by the State authorities, enable us to form a pretty correct estimate of the strength of the rebels now in the field. It is leaving off odd hundreds, as follows:

State.	Authorities.	No.
Georgia	Governor's Message	27,000
Louisiana	Governor's Message	25,000
South Carolina	Governor's Message	19,000
Virginia	Governor's Message	83,000
Tennessee	Governor's Proclamation	35,000
Kentucky	Estimated	10,000
Missouri	Price's proclamation	5,000
Alabama	Estimated	22,000
Mississippi	*Vicksburg Sun*	21,000
Florida	Estimated	10,000
Texas	Estimated	30,000
North Carolina	Governor's Message	35,000
Arkansas	Report of Adjutant of State	24,000
Maryland	Estimated	3,000
Total		349,000

STRENGTH OF CANADA AND THE STATES ON THE BORDER.

By the Canadian census of this year and the United States census of 1860, the relative strength of the Canadas and the States bordering on them is as follows:

Canada East, bordering on New England	1,003,666
Canada West on the New York and Michigan borders	1,395,222
Total	2,398,888

The States in proximity to the Canada line, according to the census of 1860, show the following population:

New York	3,851,563	
Michigan	754,391	
Maine	619,958	
New Hampshire	326,072	
Vermont	325,827	5,877,811

The number between the ages of eighteen and forty-five in Canada is 470,000; in the States on the border, 1,183,000—or nearly three to one.

BRIEF SUMMARY
—OF THE—
FORCES OF THE "GREAT POWERS."

The following statement of the Forces of the "Grea[t] Powers," at the close of 1861, is from the *Almanach Gotha*, high authority.

FRANCE.

Army on a war footing, 707,770 men, 130,000 hors[es] peace footing, 414,868 men, 72,850 horses. Navy, 6[00] vessels afloat, building and under transformation, carr[y]ing together, 13,358 guns. Out of that number there a[re] 373 steamers, of which 56 are iron-cased. The crews [of] the fleet who on a peace footing amount to 38,375 m[en] may in case of war be increased to 60,000. The seam[en] forming part of the maritime inscription are 670,000 [in] number. The effective strength of the marines is 22,4[00] men in peace, and 26,879 in war Custom-house offic[ers] or coast guard, 25,501 men.

GREAT BRITAIN.

Army 213,773 men, 21,904 horses. Navy, 893 vesse[ls] carrying 16,411 guns. The crews number 78,200 men, [of] whom 18,000 are marines, and 8,550 coast guard men.

RUSSIA.

Army, 577,859 men, regular troops; and 136 regime[nts] of cavalry, 31 battalions, and 31 batteries of irregula[r]. Navy, 313 vessels, of which 242 are steamers; carry[ing] together, 3,854 guns The Russian government has a[lso] 474 vessels acting as guardships at different places a[nd] for transports.

AUSTRIA.

Army, 587,695 men. Navy, 58 steamers and 79 sailin[g] vesssels, carrying together 895 guns.

PRUSSIA.

Army, peace footing, 212,649 men; war footing, 622[,]366 men. Navy, 34 vessels, of which 26 are steamers.

ITALY.

Official effective strength of the army on the 10th of June, 1861, 327,290 men, divided into 68 regiments of infantry, 26 battalions of bersaglieri, 17 regiments of cavalry, 9 of artillery, 2 of engineers, and 3 wagon trains. Navy, 106 vessels, carrying 1,036 guns, and 18 000 men.

PAPAL GOVERNMENT.

Ten thousand soldiers; expense of the army, ten million; subjects, one million.

OFFICIAL STATEMENT OF THE BRITISH NAVY FOR 1862.

The list shows a total of 856 vessels building, preparing or in commission, of which 702 are steamers, and comprises "81 line-of-battle ships, each amounting from 74 to 131 guns; 22 vessels, each with an armament of from 60 to 70 guns; 45 51 gun frigates, the whole, with the exception of about 10 of that number, being screw steamers; 57 ships, each mounting from 22 to 50 guns, and the majority of which have a tonnage as large as ships of the line; 29 screw corvettes or frigates, each mounting 22 guns; 317 screw and paddle-wheel steamers, each carrying less than 22 guns; and 185 screw gunboats, each provided with two Armstrong guns."

BRITISH FLEET IN AMERICAN WATERS.

The fleet in American waters comprises 14 line-of-battle steamers, ranging from 51 to 100 guns; 7 from 20 to 50, and 14 smaller vessels, exclusive of all the vessels ordered to join the same command.

WHAT ENGLAND HAS EXPENDED IN ARMAMENTS SINCE THE COMMENCEMENT OF THE REBELLION IN THE UNITED STATES.

A grant of 300 millions was voted for the navy in March last; the expenses of the fleet and of the army have been carried up to 765 millions; and the funds of 3,000 savings banks have been put into requisition to complete these immense preparations. England has sent 30,000 men to Canada, and thoroughly armed her navy.

POPULATION OF THE GLOBE.

Professor C. F. W. Dietrich, of the University of Berlin, has furnished the Academy of Sciences in that city with the most recent and reliable tables on this subject, giving the following results, with his grounds for them:—

Population of Europe		272,000,000
"	Asia	755,000,000
"	America	200,000,000
"	Africa	59,000,000
"	Australia, etc.	2,000,000
Total		1,288,000,000

or more than twelve hundred millions. Reckoning the average death as about one in every forty inhabitants, 32,000,000 die in a year; 87,671 in a day; 3653 in an hour; and 61 in a minute. Thus one human being dies on an average every second, and more than one is born.

The entire population is thus divided in point of *religion*:—

Christians—Protestants	89,000,000	
Romish Church	170,000,000	
Greek Church	76,000,000	
		335,000,000
Jews		5,000,000
Mohammedans		160,000,000
Heathen		788,000,000

Dietrich thus distributes the population of the globe according to *races*:—

Caucasian race	369,000,000
Mongolian "	522,000,000
Ethiopian "	196,000,000
American "	1,000,000
Malay "	200,000,000
Total	1,288,000,000

M. D'Halloy, in the Proceedings of the Belgian Academy, reckoning the population of the globe at 1,000,000,000, thus divides them as to races:—

WHITE RACE,	{ European branch	289,586,000	
	Aranican "	50,390,000	
	Scythian "	30,747,000	
			370,723,000
YELLOW RACE,	{ Hyperborean branch	160,000	
	Mongolian "	7,000,000	
	Sinic—Chinese "	338,300,000	
			345,460,000
BROWN RACE,	{ Hindoo branch	171,100,000	
	Ethiopian "	8,300,000	
	Malay "	25,600,000	
			205,000,000
RED RACE,	{ Southern branch	9,200,000	
	Northern "	400,000	
			9,600,000
BLACK RACE,	{ Western branch	56,000,000	
	Eastern "	1,000,005	
			57,000,000
HYBRIDS—Mulattoes, Zambos, etc.			12,217,000
Total			1,000,000,000

The population of several of the leading countries and their colonies has, according to recent censuses, been as follows:—

	Colonies.	Countries.
British Empire	5,224,477	27,435,325
" Indies	151,316,129	
France	739,496	35,400,486
Denmark	119,491	2,296,497
Holland	21,786,700	3,241,990
Portugal	1,722,140	3,412,000
Spain	3,717,433	12,386,841
Austria		35,730,112

	Colonies.	Countries.
Prussia	....	16,331,187
Russia	....	66,008,315
Bavaria	....	4,519,526
Belgium	....	4,350,090
Greece	....	637,700
Hamburg	....	188,054
Papal States	....	2,908,115
Sardinia	....	4,650,368
Sweden and Norway	....	4,645,007
Turkey in Europe	....	15,500,000
Two Sicilies	....	8,423,306
China	....	400,000,000

The population of China, that very interesting country, is very uncertain. According to the best native authority, the population should now be nearly 400,000,000; but the population is given by Gutzlaff at 367,000,000, and confirmed at about that by other late writers.

COLONIAL POPULATION IN 1715.

The following are some statistics of old colonial days. One hundred and forty-five years ago, in the reign of George I., the ascertained population of the Continental Colonies was as follows:—

	White Men.	Negro Slaves.
New Hampshire	9,500	150
Massachusetts	94,000	2,000
Rhode Island	7,500	500
Connecticut	46,000	1,500
New York	27,000	4,000
Pennsylvania	43,300	2,500
New Jersey	21,000	1,500
Maryland	40,700	9,400
Virginia	72,000	23,000
North Carolina	7,500	3,700
South Carolina	6,250	10,500
Total	375,000	58,550

THE GOVERNMENTS OF THE WORLD, 1862.

State.	Name of Ruler.	Title.	Form of Government.	Sq Miles	Populat'n	Religion.
United States	Abraham Lincoln	President	Fed Rep.—two houses Cong	2,936,166	31,429,891	Um.Tol's.
Great Britain	Victoria I	Queen	Lim Mon—Lords & Com.	116,700	29,380,205	Prot.Epis.
France	Napoleon III	Emperor	Const Mon—Senate & Legis	208,121	38,112,583	Catholic.
Russia	Alexander II	Czar	Absolute Monarchy	2,120,397	64,031,068	Greek Ch.
Austria	Francis Joseph I	Emperor	Absolute Monarchy	253,226	36,514,466	Catholic.
Sweden and Norway	Charles XV	King	Lim Mon., with Legislature	296,540	4,762,274	Lutheran.
Liechtenstein	John	Prince	Principality	53	7,530	Pro & Cath
Denmark	Frederick VII	King	Lim Mon., with Prov States	21,836	2,296,097	Lutheran.
Holland	William III	King	Lim Mon—two Chambers	13,890	3,267,638	Reformed
Belgium	Leopold I	King	Lim Mon—two Chambers	11,313	4,839,099	Catholic.
Prussia	Fred William IV	King	Lim Mon—two Chambers	107,369	16,346,625	Evangel.
Saxony	John	King	Lim Mon—two Chambers	5,763	1,894,431	Catholic.
Hanover	George V	King	Lim Mon—two Chamber.	14,040	1,758,897	Evangel.
Mecklenburg Schwerin	Fred Francis	Grand Duke	Lim Sov—one Chamber.	4,701	543,329	Lutheran.
Mecklenburg-Strelitz	Fred William	Grand Duke	Lim Sov—one Chamber	997	96,292	Lutheran.
Oldenburg	Peter	Grand Duke	Lim Sov—two Chambers.	2,470	279,039	Lutheran.
Brunswick	William	Duke	Lim Sov—one Chamber.	1,525	269,913	Lutheran.
Nassau	Adolphus	Duke	Lim Sov—two Chambers	1,736	428,218	Evangel.
Saxe-Weimar-Eisenach	Charles Alexander	Duke	Lim Sov—one Chamber.	1,403	261,376	Lutheran.
Saxe-Coburg-Gotha	Ernest II	Duke	Lim Sov—one Cha to Duchy	790	149,753	Lutheran.
Saxe-Meiningen	Bernard	Duke	Lim Sov—one Chamber.	956	163,323	Lutheran.
Saxe-Altenburg	Ernest	Duke	Lim Sov—one Chamber.	431	131,780	Lutheran.
Anhalt-Dessau	Leopold	Duke	States with Limited Powers	350	63,700	Evangel.
Anhalt-Bernburg	Alexander	Duke	States with Limited Powers	339	50,411	Evangel.
Schwarzburg Rudolstadt	Fred Ganther	Prince	Lim Sov—one Chamber.	405	69,656	Lutheran.
Schwarzburg Sondershn	Gunther	Prince	Lim Sov—one Chamber.	333	60,002	Lutheran.
Reuss—Elder Line	Henry XXII	Prince	Lim Sov } —one Chamber	588	112,175	Lutheran.
Reuss—Younger Line	Henry LXVII	Prince	Lim Sov } —one Chamber			
Lippe-Detmold	Leopold	Prince	Lim Mon—one Chamber	435	104,674	Reformed.
Lippe-Schaumburg	George	Prince	Lim Mon—one Chamber.	203	28,837	Reformed.
Waldeck	George Victor	Prince	Lim Sov—one Chamber	455	58,219	Evangel.

THE GOVERNMENTS OF THE WORLD, 1862.

States	Name of Ruler	Title	Form of Government	Sq Miles	Populat'n	Religion
Thibet		Tale Lama	Hierarchy		30,000,000	Buddhic
Burmah	Sera-wa	King	Absolute Despotism	200,000	3,000,000	Buddhic
Abyssinia		Emperor	Federate Monarchy	282,000	3,500,000	Coptic Ch.
Madagascar	Rakout Radama	King	Despotic Monarchy	240,000	4,500,000	M.&Chris.
Morocco	Sidi Mohammed	Em-er	Despotic Sovereignty	222,500	6,000,000	Mohan.
Brazil	Don Pedro II	Emperor	Hereditary Monarchy	3,094,400	6,035,000	Catholic
Argentine Confederation	Santiago Derqui	President	Federate Republic	371,450	1,030,000	Catholic
Buenos Ayres	Bartolomo Mitre	Acting Pres.	Republic	620,000	1,000,000	Catholic
Uruguay	Bernardo P. Berio	President	Republic	75,000	600,000	Catholic
Paraguay	Carlos A. Lopez	Pres. for life	Republic	81,000	1,000,000	Catholic
Bolivia	J. M. Linares	President	Republic	337,500	303,255	Catholic
Chili	Manuel Montt	President	Republic	170,000	1,558,453	Catholic
Costa Rica	Monica-rc	Provis. Pres	Republic	16,740	1,30 ,000	Catholic
Ecuador	Gabriel Gar. Moreno	President	Republic	240,000	800,000	Catholic
Guatemala	Rafael Carrera	President	Republic	44,500	600,000	Catholic
Honduras	Santos Guardeola	President	Republic	33,000	325,000	Catholic
Mexico	Benito Juarez	President	Republic	831,140	7,853,391	Catholic
New Granada	T. C. De Mosquera	President	Republic	480,000	2,363,054	Catholic
Nicaragua	Thomaso Martinez	President	Republic	35,000	257,000	Catholic
Peru	Ramon Castilla	President	Republic	370,000	2,279,093	Catholic
San Salvador	Gen. G. Barrios	President	Republic	7,500	250,000	Catholic
Venezuela	Jose A. Valverde	President	Republic	400,000	1,419,259	Catholic
Hayti	Gen. Geffard	President	Republic	10,081	550,000	Catholic
Da 'nica	J. Des Valverde	President	Republic	17,500	126,000	Catholic
Sandwich Islands	L. Kamehameha IV	King	Monarchy	6,500	72,984	Protestant
Society Islands	Pomare	Queen	Monarchy		200,000	Pagan
Liberia	Stephen A. Benson	President	Republic		15,000	Uni Tol'en
Dahomey	Reernee Reernee	King	Absolute Despotism	35,000	206,000	Pagan&Ca.

Country	Ruler	Government	Population	Religion
Hesse-Homburg	Ferdinand	Landgrave	206	Reformed
Baden	Frederic	Grand Duke	5,712	Evangel.
Hesse-Cassel	Frederic William	Elector	4,430	Reformed
Hesse-Darmstadt	Louis III	Grand Duke	3,361	Lutheran
Wurtemberg	William I	King	7,958	Lutheran
Bavaria	Maximilian II	King	28,433	Catholic
Spain	Isabella	Queen	176,980	Catholic
Portugal	Pedro V	King	31,500	Catholic
Italy	Victor Emanuel II	King	97,703	Catholic
States of the Church	Pius IX	Pope	17,018	Catholic
Greece	Otho I	King	18,444	Catholic
Turkey	Abdul Aziz	Sultan	189,920	Moham.
Monaco	Chas Honore	Prince	50	Catholic
Bremen—Free City	Chas Fred G Mohr	Burgomaster	112	Prot.Cath
Frankfort—Free City	Dr. S. Gottl. Muller	Burgomaster	90	Pro.& Cath
Hamburg—Free City	Dr. H. Kellinghusen	Burgomaster	151	Pro.& Cath
Lubec—Free City	C. L. Roeck	Burgomaster	114	Pro.& Cath
Andorra		24 Consuls	200	Catholic
Switzerland	Dr. J. B. Weder	Pres. Nat. Con. Federate Republic	15,161	Prot.Cath
San Marino	Giuseppe Fillippi, Pietro Righi	Captains Regents } Republic.—Senate and Executive Council	22	Catholic
Servia	Obrenovich II	Hospodar	20,600	Greek Ch.
Montenegro	Mirko	Prince	430	Greek Ch.
Egypt	Said Pasha	Viceroy	11,900	Moham.
China	Hienfung	Hoang Ti	1,207,299,387	Confuc. & Bud.
Persia	Naser ed Din	Sohah	450,000	Moham.
Japan		Siogoon	160,000	Buddhic.
Annam (Cochin China)		King	78,035	Buddhic.
Siam	Somdetch Phra	King	204,720	Buddhic.
Afghanistan	Dost Mohammed	Shah	225,000	Moham.
Bokhara		Khan	245,000	Moham.
Khokan		Khan	130,000	Moham.
Yemen		Imaum		Moham.
Beloochistan		Khan	160,000	Moham.

Dimensions of Big Ships.

	Breadth of Beam. Feet.	Depth. Feet.	Length. Feet.	Tonnage.
Great Eastern	83	58	680	18,000
General Admiral	55	34	307	6,000
Niagara	55	31½	345	5,800
Adriatic	50	33	354	5,888
Vanderbilt	49	33	340	5,100
Pennsylvania	56.9	54.9	247	6,000
Munster			378	4,069
Leinster (Galway			375	4,000
Connaught { Line			375	4,000
Ulster ((new)			375	4,000
Persia			375	3,300
Himalaya			360	5,000
City of Baltimore			340	2,367
City of Washington			325	2,380
Orlando			337	3,727

Length of American Steam Frigates.

Minnesota	264 feet	8½ inches
Wabash	262 "	4 "
Merrimac	255 "	9 "
Roanoke	263 "	8¼ "
Colorado	263 "	8¼ "

LENGTH OF STEAMSHIP ROUTES.

	Geographical miles.
New York to Southampton	2980
" Liverpool	2880
" Glasgow	2800
" Galway	2680
Boston to Liverpool	2720
" Belfast	2620
" Galway	2520
Philadelphia to Liverpool	3090
" Glasgow	3010
New York to San Francisco via Tehuantepec	4168
" " " Nicaragua	4852
" " " Panama	5255
New Orleans to San Francisco via Tehuantepec	3071
" " " Nicaragua	4100
" " " Panama	4068
Land's End (England) to San Francisco via Tehuantepec	6808
" " " Nicaragua	7252
" " " Panama	7810

Quick Passages of Ocean Steamships.

1851, Aug. 6, Baltic, Liverpool to New York, nine days, nineteen hours.
1853, Aug. 13, Arabia, Liverpool to New York, nine days, twenty-two hours, fifty-five minutes.
1854, June 28, Baltic, Liverpool to New York, nine days, seventeen hours, fifteen minutes.
1856, July 8, Baltic, Liverpool to New York, nine days, sixteen hours, thirty-three minutes.
1857, June 23, Persia, nine days, twenty-one hours, twenty-nine minutes.
1857, June 3, Vanderbilt, Cowes to New York, ten days, eighteen hours.
1857, July 8, Vanderbilt, Cowes to New York, ten days, twelve hours.
1858, June 9, Vanderbilt, Southampton to New York, nine days, thirteen hours.
1859, May 21, Vanderbilt, Southampton to New York, nine days, nine hours, twenty-six minutes.
1860, Aug. 26, Great Eastern, New York to Milford Haven, nine days and four hours,—the shortest eastern passage yet made.
1861, April, Persia, Liverpool to New York, nine days, eight hours, seven minutes.

RATES OF POSTAGE.

Letters within the United States not over 3000 miles, three cents each 1-2 oz.; over 3000 miles, 10 cents; must be prepaid. To the British N. A. Provinces, under 3000 miles, 10 cents; over 3000, 15 cents. Drop letters, 1 cent, prepaid or not; advertised letters, 1 cent. Letters to two or more persons in one envelope are illegal. Ship-letters to any United States port, 6 cents; if forwarded inland, 2 cents, and the usual United States postage.

Every letter or parcel not exceeding half an ounce in weight shall be deemed a single letter, and every additional weight of half an ounce or less shall be charged with an additional single postage.

PAPERS.—Weekly papers within the county where published, free; otherwise, on the regular numbers of a newspaper published weekly, for not exceeding 50 miles, 5 cents per quarter; for over 50 and under 300 miles, 10 cents per quarter; for over 300 and under 1000 miles, 15 cents per quarter; for over 1000 and under 2000 miles, 20 cents per quarter; for over 2000 and under 4000 miles, 25 cents per quarter; for over 4000 miles, 30 cents per quarter. Monthly newspapers sent to subscribers, one quarter; semi-monthly, one half; semi-weekly, twice; tri-weekly, treble; and oftener, five times those rates. Upon every other newspaper, and each circular not sealed, handbill, engraving, pamphlets, periodical, magazine, book, and every other description of printed matter, of no greater weight than one ounce, for any distance not exceeding 500 miles, 1 cent; and for each additional ounce or fraction of an ounce, 1 cent; for over 500 and under 1500 miles, double those rates; for over 1500 and under 2500 miles, treble those rates; for over 2500 and under 3500 miles, four times those rates; for over 3500 miles, five times those rates.

Books, prepaid, not weighing over 4 pounds, 1 cent per oz. for any distance in the United States under 3000 miles, and 2 cents an oz. over 3000 miles, pre-payment required,—all fractions over the oz. being counted as an additional oz.

Rates of Letter-Postage to Foreign Countries.

To England, Ireland, and Scotland, (California, Oregon, and Washington excepted,) 24 cents, 1-2 oz. From California, Oregon, or Washington 29 cents 1-2 oz.

To France and Algeria, by French mails, 15 cents 1-4 oz., 30 cents 1-2 oz.

To German States, by Prussian closed mail, 30 cents 1-2 oz.

" " by French mail, 21 cents 1-4 oz., 42 cents 1-2 oz.

" " by Bremen mail, (except Bremen, Baden, and Luxenburg,) 15 cents 1-2 oz.; newspapers, 3 cents each.

To German States, by Hamburg mail, (except Hamburg and Luxemburg,) 15 cents oz.
To Holland, by French mail, 42 cents 1-2 oz.
" via England on American ships, 21 cents 1-2 1-2 oz.
To Bremen, by Bremen mail, 10 cents 1-2 oz.
To Hamburg, by Hamburg mail, 10 cents 1-2 oz.
To Hanover, by Prussian mail, 60 cents 1-2 oz.
" by Bremen or Hamburg, 15 cents 1-2 oz.
To Luxemburg, by Bremen ordinary mail, 22 cents 1-2 ounce.
To Holland and the Netherlands, by French mail, 21 cents 1-4 oz., 42 cents 1-2 oz.
To Austria and its States, by Prussian closed mail, 30 cents 1-2 oz.
" " " by Bremen or Hamburg mail, 15 cents 1-2 oz.
To Austria and its States, by French mail, 21 cents 1-4 oz., 42 cents 1-2 oz.
To Russia, by Prussian closed mail, 37 cents 1-2 oz.
" by Bremen or Hamburg mail, 29 cents 1-2 ounce.
To Prussia, by Prussian closed mail, 30 cents 1-2 oz.
" by Bremen or Hamburg mail, 15 cents 1-2 oz.
" by French mail, 21 cents 1-4 oz., 42 cents 1-2 oz.
To Sardinian States, by Prussian closed mail, 42 cents 1-2 oz.
" " by French mail, 21 cents 1-4 oz., 42 cents 1-2 oz.
" " by Bremen or Hamburg mail, 23 cents 1-2 oz.
To Lombardy, by Prussian closed mail, 42 cents 1-2 oz.
" by French mail, 21 cents 1-4 oz., 42 cents 1-2 oz.
" by Bremen or Hamburg mail, 15 cents 1-2 oz.
To Parma and Madena, by Prussian closed mail, 42 cents 1-2 oz.

To Parma and Madena, by French mail, 27 cents 1-4 oz., 54 cents 1-2 oz.
" " by Bremen or Hamburg mail, 25 cents 1-2 oz.
To the Papal States, by Prussian closed mail, 46 cents 1-2 oz.
" by French mail, 27 cents 1-4 oz., 54 cents 1-2 oz.
" by Bremen or Hamburg mail, 28 cents 1-2 oz.
To the Two Sicilies, by Prussian closed mail, 49 cents 1-2 oz.,—*prepaid.*

PUBLIC LIBRARIES IN THE U. S.

The Manual of Public Libraries and Institutions, by Wm. J. Rhees, lately published, contains some very interesting statistics, from which are condensed the following statement of leading facts. In the entire Union the reported and estimated results were as follows in 1859 :—

	No.	Vols.
Libraries with volumes reported	1,207	4,220,686
" " estimated.	1,593	500,000
" of Common Schools	18,000	2,000,000
" of Sunday Schools	30,000	6,000,000
Grand aggregate	50,890	12,720,686

Largest Public Libraries.

	Vols.
Astor Library, New York	80,000
Mercantile Library, New York	51,000
Society Library, New York	40,000
Union Theological, New York	24,000
Athenæum, Boston	70,000
Public Library, Boston	70,000
Harvard University, Cambridge	74,000
Yale College, New Haven	36,000
Philadelphia and Loganian Library	64,900
Academy of Natural Sciences, Philadelphia	25,000
American Philosophical Society, Philadelphia	20,000
University of Virginia, Charlottesville	30,000
Georgetown College, Georgetown, D. C	26,000
Library of Congress, Washington	50,700
Smithsonian Institute, Washington	25,000
Force Library, Washington	20,000

Public Libraries in the States.

	Vols.		Vols.
Alabama	36,529	New Jersey	89,520
Arkansas	1,000	New York	7,50,421
California	70,428	North Carolina	36,344
Connecticut	145,058	Ohio	212,642
Delaware	31,085	Pennsylvania	467,716
Florida	9,687	Rhode Island	154,842
Georgia	64,236	South Carolina	106,080
Illinois	58,501	Tennessee	94,251
Indiana	81,851	Texas	3,050
Iowa	11,431	Vermont	32,800
Kentucky	112,293	Virginia	142,767
Louisiana	58,680	Wisconsin	59,600
Maine	114,112	Dist. of Columbia	272,835
Maryland	194,671	Kansas	7,000
Massachusetts	632,800	Nebraska	800
Michigan	35,986	New Mexico	—
Minnesota	5,700	Oregon	2,051
Mississippi	25,323	Washington	4,352
Missouri	69,509		
New Hampshire	84,915	Total	4,280,866

Public Libraries in Cities.

	Vols.		Vols.
New York	346,185	St. Louis	47,590
Philadelphia	271,981	Charleston	38,690
Boston	258,079	Chicago	20,573
Baltimore	95,644	New Orleans	20,360
Cincinnati	70,407	Louisville	18,773

COTTON RAISED IN THE UNITED STATES,

From 1820 to 1859, also giving the quantity purchased by Great Britain during that time.

	CROP. Bales.	PURCHASED BY GRAET BRITAIN. Bales.
1820 to 1824	501,852	357,066
1825 to 1829	849,032	513,724
1830 to 1834	1,111,297	677,833
1835 to 1839	1,624,703	957,264
1840 to 1844	2,024,588	1,211,840
1845 to 1849	2,210,425	1,168,680
1850 to 1854	2,882,117	1,600,840
1855 to 1859	3,358,202	1,797,475

STATISTICAL POCKET MANUAL.

PART II.

GENERALS AND THEIR STAFFS.
UNITED STATES ARMY, 1862.
REGULAR AND VOLUNTEER SERVICE

REGULAR SERVICE.

MAJOR GENERAL GEORGE B. McCLELLAN.

STAFF.

Assistant Adj. General	Brig. Gen. Seth Williams.
Act. Ass. Adj. General	Lieut. Col. A. V Colburn.
Inspector General	} Brig. Gen. R. B. Marcy.
Chief of Staff	
Assistant do.	Lieut. Col. E. McK. Hudson.
Assistant do.	Lieut. Col. N. B. Sweitzer.
Chief Quartermaster	Brig. Gen. Stewart Van Vleit.
Assistant do.	Lieut. Col. Rufus Ingalls.
Inspecting do.	Lieut. Col. C. D. Blanchard.
Chief Engineer	Brig. Gen. J. G. Barnard.
Chief Commissary	Lieut. Col. H. F. Clark.
Chief of Cavalry	Brig. Gen. Geo. Stoneham.
Inspector of do.	Col. Charles F. Havelock.
Chief of Artillery	Brig. Gen. W. F. Barry
Assistant to do.	Lieut. Col. Abner Doubleday.
Chief Topograph. Engineer	Lieut. Col. J. N. Macomb.
Assistant do.	Capt. G. M. Poe.
Medical Director	Lieut. Col. Chas. S. Tripler.
Signal Officer	Lieut. Col. A. J. Meyer.

(3)

Chief of Ordnance . . . . Col. C. P. Kingsbury.
Assistant to do. . . . . Major George C. Strong.
Aid . . . . Col. Thos. J. Gant.
Aid . . . . Col. H. J. Hunt.
Aid . . . . Col. Henry Wilson, Mass.
Aid . . . . Col. Wm. McKee Dunn, Ind.
Aid . . . . Col. Le Comte de Villaneau.
Aid . . . . Col. S. Hamilton.
Aid . . . . Col. John Jacob Astor.
Aid . . . . { Lieut. Col. L. A. Williams, 10th U S. Infantry.
Aid . . . . Lieut. Col. Richard B. Irwin.
Aid . . . . { Lieut. Col. James A. Hardee, 5th Artillery.
Aid . . . . { Lieut. Col. William Hays, 2d Artillery.
Aid . . . . { Capt. Louis Philippe d'Orleans, Comte de Paris.
Aid . . . . { Capt. Robert d'Orleans, Duc de Chartres.
Aid . . . . Capt. Le Comte de Villarcau.
Aid . . . . Capt. E. A. Raymond, Boston.
Aid . . . . Capt. W. P. Mason, Boston.
Aid . . . . Capt. Hammerstein, N. Y.
Aid . . . . Capt. Harry W. Powers, N. Y.

BODY GUARD.

Major . . . . S. G. Barker.
Captain . . . . G. W. Shea.
Captain . . . . D. C. Brown.
Lieutenant . . . . G. H. Sitts.
Lieutenant . . . . G. S. Phelps.
Lieutenant . . . . E. A. Webster.
Lieutenant . . . . P. Purley Page.

This squadron now numbers two hundred men, part of which served with the General in Western Virginia. They are armed with Sharp's breech-loading rifles, with sabre bayonets.

Gen. McClellan has found it necessary to organize a staff of experienced army officers, several of them ranking as brigadier generals, that they can, if necessary, take command at a critical moment, should colonels not be equal to an emergency.

MAJOR GENERALS.

MAJOR GENERAL JOHN C. FREMONT.

General Fremont is appointed to the command of the Mountain Department. His staff has not been officially announced.

STATISTICAL POCKET MANUAL. 5

MAJOR GENERAL HENRY W. HALLECK.*
DEPARTMENTAL STAFF.

Chief of Staff and Chief Eng...	Brig. Gen. Geo. W. Cullum.
Assistant Chief of Staff at Headquarters	Brig. Gen. Schuyler Hamilton.
Assistant Adj. Gen. at Headquarters	Capt. J. C. Kelton.
Assistant Adj. General	Capt. William McMichael.
Assistant Adj. General	Capt. S. M. Preston.
Chief Quartermaster	Major Robert Allen.
Assistant Quartermaster	Capt. J. M. Bradshaw.
Chief of Subsistence	Capt. Thomas J. Haines.
Chief Medical Director	Surgeon J. J. B. Wright.
Chief Paymaster	Lieut. Col. T. P. Andrews.
Assistant Eng. and A. D. C.	Lieut. Col. J. B. McPherson.
Chief of Topographical Eng. and A. D. C.	Col. George Thom.
A. D. C. on Topographical duty	Col. Richard D. Cutts.
Chief of Ordnance	Capt. Franklin D. Callender.
Chief of Artillery	Lieut. Col. James Totten.
Chief of Cavalry	Lieut. Col. E. Steen, U. S. A.
Acting Aid	Capt. John Hoskin.
Volunteer Aid	Col. J. C. McKibbon, California.
Aid	Capt. A. J. Halleck.
Commissary	Major W. W. Leland.
Provost Marshal General	Bernard G. Farrar.

STATE MILITIA STAFF.

Assistant Adj. General	Lieut. Col. Calvin W. Marsh.
Aid-de-Camp	Lieut. Col. Bernard G. Farrar.
A. D. C. and Asst. Ins. Gen.	Lieut. Col. John B. Gray.

BREVET MAJOR GENERAL JOHN E. WOOL.
STAFF.

Asst. Adj. Gen., Chief of Staff.	Major W. D. Whipple.
Acting Assistant Adj. Gen.	Capt. Chas. C. Churchill.
Inspector General	Col. T. J. Crane.
Chief Quartermaster	Capt. Grier Tallmadge.
Chief Commissary	Capt. J. McL. Taylor.
Medical Director	Major J. M. Cuyler, M. D.
Surgeon	Capt. R. H. Gilbert, M. D.
Surgeon	Capt. Josiah Curtis, M. D.
Topograph Engineer-in-Chief, Acting A. D. C.	Capt. W. F. Reynolds.
Provost Marshal	Major Jones.
Signal Officer	Capt. J. H. Quackenbush.
Harbor Master	Capt. James Milward, Jr.
Aid	Major Le Baron Von Vegesak, Sweden.
Aid	Major Le Baron Von Hermann, Prussia.
Aid	Major A. Hamilton, Jr.
Aid	Major Le Grand B. Cannon, New York.

* General Halleck is now Commander in-chief.

6   STATISTICAL POCKET MANUAL.

Aid . . . . Major Henry Z. Hayner.
Aid . . . . Capt. W. Jay, Bedford, N. Y.
Aid . . . . Capt. —— Spencer.

BODY GUARD.

This squadron, two hundred strong, is formed of two companies of the Mounted Rifles, under command of
Major . . . . B. F. Onderdonk.

BRIGADIER GENERALS ACTING AS MAJOR GENERALS.

BRIGADIER GENERAL WM. S. ROSECRANS.

STAFF.

Asst. Adj. Gen., Chief of Staff . Major Geo. S. Hartsuff, U. S. A.
Asst. Adj. Gen. Volunteers . . . Capt. H. Thrall.
Provost Marshal . . . . Major Jos. Darr, Jr., 1st Va. Cav.
Inspector General . . . . Major A. J. Slemmer.
Acting Inspector General and }
  Mustering Officer . . . . } Major Samuel W. Crawford.
Chief Quartermaster . . . . . . Major R. E. Clary.
Asst. Quartermaster, U. S. A. . Capt. John G. Chandler.
Asst. Quartermaster of Vols. . . Capt. C. N. Goulding.
Chief Commissary . . . . Capt. John W. Barriger.
Asst. do. of Subsistence . . . . Capt. Francis Darr.
Medical Director . . . . Major H. R. Wirtz, M. D.
Staff Surgeon . . . . Capt. A. Hartsuff.
Chief Paymaster . . . . Major D. H. McPhail, U. S. V.
Topographical Engineer . . . . Capt. W. F. Reynolds.
Judge Advocate General . . . . Capt. T. Gaines, 5th O. V. M.
Engineer . . . . Capt. W. F. Reynolds, U. S. A.
Engineer . . . . Capt. W. Morgadante, O. V. M.
Engineer Aid . . . . Capt. W. A. Powell.
Aid . . . . Capt. H. H. Clements, O. V. M.

BRIGADIER GENERAL JOS. K. F. MANSFIELD

STAFF.

Assistant Adjutant General . . —— ——
Aid . . . . Capt. Drake DeKay.
Aid . . . . Clarence H. Dyer.

BRIGADIER GENERAL IRVIN McDOWELL.

STAFF.

Assistant Adjutant General . . —— ——
Aid . . . . —— ——
Aid . . . . —— ——

BRIGADIER GENERAL EDWIN V. SUMNER.
STAFF.
Assistant Adjutant General . . ——— ———
Chief Aid . . . . Capt. Lawrence Kip, U. S. Art.
Aid . . . . Capt. J. H. Taylor, U. S. Cav.
Aid . . . . Lieut. S. Sumner, U. S. Cav.

BRIGADIER GENERAL PHILIP ST. GEO. COOKE.
STAFF.
Assistant Adjutant General . ——— ———

Brigadier General Philip St. George Cooke, U. S. A., has been appointed to the command of all the regular cavalry in the army of the Potomac.

BRIGADIER GENERAL LORENZO THOMAS.
STAFF.
Colonel . . . . Edward D. Townsend.
Lieutenant Colonel . . . . . . Wm. A. Nichols.
Captain . . . . Thomas M. Vincent.

General Thomas is Adjutant General of the complete army of the United States, and the whole corps of the Adjutant General's department may be considered as belonging to his staff in addition to those above named.

BREVET BRIG. GEN. SYLVESTER CHURCHILL.
STAFF.
Colonel . . . . Henry V. Rensselaer.
Major . . . . N. H. Davis.

General Churchill is chief of the department of the Inspector General of the United States army, and in like manner to the Adjutant General. The whole corps of the department indirectly forms his staff.

BRIG. GENERAL MONTGOMERY C. MEIGS.
STAFF.
Colonel . . . . C. Thomas.
Colonel . . . . D. Tompkins.

General Meigs is chief of the Quartermaster's Department of the American army, and the like remarks will apply to his staff as in the two preceding cases.

BRIGADIER GENERAL JAMES W. RIPLEY.
STAFF.
Lieutenant Colonel . . . . . . G. D. Ramsey.
Major . . . . William A. Thornton.
Captain . . . . Alexander B. Dyer.

General Ripley is the chief officer of the United States Ordnance Department. His staff embraces the whole corps.

BREVET BRIG. GEN. JOSEPH G. TOTTEN.
STAFF.
Lieutenant Colonel . . . . . . Richard Delafield.
Captain . . . . T. L. Casey.

General Totten is Chief Engineer of the United States army, and has charge of the whole engineer corps of the United States, a number of the officers of which department have recently been promoted to the rank of Brigadier General of Volunteers, on account of their efficiency as army officers.

Brigadier Generals Anderson and Harney are not in actual service, the former being in ill health, and the latter not having been detailed to a command since his removal from the Department of the West.

MAJOR GENERAL JOHN A. DIX.
STAFF.
Assistant Adjutant General, Chief of Staff . . . . Captain D. T. Van Buren.
Engineer . . . . Major D. P. Woodbury.
Quartermaster . . . .
Aid and Military Secretary . . . Lieutenant Charles Temple Dix.
Medical Director . . . .

MAJOR GENERAL DAVID HUNTER.
STAFF.
Assistant Adjutant General, Chief of Staff . . . . Major M. J. Parrott.
Medical Director . . . . Major Joseph K. Barnes.
Brigade Surgeon . . . . Major A. B. Campbell.
Adjutant . . . . Major John D. Hubbard.
Division Quartermaster . . . . Captain John W. Shaffer.
Division Commissary . . . . . Captain John W. Turner.
Aid . . . . Captain Ed. Lynde.
Aid . . . . Lieut. Col. Lanke, U. S. V.
Aid . . . . Lieut. E. W. Smith.
Aid . . . . Lieut. Samuel W Stockton.

STATISTICAL POCKET MANUAL. 9

MAJOR GENERAL EDWIN D. MORGAN.
STAFF.

Adjutant General of the State . Col. Thomas Hillhouse.
Assistant do. . . . . Col. D. Campbell.
Inspector General . . . . Col. R. M. Patrick.
Chief Engineer . . . . Col. Chester Arthur.
Judge Advocate General . . . . Col. W. H. Anthon.
Surgeon General . . . . Col. S. O. Vanderpool.
Quartermaster General . . . . . Col. C. Van Vechten.
Assistant do. . . . . Lieut. Col. C. A. Arthur.
Commissary General . . . . . . Brig. Gen. B. H. Welsh, Jr.
Assistant do. . . . . Lieut. Col. Wm. G Welch.
Paymaster General . . . . Col. T. B. Van Buren.
First Aid . . . . Capt. Thomas Arden.
Second Aid . . . . Capt. S. D. Bradford, Jr.
Third Aid . . . . Capt. E. F. Sheppard.
Volunteer Aid . . . . Capt. G. Bliss, Jr
Military Secretary . . . . Capt. J. H. Linsley.

The staff of this General has not been officially announced, and it is not known whether it differs materially or not from that of the Commander-in-Chief of the State of New York, and which we give above. The department embraces the State of New York only, and the present head-quarters is located at Albany.

ACTING MAJOR GENERAL,
BRIGADIER GENERAL DON CARLOS BUELL.
STAFF.

Assistant Adjutant General, Chief of Staff . . . . Capt. James B. Fry.
Assistant Adjutant General . . Capt. N. H. McLean.
Assistant Adjutant General . . Capt. O. D. Greene.
Assistant Adjutant General, Aid-de-Camp . . . . Capt. James M. Wright.
Aid . . . . First Lieut. C. S. Fitzhugh.
Aid . . . . First Lieut. A. W. Rockwell.
Assistant Quartermaster Gen. . Col. Thomas Swords.
Commissary . . . . Capt. H. C. Symonds.
Medical Director . . . . Major Robert Murray.
Paymaster . . . . Major Charles T. Larned.
Chief Engineer . . . . Capt. F. E. Prime.
Chief Topographical Engineer . Capt. Nathaniel Michler.
Aid . . . . Capt. Clifton Wharton.

BODY GUARD.
Captain . . . . W. J. Palmer.

This corps numbers over one hundred rank and file. Nearly every State has a representative in the guard, and, taken altogether, there is not a finer looking body of men in the service.

ACTING MAJOR GENERAL,
BRIGADIER GENERAL THOMAS W. SHERMAN.

STAFF.

Assistant Adjutant General	Capt. Louis Pelouze, Fifteenth Infantry.
Chief Quartermaster	Capt. Rufus Saxton, Assistant Quartermaster United States Army.
Assistant Quartermaster	Capt. H. A. Hascall, Assistant Quartermaster United States Army.
Assistant Quartermaster	Capt. Charles E. Fuller, Assistant Quartermaster United States Army.
Chief Commissary	Capt. Michael Morgan, Assistant Commissary of Subsistence United States Army.
Chief Engineer	Capt. Quincey A. Gilmore, United States Engineers.
First Assistant Engineer	First Lieut. John A. Tardy, Jr., United States Engineers.
Second Assistant Engineer	Second Lieut. Patrick O'Rorke, United States Engineers.
Topographical Engineer	Second Lieut. James H. Wilson, United States Engineers.
Chief of Ordnance	Capt. John McNutt, Ordnance Department United States Army.
Assistant Chief of Ordnance	First Lieut. Francis J. Shunk, Ordnance Department United States Army.
Medical Director	Surgeon George E. Cooper, United States Army Medical Department.
Signal Officer	First Lieut. Theodore L. Dumont, United States Volunteers.
Aid-de-Camp	Lieut. George Merrill, United States Volunteers.
Aid-de-Camp	Lieut. James Magner, Twenty eighth Massachusetts Volunteers.
Additional Paymaster	Major Z. K. Pangborn.
Additional Paymaster	Major J. L. Hewitt.

SIGNAL CORPS.

Chief Officer in charge, attached to the Staff of General Sherman	Lieut. Theodore L. Dumont.
Attached to the Staff of Brigadier General Viele	Lieut. E. J. Keenan.
	Lieut. O. H. Howard.
Attached to the Staff of Brigadier General Stevens	Lieut. W. L. Taft.
	Lieut. W. S. Coggswell.
Attached to the Staff of Brigadier General Wright	Lieut. H. Clay Snyder.
	Lieut. Franklin E. Town.

STATISTICAL POCKET MANUAL. 11

MAJOR GENERALS OF VOLUNTEERS.

MAJOR GENERAL LOUIS A. BLENKER.

STAFF

Assistant Adjutant General	Major Tinklemeyeo.
Aid	Col. Prince Salm Salm, of Prussia.
Aid	Major Foster.
Aid	Capt. Trzeciak.
Aid	Capt. Wiedehold.
Aid	Capt. Von Zchuschen.
Aid	Rittmeister Heintz.

MAJOR GENERAL GEORGE A. McCALL.

STAFF.

Assistant Adjutant General	Col. H. J. Biddle.
Medical Director	Major James King.
Aid	Capt. Hon. Edward McPherson.

ACTING MAJOR GENERALS.

ACTING MAJOR GENERAL, BRIGADIER GENERAL AMBROSE E. BURNSIDE.

STAFF

Assistant Adjutant General	Capt. Lewis Richmond.
Division Quartermaster	Capt. Herman Biggs.
Assist. Division Quartermaster	Capt. William Cutting.
Acting Division Commissary	Capt. E. R. Goodrich.
Medical Director, Acting Division Surgeon	Major W. H. Church, M. D.
Aid-de-Camp	Lieut. Duncan C. Pell.
Aid-de-Camp	Lieut. George R. Fearing.
Naval Officer	Com. S. F. Hazard, U. S. N.

This command forms another naval expedition similar to General Sherman's.

ACTING MAJOR GENERAL, BRIGADIER GENERAL WILLIAM B. FRANKLIN

STAFF.

Assistant Adjutant General	Capt. E. Sparrow Purdy.
Act. Assist. Adjutant General	Capt. Walworth Jenkins.
Medical Director	Major Frank H. Hamilton, M. D.
Assistant Quartermaster, Commissary	Capt. C. W. Towles, U. S. A.
Aid	Lieut. J. P. Baker, First Cavalry.

ACTING MAJOR GENERAL,
BRIGADIER GENERAL ULYSSES S. GRANT.
Staff.

Chief of Staff	Col. J. D. Webster.
Chief of Engineers	
Assistant Adjutant General	Capt. John A. Rawlings.
Chief Quartermaster	Capt. R. B. Hatch.
Chief Commissary	Capt. W. W. Leland.
Ordnance Officer	Capt. W. F. Brinck.
Medical Director	Surgeon James Simons, U. S. A.
Medical Purveyor	Asst. Sur. J. P. Taggart, U. S. A.
Paymaster	Major I. N. Cook.
Aid	Capt. Clark B. Lagow.
Aid	Capt. William S. Hillyer.
Volunteer Aid	Major John Riggin, Jr.

ACTING MAJOR GENERAL,
BRIGADIER GENERAL SILAS CASEY.
Staff.

Assistant Adjutant General	Capt. Henry W. Smith.
Aid	Lieut. E. Walter West.
Aid	Lieut. C. H. Raymond.

ACTING MAJOR GENERAL,
BRIGADIER GENERAL S. P. HEINTZELMAN.
Staff.

Assistant Adjutant General	—— ——
Quartermaster	—— ——
Medical Director	
Aid	Capt. Isaac Moses.
Aid	Capt. Leavitt Hunt.
Aid	Capt. Granville E. Johnson.

ACTING MAJOR GENERAL,
BRIGADIER GENERAL JOSEPH HOOKER.

Some changes have taken place in the staff of this division recently. We refrain from giving it until we hear from the division.

ACTING MAJOR GENERAL D. E. KEYES.
Staff.

Assistant Adjutant General	Capt. John Murray
Quartermaster	Capt. Justin Hodge.
Commissary	Capt. Woodruff.
Medical Director	Major Rauch, M. D.
Aid	Lieut. E. P. Chetwood.

ACTING MAJOR GENERAL —— LOVE.

General Love is to have the charge of the Indiana Legion as soon as it is ready for the field. His staff is not yet appointed. The Legion is to be held in reserve for any emergency that may arise in Kentucky.

ACTING MAJOR GENERAL A. D. McCOOK.
STAFF.
Assistant Adjutant General . . Capt. Daniel McCook.
Aid . . . . Capt. J. H. Gilman, U. S. A.
Surgeon . . . . —— ——

ACTING MAJOR GENERAL JOHN POPE.
STAFF.
Assistant Adjutant General . . Capt. Speed Butler.
Quartermaster . . . . —— ——
Surgeon . . . . —— ——

ACTING MAJOR GENERAL, BRIGADIER GENERAL FITZ JOHN PORTER.

The staff of this division has undergone a revision; therefore we do not publish the names until further advised.

ACTING MAJOR GENERAL, BRIGADIER GENERAL JOSEPH J. REYNOLDS.
STAFF.
Aid-de-Camp . . . . Lieut. Isaiah B. McDonald.
Assistant Adjutant General . . Capt. George S. Rose.
Assistant Quartermaster . . . . Capt. John Lovering.
Commissary of Subsistence . . Capt. William C. Tarkington.

ACTING MAJOR GENERAL W. T. SHERMAN.
STAFF.
Assistant Adjutant General . . Capt. J. W. Hammond.
Commissary . . . . Capt. George S. Roper.
Surgeon . . . . —— ——

ACTING MAJOR GENERAL FRANZ SIGEL.
STAFF.
Assistant Adjutant General . . Major Scote.
Commissary . . . . —— ——
Surgeon . . . . —— ——

ACTING MAJOR GENERAL,
BRIGADIER GENERAL CHARLES F. SMITH.
STAFF.
Assistant Adjutant General . . Capt. Thos. J. Newsham.
Aid . . . . Lieut. Price.
Surgeon . . . .
Quartermaster . . . . Capt. G. A. Pierce.

ACTING MAJOR GENERAL,
BRIGADIER GENERAL WILLIAM F. SMITH.
STAFF.
Assistant Adjutant General . . Capt. Mundee.
Surgeon . . . .
Aid . . . . Lieut. Wm. F. Burrows.
Quartermaster . . . .

ACTING MAJOR GENERAL,
BRIGADIER GENERAL CHARLES P. STONE.
STAFF.
Assistant Adjutant General . . Capt. C. Smith.
Assistant Acting Adj. Gen. . . Capt. Stewart.
Surgeon . . . .
Aid . . . . Lieut. James T. Mackie.
General Stone is under arrest.

ACTING MAJOR GENERAL,
BRIGADIER GENERAL J. B. S. TODD.
STAFF.
Assistant Adjutant General . . Capt. J. Shaw Gregory.
Surgeon . . . . Major G. H. Hubbard, M. D.
Aid . . . . Lieut. Edgertin.

VOLUNTEER FORCE.

MAJOR GENERALS OF VOLUNTEERS.

	Name.	Appointed from
1.	Banks, Nathaniel P.	Massachusetts.
2.	Blenker, Louis.	New York.
3.	Butler, Benjamin F.	Massachusetts.
4.	Dix, John A.	New York.
5.	Hunter, David.	Illinois.
6.	McCall, George A.	Pennsylvania.
7.	Morgan, Edwin D.	New York.

STATISTICAL POCKET MANUAL. 15

ACTING MAJOR GENERALS OF VOLUNTEERS.

Buell, Don Carlos.
Burnside, Ambrose E.
Franklin, Wm. B.
Grant, Ulysses S.
Heintzelman, S. P
Hooker, Josiah J.
Keyes, Erasmus D.
Love, ——.
McCook, A. D.
Pope, John.

Porter, Fitz John.
Reynolds, Joseph A.
Sherman, Thomas W.
Sherman, Wm. T.
Sigel, Franz.
Smith, Charles F.
Smith, Wm. F.
Stone, Charles P.
Todd, John B. S.

BRIGADIER GENERALS OF VOLUNTEERS.

Abercrombie, John J.
Anger, Christopher C.
Barnard, J. G.
Barry, Wm. F.
Benham, H. W.
Biddle, Charles J.
Blythe, James E.
Bohlem, ——.
Boyle, Jere. T.
Brannan, J. M.
Brooks, Wm. F. H.
Burns, ——.
Butterfield, Daniel.
Burnett, Ward B.
Carlin, W. P.
Carr, Eugene A.
Casey, Silas.
Cooper, James.
Couch, Darius N.
Cox, James D.
Crittenden, Thos. L.
Cullum, George W.
Curtis, Samuel R.
Davis, Jefferson C.
Denver, James W.
De Villiers, Charles.
Doane, ——.
Downey, Alex. C.
Duryea, Abram.
Dumont, ——.
Fitch, Graham N.
Foster, John G.
Gorman, Willis A.
Graham, Lawrence P.
Hamilton, Schuyler.
Hamilton, Charles S.
Hamilton, Frank H.
Hancock, W. S.
Hatch, John P.
Hill, ——, (not at present in service.)
Howard, O. O.

Huger, Charles C.
Hunter, Morton C.
Hurlburt, S. A., (not in service.)
Jameson, Charles D.
Johnson, Richard W.
Kearney, Philip.
Keim, Wm. H.
Kelly, Benj. F.
King, Rufus.
Lander, Fred'k W., (deceased.)
Lockwood, Henry H.
Mansfield, John L.
Martindale, John H.
Marcy, R. B.
McClernand, John A.
McKean, Thomas J.
McKinistry, Justus, (under arrest.)
Meade, George C.
Meagher, Thomas Francis.
Milroy, H. R.
Mitchell, Ormsby M.
Montgomery, Wm. R.
Morrell, George W.
Morgan, George W
Negley, J. B. S.
Nelson, Wm.
Newton, John.
Oakes, James.
Ord, Edward O C.
Oude, ——.
Paine, Eleazar A.
Palmer, J. N.
Parke, John G.
Peck, John J.
Phelps, John Wolcott.
Pope, Hamilton.
Porter, Andrew.
Prentiss, Benj. M.
Price, Thos. L., (not in service.)
Rathbone, J. F.
Reno, Jesse L.

Reynolds, John F.
Richardson, Israel B.
Robinson, John H.
Rosseau, Lovell H
Scroggs, Gustavus Adolphus.
Schenck, Robert C.
Schoepff, Alvin.
Schofield, John M.
Sedgwick, John.
Shields, James.
Sickles, Daniel E.
Simmons, S. G.
Slocum, Henry W
Sprague, William.
Stahel, Julius.
Stanley, D. S.
Stevens, Isaac I.
Stoneham, George.
Strong, Wm. K.
Sturgiss, Samuel D.
Sykes, George.
Thomas, Geo. H.
Thompson, R. W.
Thurston, Chas. L.
Turner, ——.
Van Vleit, Stewart.
Viele, Egbert L.
Von Steinwehr, Adolph.
Wade, Melancthon S.
Wadsworth, James S.
Wallace, Lewis.
Ward, Wm. T.
Williams, A. S.
Williams, Seth.
Williams, Thomas.
Wood, Thomas J.
Wright, Horatio G.
Wyman, John B.

ACTING BRIGADIER GENERALS, NOT COMMISSIONED.

Carrington, Henry B., Colonel 18th United States Infantry.
Carter, ——, Colonel commanding Tennessee troops.
Cook, John, Colonel 7th Illinois Volunteers.
Cowdin, Robert, Colonel 1st Massachusetts Volunteers.
Cruft, Chas., Colonel 31st Indiana Volunteers.
D'Utassi, Fred. George, 39th New York Volunteers.
Garfield, J. A., Colonel 42d Ohio Volunteers.
Gordon, George H., Colonel 2d Massachusetts Volunteers.
Harland, Edward, Colonel 8th Connecticut Volunteers.
Hinks, E. W., Colonel 19th Massachusetts Volunteers.
Hovey, Aldin V, Colonel 24th Indiana Volunteers.
Kelton, L. C., Colonel 9th Missouri Volunteers.
Lamon, Ward H., Virginia Cavalry.
Lane, James, Kansas Volunteers.
Leonard, Samuel H., Colonel 13th Massachusetts Volunteers.
Loan, Benj., Missouri State Militia.
Lythe, W. H., Colonel 10th Ohio Volunteers.
Manson, M. D., Colonel 10th Indiana Volunteers.
Oglesby, R. J., Colonel 8th Illinois Volunteers.
Osterhaus, ——, Missouri Volunteers.
Palmer, ——, Colonel Missouri Volunteers.
Plummer, J. B., 11th Missouri Volunteers.
Sill, Joshua A., Colonel 33d Ohio Volunteers.
Steele, Frederick, Lieutenant Colonel U. S. A.
Starr, Samuel H., Colonel 5th New Jersey Volunteers.
Sweeny, T. W., Captain U. S. A.
Taylor, Robt. T., Colonel 33d New York Volunteers.
Totten, James, Lieutenant Colonel 1st Missouri Artillery.
Turchin, J. B., Colonel 19th Illinois Volunteers.
Turner, ——, Colonel Missouri Volunteers.
Veatch, James C., Colonel 25th Indiana Volunteers.
Wallace, W. H. L., Colonel 11th Illinois Volunteers.
Weber, Max, Colonel 20th New York Volunteers.

STATISTICAL POCKET MANUAL. 17

GENERALS OF VOLUNTEERS IN COMMAND OF DEPARTMENTS.

MAJOR GENERAL NATHANIEL P. BANKS.
STAFF.

Inspector General, Chief of Staff . . . . } Major D. D. Perkins, 4th Artillery U. S. A.
Medical Director . . . . Surgeon Wm. S. King, U. S. A.
Assistant Adjutant General . . Major R. Morris Copeland, Vol.
Aid . . . . Col. John S. Clark, Vol.
Aid . . . . } Capt. William Sheffler, late of Prussia.
Aid . . . . } Capt. R. C. Shribor, late of Prussia.
Aid . . . . Capt. De Hautville, Vol.
Engineer . . . . Capt. J. W. Abert.
Topographical Engineer . . . . D. H. Strother ("Porte Crayon.")
Assistant Quartermaster . . . . Capt. S. B. Holabird, U. S. A.
Assistant Quartermaster . . . } Capt. J. D. Bingham, 2d Artillery U. S. A.
Assistant Quartermaster . . . Capt. Flagg, U. S. A.
Assistant Commissary . . . . } Capt. E. G. Beckwith, 3d Artillery U. S. A.
Assistant Commissary . . . . Capt. C. B. Penrose, Vol.
Signal Officer . . . . Lieut. W. W. Rowley, Vol.
Ordnance Officer . . . . . . Lieut. Warren Thompson, Vol.

General Banks has command of the division whose head-quarters is at Frederick, Md. The following three Generals have brigades under him, in the order in which they stand:—

BRIGADIER GENERAL J. J. ABERCROMBIE.
STAFF.

Acting Asst. Adj. General . . . Major G. B. Drake, U. S. A.
Quartermaster . . . . Lieut. Wm. U. Greer, Vol.
Commissary . . . . Lieut. J. M. Ellis, Vol.
Aid . . . . Lieut. Sam'l Appleton, Vol.
Surgeon . . . . Dr. N. R. Moseley, Vol.

BRIGADIER GENERAL CHAS. S. HAMILTON.
STAFF.

Acting Asst. Adj. General . . . Major S. H. D. Crane, Vol.
Quartermaster . . . . Lieut. S. E. Lefferts, Vol.
Assistant Commissary . . . . Lieut. Pierce, Vol.
Aid . . . . Lieut. T. J. Wildrey, Vol.
Surgeon . . . . Dr. G. L. Pancoast.

BRIGADIER GENERAL A. S. WILLIAMS.
STAFF.

Acting Asst. Adj. General . . . Capt. W. D. Wilkins.
Quartermaster . . . . Lieut. Edw. V. Preston, Vol.

Assistant Commissary . . . . . Lieut. Edgar C. Beaman, Vol.
Aid . . . . Lieut. S. E. Pitman, Vol.
Surgeon . . . . Dr. Thomas Antisel.

ACTING BRIG. GEN., COL. WM. LINN TIDBALL.
Staff.

Assistant Adjutant General . . Lieut. N. L. Jeffries.
Commissary . . . . Capt. John Hall.
Acting Aid . . . . Lieut. W. W. Kerr.

Colonel Tidball commands the Second Brigade of General Casey's division. The composition of the brigade is as follows : —

Fifty-ninth regiment N. Y. V. . Colonel Tidball.
Eighty-sixth do. do. . Colonel Bailey.
Eighty-fifth do. Pa. V. . Colonel Howell.
Ninety-third do. do. . Colonel McCarter.

ACTING BRIG. GEN., COLONEL W. W. H. DAVIS.
Staff.

Not yet received.

Colonel Davis has charge of the First Brigade to the same division.

MAJOR GENERAL BENJ. F. BUTLER.
Staff.

Assistant Adjutant General, Acting Officer of Ordnance, and Chief of Staff	Major George E. Strong.
Acting Asst. Adjutant General and Aid-de-camp	Capt. Peter Haggerty.
Aid-de-camp	Lieut. Wm. H. Wiegel.
Brigade Surgeon and Medical Director	Gilman Kimball.
Brigade Quartermaster and Assistant Quartermaster . . .	Capt. Paul R. George.
Chief of the Engineer Corps . .	Capt. J. N. Turnbull.
Chief of Artillery	Capt. George A. Kensel.
Engineer of Fortifications . . .	Moses Bates.

Recruiting Staff.*

Recruiting Officer-in-chief . . . Brig. Gen. Wm. W. Bullock.
Brigade Major and Inspector . . Solon Fisher.
Engineer . . . . Wm. J. Faulkner
Aid-de-camp . . . . John Federhen.
Inspecting Surgeon . . . . Frederick S. Ainsworth.
Lieutenant . . . . James C. Singleton.
Lieutenant . . . . Charles Franklin Jones.
Sergeant . . . . B. Frank Dexter.
Sergeant . . . . W. W. Bullock, Jr.

* This list of officers properly belongs to the Militia of Massachusetts.

STATISTICAL POCKET MANUAL. 19

BRIGADIER GENERALS.

BRIGADIER GENERAL JOHN J. ABERCROMBIE.
STAFF.
Assistant Adjutant General . . Capt. Chappen.
Quartermaster . . . . Lieut. D. W. Keyes.
Brigade Surgeon . . . . Capt. J. H. Baxter, M. D.
Aid . . . . Lieut. Matthews.

General Abercrombie's brigade is the second in the division under General Banks.

BRIGADIER GENERAL JOHN H. MARTINDALE.
STAFF.
Assistant Adjutant General . . Capt. Charles J. Powers.
Aid . . . . Lieut. John Williams.

General Martindale's brigade forms a portion of one of the divisions of General McClellan's grand army before Washington.

BRIGADIER GENERAL JOHN A. McCLERNAND.
STAFF.
Assistant Adjutant General . . Capt. M. Brayman.
Quartermaster . . . . Capt. Dunlap.
Medical Director . . . . Dr. Simmous.
Associate Director . . . . Dr. Brenton.
Hospital Surgeon . . . . Capt. J. S. Young, M. D.
Commissary . . . . Capt. Spencer C. Benham.
First Aid . . . . Capt. Dresser.
Second Aid . . . . Lieut. C. S. Cooper.

BRIGADIER GENERAL EGBERT L. VIELE, U. S. A.
STAFF.
Acting Assist. Adjutant General Capt. Pierre C. Kane.
Brigade Quartermaster . . . .
Assistaut Commissary General Capt. Gideon Seull.
Brigade Surgeon . . . . Major J. C. D. Dalton. Jr.
Aid-de-Camp . . . . Capt. C. H. Farrell.
Aid-de-Camp . . . . Lieut. J. D. Gould.
Aid-de-Camp . . . . Lieut. Davis.

BRIGADIER GENERAL HORATIO G. WRIGHT.
STAFF.
Assistant Adjutant General . . Capt. C. W. Foster.
Assist. Quartermaster General . Capt. H. P. Goodrich.
Assistant Commissary General Capt. Abijah Keith.
Brigade Surgeon . . . . Major Craven.
Aid . . . . Lieut. J. Stotler.
Aid . . . . Lieut. T. L. Nayden.

BRIGADIER GENERAL JOHN M. SCHOFIELD.
Staff.

Assistant Adjutant General . . Major Henry Hiscock.
Acting Inspector General at St. Joseph . . . . } Capt. Thomas B. Biggers.
Acting Assistant Quartermaster at St. Joseph . . . . . . } T. W. Southack.
Aid-de-Camp . . . . Major Henry L. McConnell.
Aid-de-Camp . . . . Major John F. Tyler.

BRIGADIER GENERAL GEORGE W. MORELL.
Staff.

Assistant Adjutant General . . Capt. Richard T. Auchmuty.
Commissary . . . . Capt. Samuel McKelvey.
Quartermaster . . . . Capt. George N. Smith.
Aid-de-Camp . . . . Lieut. J. Elliott Williams.
Aid-de-Camp . . . . Lieut. Isaac Seymour, Jr.
Brigade Surgeon . . . . Dr. W. E. Waters.

BRIGADIER GENERAL H. W. BENHAM.
Staff.

Acting Assist. Adjutant General Lieut. J. O. Strange.
Acting Quartermaster . . . . . Lieut. Hawkes.
Commissary . . . . Capt. W. L. Mallory.
Brigade Surgeon . . . . Capt. George Schumard, M. D.
Aid . . . . Lieut. S. P. Warren.

BRIGADIER GENERAL JOHN J. PECK.
Staff.

Assistant Adjutant General . . Capt. William H. Morris.
Surgeon . . . . Capt. T. R. Spencer, M. D.
Commissary of Subsistence . . Capt. M. J. Green.
Acting Aid . . . . Lieut. Charles R. Sterling.

BRIGADIER GENERAL O. O. HOWARD.
Staff.

Assistant Adjutant General . . Capt. Frederick D. Sewell.
Quartermaster . . . .
Senior Aid . . . . Capt. Nelson A. Miles.
Surgeon . . . .

BRIGADIER GENERAL JOHN W. PHELPS.
Staff.

Assistant Adjutant General . . Capt. Hiram Stevens.
Commissary . . . . Capt. Bowdish.
Brigade Surgeon . . . . Capt. Josiah Curtis, M. D.
Aid . . . . Capt. Christian T. Christensen.

BRIGADIER GENERAL ISAAC I. STEVENS.
STAFF
Assistant Adjutant General . . Capt. Stevens, (son of Gen.)
Assist. Quartermaster General . Capt. William Lilley.
Assistant Commissary General Capt. L. A. Warfield.
Surgeon . . . . Dr. George S. Kemble.

BRIGADIER GENERAL LEWIS WALLACE.
STAFF.
Assistant Adjutant General . . Capt. Frederick Krepler.
Commissary . . . . Robert H. Bryant.
Surgeon . . . . Capt. Thomas W. Fry, M. D.
Aid . . . . Capt. Edwin R. Lewis.

BRIGADIER GENERAL SAMUEL R. CURTIS.
STAFF.
Assistant Adjutant General . . Capt. F. F. Burlock.
Acting Assist. Adjutant General and Aid-de-Camp . . . } Major N. P. Shipman.
Assistant Quartermaster . . . . Capt. P. T. Turnley.

BRIGADIER GENERAL J. D. COX.
STAFF.
Acting Assist. Adjutant General Lieut. James W. Conine.
Commissary . . . . Capt. Ira Gibbs.
Quartermaster . . . . Capt. M. D. W. Loomis.
Aid . . . . Lieut. Christy.

BRIGADIER GENERAL LAWRENCE P. GRAHAM.
STAFF.
Assistant Adjutant General . . Capt. Augustus Wroan.
Quartermaster . . . .
Aid . . . . Lieut. William D. Morton.
Surgeon . . . .

BRIGADIER GENERAL JOHN G. FOSTER.
STAFF.
Assistant Adjutant General . . Capt. Charles F. Hoffman.
Quartermaster . . . . Capt. Daniel Messenger.
Surgeon . . . . Capt. A. Hitchcock, M. D.

BRIGADIER GENERAL WILLIS A. GORMAN.
STAFF.
Assistant Adjutant General . . Capt. Daniel Hibberd.
Quartermaster . . . . Capt. G. N. Woods.
Aid . . . . Capt. Andrew Levering.

BRIGADIER GENERAL ABRAM DURYEE.
STAFF.
Assistant Adjutant General . . Capt. William Von Dohn.
Surgeon . . . . —— ——
Quartermaster . . . . —— ——

BRIGADIER GENERAL W. P. CARLIN.
STAFF.
Acting Assist. Adjutant General A. L. Bailhache.
Brigade Surgeon . . . . Capt. Casselbury, M. D.
Quartermaster . . . . —— ——

BRIGADIER GENERAL EUGENE A. CARR.
STAFF.
Assistant Adjutant General . . Col. Louis D. Hubbard.
Surgeon . . . . Capt. William Thomas, M. D.
Quartermaster . . . . Capt. Byron O. Carr.

BRIGADIER GENERAL DARIUS N. COUCH.
STAFF.
Assistant Adjutant General . . —— ——
Aid . . . . Capt. Hon. James Buffington.
Surgeon . . . . —— ——

BRIGADIER GENERAL JOHN B. WYMAN.
STAFF.
Assistant Adjutant General . . —— ——
Acting Assist. Quartermaster, } Capt. M. P. Small.
  Commissary of Subsistence }

BRIGADIER GENERAL THOMAS L. PRICE.
STAFF.
Assistant Adjutant General . . Capt. John Pound, U. S. A.
Surgeon . . . . —— ——
Aid . . . . Capt. Eno.

BRIGADIER GENERAL J. N. PALMER.
STAFF.
Assistant Adjutant General . . Capt. Nathan Reeve.
Acting Assist. Adjutant General Lieut. William A. Scott.
Aid . . . . Lieut. Childs.

BRIGADIER GENERAL J. S. NEGLEY.
STAFF.
Assistant Adjutant General . . —— ——
Aid . . . . Capt. Henry L. Vancleire.
Aid . . . . Lieut. Miller.

BRIGADIER GENERAL BEN. T. KELLEY.
STAFF.

Assistant Adjutant General . . Capt. Ben. T. Hawkes.
Brigade Inspector . . . . Col. George H. Crossman.
Aid . . . . Major Frothingham.

BRIGADIER GENERAL WINFIELD S. HANCOCK.
STAFF.

Assistant Adjutant General . . Capt. John Hancock.
Surgeon . . . .
Quartermaster . . . .

BRIGADIER GENERAL BENJ. M. PRENTISS.
STAFF.

Assistant Adjutant General . . Capt. Henry Binmore.
Aid . . . . Major Benjamin H. Grierson.
Aid . . . . Lieut. R. G. Jones.

BRIGADIER GENERAL HENRY W. SLOCUM.
STAFF.

Assistant Adjutant General . . Capt. James Howland.
Surgeon . . . . Capt. S. L. Herrick, M. D.
Assistant Surgeon . . . . Capt. George Buer.

BRIGADIER GENERAL WILLIAM NELSON.
STAFF.

Assistant Adjutant General . .
Brigade Surgeon . . . . Major Bradford.

BRIGADIER GENERAL E. DUMONT.
STAFF.

Assistant Adjutant General . . Capt. Ferry.
Aid . . . . Capt. Blair.

BRIGADIER GENERAL SILAS CASEY.
STAFF.

Assistant Adjutant General . . Capt. Henry W. Smith.
Commissary . . . . Capt. John Hall.

BRIGADIER GENERAL W. R. MONTGOMERY.
STAFF.

Assistant Adjutant General . . Capt. Jacob R. Wilson.
Aid . . . . Lieut. Freese

BRIGADIER GENERAL FRANK H. HAMILTON.
STAFF.
Assistant Adjutant General . . —— ——
Surgeon . . . . Alexander N. Dougherty.

BRIGADIER GENERAL PHILIP KEARNEY.
STAFF.
Assistant Adjutant General . . —— ——
Surgeon . . . . Capt. J. C. Dalton, M. D.

BRIGADIER GENERAL —— TURNER.
STAFF.
Assistant Adjutant General . . —— ——
Aid . . . . Lieut. F. Deweese.

BRIGADIER GENERAL A. S. WILLIAMS.
STAFF.
Assistant Adjutant General . . Capt. Wm. D. Wilkins.
Quartermaster . . . . Capt. Henry M. Whittlesey.

BRIGADIER GENERAL MELANCTHON S. WADE.
STAFF.
Assistant Adjutant General . . Capt. Andrew C. Kemper.

BRIGADIER GENERAL JAMES S. WADSWORTH.

BRIGADIER GENERAL THOMAS J. WOOD.
STAFF.
Assistant Adjutant General . . Capt. Wm. H. Scheater.
Acting Asst. Adj. General . . . Lieut. Geo. W. Leonard.

BRIGADIER GENERAL FRED'K W. LANDER.
STAFF.
Assistant Adjutant General . . Capt. Candla.
Aid . . . . Lieut. George H. Butler.

BRIGADIER GENERAL —— DOANE.
STAFF.
Assistant Adjutant General . . Major Samuel C. Ellis.
Brigade Inspector . . . . Major John Hill.

BRIGADIER GENERAL THOMAS WILLIAMS.
STAFF.
Assistant Adjutant General . . —— ——
Aid . . . . Lieut. George C. D. Kay.

BRIGADIER GENERAL ELEAZAR A. PAINE.
STAFF.
Assistant Adjutant General . . Capt. Leonard Scott.
Surgeon . . . . —

BRIGADIER GENERAL RICHARD W. JOHNSON.
STAFF.
Assistant Adjutant General . Capt. Henry Clay.
Aid. . . . . Lieut. Thos. Johnson.

BRIGADIER GENERAL R. H. MILROY.
STAFF.
Assistant Adjutant General . . Capt. W. G. George.
Aid. . . . . Lieut. Zeb. Baird.

BRIGADIER GENERAL ANDREW PORTER.
STAFF.
Assistant Adjutant General . . Lieut. James McMillan.
Surgeon . . . . Capt. W D. Stewart, M. D.

BRIGADIER GENERAL EDWARD O. C. ORD.
STAFF.
Assistant Adjutant General . . Capt. Placidus Ord.
Quartermaster . . . . Capt. Anson Stager.

BRIGADIER GENERAL DANIEL BUTTERFIELD
STAFF.
Assistant Adjutant General . . Capt. Thomas J. Hoyt.

BRIGADIER GENERAL WILLIAM W. BURNS.
STAFF.
Assistant Adjutant General . . Capt. George A. Hicks.

BRIGADIER GENERAL JAMES W. DENVER.
STAFF.
Acting Asst. Adj. General . . . Capt. F. Clarke.

BRIGADIER GENERAL C. D. JAMESON.
STAFF.
Assistant Adjutant General . Capt. Corall N. Porter.

BRIGADIER GENERAL GEORGE STONEMAN.
STAFF.
Aid. . . . . Lieut. A. V. Sumner, Jr.

BRIGADIER GENERAL GEORGE H. THOMAS.
STAFF.
Assistant Adjutant General . . Capt. George G. Flint.

BRIGADIER GENERAL D. S. STANLEY.
STAFF.
Assistant Adjutant General . . Capt. George D. Kellogg.

BRIGADIER GENERAL JOHN F. REYNOLDS.
STAFF.
Assistant Adjutant General . . Capt. Charles Kingsbury.

BRIGADIER GENERAL ALVIN SCHOEPFF.
STAFF.
Assistant Adjutant General . . Major Helveti.

BRIGADIER GENERAL WILLIAM F. H. BROOKS.
STAFF.
Assistant Adjutant General . . Capt. Theodore Reed.

BRIGADIER GENERAL GEORGE SYKES.
STAFF.
Assistant Adjutant General . . Capt. J. P. Drouillard.

BRIGADIER GENERAL GEORGE C. MEADE.
STAFF.
Assistant Adjutant General . . Edward C. Baird.

BRIGADIER GENERAL DANIEL E. SICKLES.
STAFF.
Assistant Adjutant General . . Capt. J. H. Liebeneau.

BRIGADIER GENERAL JOHN SEDGWICK.
STAFF.
Assistant Adjutant General . . Capt. Wm. D. Sedgwick.

BRIGADIER GENERAL LOVELL H. ROSSEAU.
STAFF.
Assistant Adjutant General   Capt. Henry Clay McDowell.

BRIGADIER GENERAL JOHN NEWTON.
STAFF.
Assistant Adjutant General . . Capt. James E. Montgomery.

BRIGADIER GENERAL ROBERT C. SCHENCK.
STAFF.
Assistant Adjutant General . . Capt. Donn Piatt.

ACTING GENERALS.
ACTING GENERAL A. ASBOTH.
ACTING BRIG. GEN., COLONEL JAMES LANE.
STAFF.
Assistant Adjutant General . . Capt. T. J. Weed.
Quartermaster . . . . Capt. M. H. Insley.
Commissary . . . . Capt. A. C. Wilder.
Paymaster . . . . Capt. H. J. Adams.
Paymaster . . . . Capt. W W Updegraff.
Surgeon . . . . Capt. R. Gilpatrick, M. D.
Engineer . . . . Lieut. T. T. Anderson.
Military Secretary . . . . Lieut. H. Gray Loring.
Aid . . . . Lieut. R. H. Kerr.
Aid . . . . Lieut. Lyman Scott.
Wagon Master . . . . Gen. J. N. McCall.

ACTING BRIG. GEN., COL. ALDIN P. HOVEY.
STAFF.
Assistant Adjutant General . . Capt. Richard F. Bester.
Commissary . . . . Lieut. Mon. P. Schmuck.
Assistant Commissary . . . . . Lieut. Flem. Dunham.

ACTING BRIG GEN., COL. J. A. GARFIELD.
STAFF
Acting Asst. Adj. General . . . ———
Acting Quartermaster . . . . . Capt. Ralph Plumb.
Acting Commissary . . . . . . Capt. Jacob Heaton.

ACTING BRIG. GEN., COLONEL ——— TURNER.
STAFF.
Assistant Adjutant General . . ———
Aid . . . . Lieut. Deweese.

ACTING BRIG. GEN., COLONEL. E. W. HINKS.
STAFF.
Assistant Adjutant General   Capt. Chadwick.

There may have been, and doubtless are, several officers who have acted as temporary generals, whose names are not recorded, in consequence of the information not having reached us. We have made the list as complete as possible with the data we have already collected.

BURNSIDE EXPEDITION.

The following is a full statement of the force of the Burnside Expedition:—

BRIGADIER GENERAL COMMANDING,
AMBROSE E. BURNSIDE.

STAFF.

Assistant Adjutant General . . Capt. Lewis Richmond.
Division Quartermaster . . . . Capt. Herman Biggs.
Assistant Quartermaster . . . . Capt. T. C. Slaight.
Commissary of Subsistence . . Capt. E. R. Goodrich.
Assist. Commis. of Subsistence Capt. William Cutting.
Ordnance Officer . . . . Lieut. D H. Plagler.
Division Surgeon . . . . Major W H Church.
Aid-de-Camp . . . . Lieut. Duncan C. Pell.
Aid-de-Camp . . . . Lieut. George Fearing.

FIRST BRIGADE—GEN. JOHN C. FOSTER.

STAFF.

Assistant Adjutant General . . Capt. S. Hoffman.
Brigade Quartermaster . . . . Capt. David Messenger.
Commissary of Subsistence . . Capt. E. E. Potter.
Aid-de-Camp . . . . Capt. P. W. Hudson.
Volunteer Aid . . . . Lieut. E. N. Strong.
Volunteer Aid . . . . Lieut. G. N. Pendleton.
Volunteer Aid . . . . Lieut. Anderson.

REGIMENTS.

Twenty-fifth Massachusetts.   Tenth Connecticut.
Twenty-third Massachusetts.   Twenty-fourth Massachusetts.
Twenty-seventh Massachusetts.

SECOND BRIGADE—GEN. JESSE L. RENO.

STAFF.

Assistant Adjutant General . . Capt. E. M. Neill.
Brigade Quartermaster . . . . Capt. C. G. Loring.
Aid-de-Camp . . . . Lieut. John A. Morris.
Aid-de-Camp . . . . Lieut. B. F. Reno.

REGIMENTS.

Fifty-first New York.   Sixth New Hampshire.
Fifty-first Pennsylvania.   Ninth New Jersey.
Twenty-first Massachusetts.

THIRD BRIGADE—GEN. JOHN G. PARKE.

STAFF.

Assistant Adjutant General . . Capt. C. T. Gardner.
Aid-de-Camp . . . . Lieut. M. A. Hill.
Volunteer Aid . . . . Lieut. Philip Lyding.

STATISTICAL POCKET MANUAL. 29

REGIMENTS.

Eighth Connecticut.
Eleventh Connecticut.
Fifty third New York.
Fifth Rhode Island, (battalion.)
Fourth Rhode Island.
Eighty-ninth New York.

It is proper to state that the staff officers of Generals Reno and Parke are not yet all appointed, and the staffs are therefore incomplete. We give all that are known at the present time.

REGIMENTAL ROSTERS.

TWENTY-FIFTH MASSACHUSETTS.

Colonel, Edwin Upton; Lieutenant Colonel, A. B. R. Sprague; Major, M. J. McCafferty; Quartermaster, William O. Brown; Surgeon, J. M. Rice; Assistant Surgeon, Therou Semple.

Co.	Captains.	First Lieuts.	Second Lieuts.
A	J. Pickets	T. E. Goodman	M. B. Bassy.
B	W. Clark	William Emery	W. F. Draper.
C	C. A. Atwood	James Tucker	M. F. Prouty.
D	A. H. Foster	G. S. Campbell	G. H. Spaulding.
E	Thomas O'Neill	William Daly	H. McConville.
F	G. H. Foss	L. Lawrence	J. H. Richardson.
G	Lewis Wagely	H. M. Richter	F. R. Wiegand.
H	O. Moulton	D. M. Woodward	N. H. Foster.
I	O. P. Parkhurst	James B. Smith	A. Buffam.
K	J. W. Denny	S. Harrington	J. M. Drennan.

TWENTY-THIRD MASSACHUSETTS.

Colonel, John Kurtz; Lieutenant Colonel, Henry Merritt; Major, A. Elwell; Adjutant, John G. Chambers; Quartermaster, J. A. Goldthwaits; Surgeon, George Derby; Assistant Surgeon, S. E. Stone; Chaplain, J. B. Clark.

Co.	Captains.	First Lieuts.	Second Lieuts.
A	E. A. Brewster	C. S. Emmerton	G. A. Fisher.
B	K. V. Martin	T. Russell	J. Goodwin, Jr
C	A. Center	E. A. Story	Fitz J. Babson.
D	C. Howland	S. E. Hart	Anthony Lang
E	W. B. Alexander	O. Rogers	T. B. Atwood.
F	G. M. Whipple	C. H. Bates	G. R. Emmerton.
G	J. W. Raymond	N. T. Woodbury	D. W. Hammond.
H	W. C. Sawyer	William L. Kent	P. H. Niles.
I	J. Hobbs	W. J. Creary	D. P. Muzzey.
K	C. A. Hart	J. Littlefield	B. F. Barnard.

TWENTY-SEVENTH MASSACHUSETTS.

Colonel, Horace C. Lee; Lieutenant Colonel, Luke Lyman; Major, W. G. Bartholomew; Adjutant, George W. Bartlett; Quartermaster, ———; Surgeon, George A. Otis; Assistant Surgeon, Samuel Camp; Chaplain, Miles Sanford.

Co.	Captains.	First Lieuts.	Second Lieuts.
A	I. C. Vance	M. H. Spaulding	E. Clark.
B	A. W. Caswell	P. W. McManus	L. H. Horton.
C	W. A. Walker	J. H. Nutting	William F. Bassett.
D	T. W. Sloan	A. R. Dennison	J. P. Atcheson.

Co.	Captains.	First Lieuts.	Second Lieuts.
E	G. A. Fuller	J. W. Trafton	L. Bradley.
F	L. F. Thayer	John W. Moore	James H. Fowler.
G	R. R. Swift	P. S. Bailey	F. C. Wright.
H	C. D. Sanford	W. H. H. Briggs	— —
I	H. A. Hubbard	E. K. Wilson	C. A. Goodale.
K	H. H. Coolsey	George Warner	W. C. Hunt.

TENTH CONNECTICUT.

Colonel, Charles L. Russell; Lieutenant Colonel, A. W. Drake; Major, J. W. Pettibone; Adjutant, H C. Pardee; Quartermaster, B. A. Fowler; Surgeon, A. P. Douglass; Assistant Surgeon, M T. Newton; Chaplain, H. L. Hall.

Co.	Captains.	First Lieuts.	Second Lieuts.
A	B. S. Pardy	— Wiley	H. M. Stillman.
B	J. L. Otis	— Jennings	— Palmer.
C	E. D. S. Goodyear	— Hurlbut	G. M. Kew.
D	George M. Coit	C. C. Brewster	— Kingsbury.
E	Henry A. Wells	C. Gatewood	John C. Coffing.
F	J. W. Branch	T. R. Mead	W. W. Perkins.
G	J. L. Hoyt	H. Quinn	H. W. Camp.
H	R. Leggett	J. O. Close	S. M. Smith.
I	O. M. Mead	G. W. Atherton	— —
K	B. Jepson	— —	— —

TWENTY-FOURTH MASSACHUSETTS.

Colonel, Thomas G. Stevenson; Lieutenant Colonel, F. A. Osborn; Major, B. H. Stevenson; Adjutant, N. L. Horton; Quartermaster, N. L. Hutchings; Surgeon, Samuel A. Greene; Assistant Surgeon, Hall Curtis; Chaplain, W. R. G. Mellen.

Co.	Captains.	First Lieuts.	Second Lieuts.
A	C. G. Hooper	G. M. Gardner	W. L. Horton.
B	W. F. Reading	C. B. Amory	Thos. L. Edmonds.
C	E. C. Richardson	J. B. Ball	John C. James, Jr.
D	J. C. Maker	Charles A. Folsom	A. S. Barstow.
E	J. F. Prince, Jr.	J. B. Nichols	D. T. Sargent.
F	George T. Austin	J. A. Partridge	C. S. Ward.
G	R. F. Clark	A. Ordway	T. M. Sweet.
H	J. L. Stackpole	James A. Perkins	J. M. Barnard.
I	J. Deland	J. H. Turner	H. D. Jarvis.
K	William Pratt	M. A. Rice	D. Jarvis, Jr.

TWENTY-FIRST MASSACHUSETTS.

Colonel, Augustus Morse; Lieutenant Colonel, Albert G. Maggi; Major, William S. Clark; Adjutant, T. C. Hall; Quartermaster, G. F. Thompson; Surgeon, C. Cutter; Assistant Surgeon, O. Warren; Chaplain, G. S. Ball.

Co.	Captains.	First Lieuts.	Second Lieuts.
A	Geo. T. Hawkes	C. W. Davis	J. Brooks, Jr.
B	C. W. Walcott	W. Willard	J. N. Hopkins.
C	J. M. Richardson	W. T. Harlow	J. J. Kelton.
D	T. S. Foster	Charles Barker	E. T. Hayward.
E	P. Bradford	S. Hovey, Jr.	W. Whittemore.
F	B. F. Rogers	A. P. Dawes	S. A. Taylor.
G	A. A. Walker	J. D. Frozier	S. C. Shumway.
H	J. P. Rice	F. A. Stearns	J. W. Fletcher.

STATISTICAL POCKET MANUAL. 31

Co.	Captains.	First Lieuts.	Second Lieuts.
I	H. Richardson	M. Parkhurst	—
K	O. W. Washburn	S. O. DeForest	J. B. Williams.

FIFTY-FIRST NEW YORK.

Colonel, Edward Ferero; Lieutenant Colonel, R. B. Potter; Major, Charles W. Le Gendre; Adjutant, A. J. Dayton; Quartermaster, D. H. Horton; Surgeon, E. N. Brick; Assistant Surgeon, J. L. Dodge; Chaplain, O. N. Benton.

Co.	Captains.	First Lieuts.	Second Lieuts.
A	W. Hazard	H. W. Francis	Thomas B. Marsh.
B	M. C. Mitchell	H. H. Holbrook	A. W. McKee.
C	J. S. Wright	W. N. Chapman	G. H. McKibben.
D	Samuel H. Sims	William Cuff	W. H. Leonard.
E	S. W. Chase	George D. Allen	W. H. Barker.
F	J. Stewart	James J. Johnston	John T. Rapelje.
G	George W. Merritt	David F. Wright	Frank W. Tryon.
H	W. D. Campbell	James M. Miller	C. G. Coddington.
I	Thomas Phillips	George A. Porter	L. O. Goodridge.
K	D. R. Johnson	A. L. Fowler	C. F. Springweller.

FIFTY-FIRST PENNSYLVANIA.

Colonel, J. F. Hartsauft; Lieutenant Colonel, T. S. Bell; Major, E. Schall; Adjutant, D. P. Bible; Quartermaster, J. J. Friedley; Surgeon, J. P. Hosack; Assistant Surgeon, J. D. Noble; Chaplain, D. G. Mallory.

Co.	Captains.	First Lieuts.	Second Lieuts.
A	W. G. Bolton	J. J. Bolton	A. Ostlip.
B	F. W. Bell	J. H. Genther	D. Nicholas.
C	W. Allabaugh	D. Himsicker	Thomas R. Lynch.
D	Edwin Schall	Lewis Hallman	S. Fair.
E	G. H. Hassenplug	J. A. Morris	W. R. Foster.
F	R. E. Taylor	L. S. Hart	J. C. Reed.
G	A. B. Snyder	W. H. Blair	P. A. Gamlin.
H	J. M. Liner	George Sharkley	J. G. Beaver.
I	J. E. Peechin	George W. Bisbing	George Schall.
K	J. E. Titus	J. Kelley	J. F. Beale.

NINTH NEW JERSEY.

Colonel, Joseph W. Allen; Lieutenant Colonel, C. H. Heckman; Major, James Wilson; Adjutant, A. Zabriskie; Quartermaster, Samuel Keyes; Surgeon, J. W. Weller; Assistant Surgeon, R. Brown. Chaplain, T. Drum.

Co.	Captains.	First Lieuts.	Second Lieuts.
A	F. Hayes	F. Felger	S. Wilburn.
B	C. Castner	L. Bartholomew	C. H. Scofield.
C	C. P. Hopkinson	E. Harris	T. Clift.
D	T. Middleton	George Irons	E. Kissem.
E	W. De Hart	H. Able	A. Beach.
F	W. B. Curtis	Aug. Thompson	J. V. Gibson.
G	G. P. Ritter	W. Zimmermann	C. W. Benton.
H	J. J. Henry	T. Stewart, Jr.	J. Lawrence.
I	H. T. Chew	S. Hufty	C. Pinker.
K	E. G. Drake	W. Arbuthnap	W. Townley.
L	C. Erbe	— Einholt	— Adler.
M	J. M. McChesney	T. Smith	A. Cause.

SIXTH NEW HAMPSHIRE.

Colonel, Nelson Converse; Lieutenant Colonel, S. G. Griffin; Major, Charles Scott; Adjutant, P. P. Bixley; Quartermaster, Alonzo Nute; Surgeon, Dr. Tracy; Assistant Surgeon, Dr Cooper; Chaplain, R. Stinson.

Co.	Captains.	First Lieuts.	Second Lieuts.
A	Joseph Clark	O. H. P. Craig	T. P. Cheney.
B	S. P. Adams	A. J. Roberts	S. G. Goodwin.
C	H. H. C. Pearson	D. A. Titcomb	J. P. Brooks.
D	S. D. Quarles	J. N. Jones	A. W. Haynes.
E	O. G. Dart	J. A. Cummings	G. H. Muchmore.
F	G. C. Starkweather	A. D. Combs	John S. Adams.
G	J. W. Putnam	E. D. Comings	C. Y. Gardner.
H	J. B. Saunders	A. J. Sites	Eli Wentworth.
I	Robert L. Ela	T. T. Morse	H. T. Dudley.
K	E. H. Converse	J. Whiting	C. L. Fuller.

EIGHTH CONNECTICUT.

Colonel, Edward Hartland; Lieutenant Colonel, P. L. Cunningham; Major, A. Perry; Adjutant, Charles M. Coit; Quartermaster, J. W. Alexander; Surgeon, M. Storrs; Chaplain, J. J. Woolley; Assistant Surgeons, D. W. C. Lathrop, J. V. Harrington.

Co.	Captains.	First Lieuts.	Second Lieuts.
A	H. H. Binpee	H. M. Hoyt	W. P. Marsh.
B	P. R. Ruth	A. W. Scott	F. D. Loomis.
C	Charles W. Nash	S. Glasson	R. H. Burnside.
D	J. C. Ward	James R. Moon	C. A. Breed.
E	M. B. Smith	H. N. Place	L. Wadhams.
F	E. Y. Smith	E. G. Main	J. E. Shepherd.
G	H. Appleman	T. G. Sheffield	H. E. Morgan.
H	D. Fowler	J. L. Russell	T. S. Weed
I	F. W. Jackson	W. J. Roberts	F. E. Nearing
K	C. L. Upham	N. G. Ives	R. M. Food.

ELEVENTH CONNECTICUT.

Colonel, T. H. C. Kingsbury; Lieutenant Colonel, Charles Matthewson; Major, G. A. Stedman; Adjutant, J. E. Lewis; Quartermaster, H. W. Richmond; Surgeon, James Whitcomb; Assistant Surgeon, Charles Rogers; Chaplain, Rev. Mr. Soule.

Co.	Captains.	First Lieuts.	Second Lieuts.
A	G. M. Southmaid	S. G. Bailey	O H. White.
B	G. D. Johnson	William Horton	J. H. Convers.
C	W. Meagling	N. Dietriech	F. Schlachter.
D	E. L. Lee	C. L. Hosford	H. S. Marshall.
E	J. H. Dewell	J. M. Pierpont	S. C. Barnum.
F	W. C. Clapp	J. Ries	J. Randall.
G	William Hyde	F. M. Sprague	M. P. Bray.
H	A. D. Daniels	J. H. Norris	S. W. Warner.
I	John Griswold	P. C. Cummings	William Sackett.
K	C. S. D. Dennison	J. A. Shipman	W. A. Boyce.

NINTH NEW YORK, (HAWKINS'S ZOUAVES.)

Colonel, Rush C. Hawkins; Lieutenant Colonel, George F. Betts; Major, Edgar A. Kimball; Chaplain, Rev. Thomas W. Conway; Adjutant, James W Evans; Quartermaster, Henry H.

Elliott, Jr.; Surgeon, George H. Humphreys; Assistant Surgeon, John P. P. White.

Co.	Captains.	Lieutenants.	Ensigns.
A	A. S. Graham	Charles Childs	T. S. Bartholomew.
B	W. G. Barnett	Geo. A. C. Barnett	John K. Perley.
C	Otto W. Parisen	William H. Ennis	James H. Fleming.
D	A. De Baire	John S. Harrison	James A. Greene.
E	W. W. Hammell	Henry C. Perley	Wm. S. Andrews.
F	Edward Jardine	Almar P. Webster	Robt. McKechnie.
G	J. C. Rodiques	Lawrence Lehay	Geo. W. Debevoise.
H	C. W. Prescott	Frank Silva	Edward C. Cooper
I	Leon Barnard	Wm. H. Rossell	Richard Burdett.
K	J. R. Whiting, Jr.	Richard H. Morris	George H. Herbert.
		Victor Klugsoehr.	

FOURTH RHODE ISLAND.

Colonel, J. P. Rodman; Lieutenant Colonel, G. W. Tew; Major, J. A. Allen; Adjutant, J. Y. Curtis; Quartermaster, C. S. Smith; Surgeon, H. W. Rives; Assistant Surgeon, R. Millar; Chaplain, A. B. Flanders.

Co.	Captains.	First Lieuts.	Second Lieuts.
A	J. Brown	Charles Johnson	J. W. Lyons.
B	M. P. Buffum	C. H. Greene	A. H. Burdick.
C	H. Simons	C. J. Capdore	E. Joslyn.
D	N. Kenyon	W. A. Read	O. A. Baker.
E	W. S. Chase	J. T. P. Bucklin	G. T. Crowninshield
F	L. E. Kent	W. F. Hall	G. E. Curtis.
G	J. M. Hopkins	C. W. Monroe	J. S. Smith.
H	C. Tillinghast	C. F. Bowen	F. W. Harback.
I	E. E. Lapham	E. W. West	Z. B. Smith.
K	W. C. Wood	F. A. Chase	H. L. Starkweather.

FIFTH RHODE ISLAND BATTALION.

Major, Job Wright; Adjutant, Charles H. Chapman; Quartermaster, M. Gladding; Assistant Surgeon, A. Potter; Chaplain, W. B. Noyes.

Co.	Captains.	First Lieuts.	Second Lieuts.
A	J. Wheeler	D. S. Remington	W. W. Douglas.
B	A. G. Wright	W. A. Hall	G. G. Hopkins.
C	J. M. Eddy	John C. Snow	J. Moran.
D	George H. Grant	H. R. Pearce	J. M. Wheaton.
E	Job Arnold		

EIGHTY-NINTH NEW YORK.

Colonel, H. S. Fairchild; Lieutenant Colonel, J. C. Robie; Major, D. T. Everts; Adjutant, J. E. Shepherd; Quartermaster, C. H. Webster; Surgeon, T. H. Squire; Assistant Surgeon, W. H. Smith; Chaplain, N. E. Pierson.

Co.	Captains.	First Lieuts.	Second Lieuts.
A	N. Coryell	F. Burt	W. A. Cahill.
B	J. B. Hagley	Henry Pratt	C. J. Read.
C	C. W. Burt	N. A. Newton	H. C. Rome.
D	J. Morrison	A. M. Bingham	W. N. Benedict.
E	S. L. Judd	W. M. Lewis	F. Davenport.
F	J. B. Vaname	E. M. Bloomer	A. Morris.
G	W. B. Guernsey	M. Ruffer	J. S. Ronk.

Co.	Captains.	First Lieuts.	Second Lieuts.
H	R. Brown	J. M. Remington	F. W. Tremain.
I	T. L. Jugland	George Ballou	— —
K	—	R. P. Cormack	— —

BATTERY F—RHODE ISLAND BRIGADE.

Captain, Charles Belgier; 156 men; 120 horses; 4 10-pounder Parrott guns; 2 12-pounder field howitzers.

THE EXPEDITIONARY VESSELS.

The transport fleet, which rendezvoused at Annapolis, consisted of upwards of fifty-five vessels, ranging in class from the small steam-tug to the huge side-wheel steamer, and from the diminutive schooner to as sturdy a ship as ever sailed under canvas. The tonnage of the fleet ranges from 100 to 1200 tons, and the draft of the vessels from three to eleven feet. The number of vessels of each class in the fleet is as follows:—

Steamers	11	Brig	1
Propellers, (gunboats,)	9	Schooners	21
Ships	4	Barges	—
Barks	4		

The steamers, to whom the burden fell of carrying the greater portion of the troops, with their masters, are as follows:—

Steamers.	Captains.	
Guide	Capt. E. E. Vaill	Purchased.
New Brunswick	Capt. Winchester	Chartered.
New York	Capt. David Clark	Chartered.
Northerner	Capt. Masson	Purchased.
Cossack	Capt. J. N. Bennett	Purchased.
Eastern Queen	Capt. Collins	Chartered.
Suwanee	Capt. Padelford	Purchased.
Eastern State	Capt. John Teale	Chartered.
Union	Capt. W. H. Chambers	Purchased.
George Peabody	Capt. — —	Purchased.
Louisiana	Capt. — —	Chartered.

GUNBOATS OR ARMED TRANSPORTS.

The following is a list of armed transports, screw propellers, all of one class, together with the armament of each, intended for the double purpose of carrying troops, covering their own landings, and assisting in an attack:—

Gunboat Picket, Capt. Thos. P. Ives, four guns; two 12-pounder Wiard guns, rifled; one 12-pounder boat howitzer; one 12-pounder mountain howitzer.

Gunboat Pioneer, Capt. Charles E. Baker, four guns; one 30-pounder Parrott rifled gun; one 12-pounder Wiard rifled gun; one 12-pounder boat howitzer; one 12-pounder mountain howitzer.

Gunboat Ranger, Capt. J. B. Childs, seven guns; two 30-pounder Parrott rifled guns; four 12-pounder Wiard rifled guns; one 12-pounder mountain howitzer.

Gunboat Sentinel, Capt. Joshua Couillard, four guns; one

30-pounder Parrott rifled gun; one 12-pounder Wiard rifled gun; one 12-pounder boat howitzer; one 12-pounder mountain howitzer.
Gunboat Zouave, Capt. Wm. Hunt, four guns; one 30-pounder Parrott rifled gun; one 12-pounder boat howitzer.
Gunboat Lancer, Capt. N. B. Mosley, four guns; one 30-pounder Parrott rifled gun; one 12-pounder Wiard rifled gun; one 12-pounder boat howitzer; one 12-pounder mountain howitzer.
Gunboat Chasseur, Capt. Wm. Wert, four guns; two 30-pounder Parrott rifled guns; two 6-pounder Wiard rifled guns.
Gunboat Vidette, Capt. Benj. Fenner, three guns; one 30-pounder Parrott rifled gun; one 12-pounder boat howitzer; one 12-pounder mountain howitzer.
Gunboat Hussar, Capt. F. Crocker, four guns; two 30-pounder Parrott rifled guns; two 6-pounder Wiard rifled guns.
Total, nine gunboats, thirty-eight guns.

SAILING TROOP SHIPS.

The following are sailing transports fitted up for carrying troops:—

Ship	Captain	Status
Ship Aracan	Capt. Kelly	Chartered.
Ship Kitty Simpson	Capt. R. Hepburn	Chartered.
Ship Ann E. Thompson	Capt. C. S. Merriman	Chartered.
Ship Marcia Greenleaf	Capt. R. Merryman	Chartered.
Bark H. D. Brookman	Capt. H. E. Cheeney	Chartered.
Bark Voltigeur	Capt. N. M. Bly	Purchased.
Bark John Trucks	Capt. Levi Collins	Chartered.
Bark Aura	———	Chartered.
Brig Dragoon	Capt. J. Liscomb	Purchased
Schooner Highlander	Capt. E. G. Dayton	Purchased.
Schooner Scout	Capt. N. Torrey	Purchased.
Schooner Skirmisher	Capt. W. H. Richardson	Purchased.

Of the above, the bark Guerilla, brig Dragoon, and schooners Highlander, Scout, and Skirmisher, each carry one gun, a 12-pounder boat howitzer.

The schooner Recruit, Capt. Coggeshall, is detailed as a hospital ship, and is under the charge of Dr. Samuel A. Greene, acting Medical Director of the Division Hospital. The Recruit carries one gun.

STORE SHIPS.

In addition to the foregoing, a fleet of a dozen or fifteen schooners, of large size, have been chartered to carry horses, provisions, ordnance, and baggage. They are as follows:—

Horse Transports. Schooner Sarah Mills, Capt. S. T. Dayton; schooner W. A. Crocker, Capt. T. D. Endicott; schooner Maria Pike, Capt. S. N. Crocker; schooner Edward Slade, Capt. G. B. Smith; schooner Sarah M. Smith, Capt. L. M. Fisk.

Pontoon Bridge Schooners. Schooner Sea Bird, Capt. Smith; schooner Mary H. Banks, Capt. Banks.

Siege Train Schooner. Schooner Col. Satterly, Capt. ——.

Supply Vessels. Schooners Plaindoine, Eliza Seegur, Glenwood, Griswold, Rotche, Emma, U. S. Rue, Jas. T. Brady.

The latter vessels are all laden with provisions, clothing, forage, ammunition, baggage wagons, ambulances, and act as tenders to the fleet. The U. S. Rue is laden with the baggage of the 51st Pennsylvania and 21st Massachusetts regiments.

THE ARMAMENT OF THE TRANSPORT FLEET.

The total number of guns distributed through the transport fleet is 45, not including those on the floating batteries, which, though fitted out at Annapolis, really belong to the naval part of the forces. The caliber of the guns ranges from 6 to 30-pounders, which consist of rifled guns, (field pieces,) boat howitzers, (rifled,) and mountain howitzers for shell. Of the whole number, all but four—the shell howitzers—are rifled, and are of the Wiard or Parrott pattern. The effective range of these pieces is from one and a half to two and a half miles. The expeditious manner in which this armament was furnished is deserving of especial mention. The whole matter was under the charge of Norman Wiard, Esq., the inventor of the steel rifled cannon. Gen. Burnside authorized him to construct the artillery, and gave him two weeks to do it in. Mr. Wiard went to work, and at the end of that time delivered to Gen. Burnside the entire number of guns ready for use, with both ship and field carriages complete, and every appliance for using the guns with equal facility on land or sea.

In addition to this he furnished 5000 rounds of shot, shell, and canister of the Hotchkiss pattern, and 800 rounds of the Parrott pattern. The efficiency of this artillery needs hardly any praise. First, these guns are a most complete armament for the transports on which they are mounted. Secondly, they are ready, whenever required, to hitch horses to, and become the most formidable field artillery. Adding the guns of Belgier's battery to these, and it will be seen that there accompanies the expedition what is every way equivalent to *fifty-one pieces of field artillery* of the most approved pattern, with but six guns in the entire lot that are not rifled.

The entire cost of the guns and ammunition, delivered under the contract with Mr. Wiard, was but $60,000. The work was done in New York and Troy, and a total of 2000 hands employed in their manufacture.

THE FLOATING BATTERIES,

Though not directly associated with the land forces or the transports, have yet been gotten up under the sole supervision of Gen. Burnside. A good idea of their character is obtained when we say that they are, in every respect, similar to the strongest and largest canal boats on the North River or Erie Canal. They are almost solid, from deck to keelson, and are divided into five water-tight compartments. They have but one deck, on which the guns are mounted; and their working is to be protected by breastworks of bales of wet hay. The caliber of the guns is 6 and 12-pounder Wiard's, rifled, with a range of two and a half miles for certain execution.

Their names, number of guns, and commanders are as follows:—

Rocket—Three guns, in command of Master's Mate James Lake; Second Mate, J. A. Wilson.

Grenade—Three guns, in command of Master's Mate W. B. Avery.

Bombshell—Two guns, in command of Second Mate —— Downey.

Grapeshot—Two guns, in command of Second Mate N. B. McKean.
Shrapnell—Two guns, in command of Master's Mate Ernest Staples; Second Mate —— Riley.

The commanders of the flotilla are Acting Master's Mates Ernest Staples and James Lake, with the former as senior officer. They each carry a crew of from twelve to eighteen gunners. They will be taken in tow by steamers, and when brought into action anchored in position. The surface they present to the enemy's guns is so extremely small that it will be very difficult to effectually damage them, unless their gunnery is much superior to what it has been on like occasions heretofore.

SIGNAL CORPS.

A signal corps of 22 lieutenants and 66 privates has been organized and instructed in the use of Major Myers's new system of signals for army and navy use, by which orders can be communicated from the deck of one ship to another, or from one division or brigade of an army to another, with great facility and reliability. The act of signaling is performed by waving, in certain directions, to represent certain combinations of figures, which in turn represent the letters of the alphabet, different colored and sized flags, and at night colored lights, on staffs sixteen feet long. The flagman knows how to make the movements when the combination of figures is announced to him, but the letter represented by the combination is only known to the signal officer, who stands by and directs him, and reads in return the signals from the opposite correspondent.

The names of the signal officers accompanying the expedition are as follows:—

Lieut. Fricker, Lieut. Thos. R. Robeson, Lieut. Thos. Foster, instructors, 8th Pennsylvania. Lieut. M. B. Bessey, Lieut. N. F. Draper, 25th Massachusetts. Lieut. N. F. Barrett, Lieut. Luther Bradley, 27th Massachusetts. Lieut. Thos. B. Marsh, Lieut. W. H. Barker, 51st New York. Lieut. J. Lyman Van Buren, Lieut. R. T. Gordon, 53d New York. Lieut. Deming Jarvis, Lieut. W. S. Barstow, 24th Massachusetts. Lieut. Sanford B. Palmer, Lieut. Samuel M. Smith, 10th Connecticut. Lieut. Peter H. Niles, Lieut. Anthony Lang, 23d Massachusetts. Lieut. George W. Warner, Lieut. Fred. Schlachter, 11th Connecticut. Lieut. Charles A. Breed, Lieut. Marvin Wait, 8th Connecticut. Lieut. J. C. Reed, Lieut. J. G. Beaver, 51st Pennsylvania. Lieut. J. W. Hopkins, Lieut. T. H. Shumway, 21st Massachusetts.

FRENCH PONTOON TRAIN.

There have been built expressly for this expedition some 300 bridge floats, or boats, to form a pontoon train of the French pattern.

To express it more definitely, they are like a fisherman's yawl, eight feet wide and about thirty feet long. They are placed two abreast in the water, stringers and plank laid upon them, and the bridge is then done. When wanted for use elsewhere, they can be placed upon wheels and axles, which accompany them, and be drawn by horses any where it is desired to go. A large portion of the train is at Fortress Monroe, and its entire length is 5440 ft.

Another pontoon train, of the regular India rubber pattern, also accompanied the expedition in charge of Mr. S. D. Field. It had been satisfactorily tested on the Severn River at Annapolis.

DIVISION HOSPITAL.

Major Church, Division Surgeon, established very excellent accommodations for the sick and wounded. The schooner Recruit, one of the best vessels in the fleet, is fitted up with four hundred and forty berths on two decks in her hold, and furnished with every appliance necessary to the care and comfort of the disabled. The Division Hospital-ship is in charge of Dr. Samuel A. Greene, of the 24th Massachusetts, assisted by Dr. Theron Trample, of the 25th Massachusetts, and Dr. Dodge, of the 51st New York.

THE NUMBER OF TROOPS.

The total number of troops is about sixteen thousand, comprising fifteen regiments of infantry, one battalion of infantry, and one battery of artillery, besides the gunners and sailors on board ship.

The assignment of the troops to the transports, after considerable figuring and consulting, was finally made in the following order:—

FIRST BRIGADE.

25th Massachusetts, steamer New York and propeller Zouave.
23d Massachusetts, propeller Hussar and schooner Highlander.
27th Massachusetts, propeller Ranger and bark Guerilla.
10th Connecticut, steamer New Brunswick and schooner Skirmisher.
24th Massachusetts, steamer Guide and propeller Vidette.

SECOND BRIGADE.

21st Massachusetts, steamer Northerner.
51st Pennsylvania, steamer Cossack and schooner Scout.
51st New York, propellers Lancer and Pioneer.
9th New Jersey, ship Ann E. Thompson and brig Dragoon.
6th New Hampshire, steamer Louisiana.

THIRD BRIGADE.

4th Rhode Island, steamer Eastern Queen.
53d New York, bark John Trucks.
8th Connecticut, propeller Chasseur and bark H. D. Brookman.
11th Connecticut, propeller Sentinel and bark Voltigeur.
5th Rhode Island, (battalion,) ship Kitty Simpson.
89th New York, ship Aracan.
Belger's Battery, steamer George Peabody.

The steamer New York is the flag-ship of the First Brigade, Gen. Foster; the Northerner of the Second Brigade, Gen. Reno; the Eastern Queen of the Third Brigade, Gen. Parke.

SHERMAN'S PORT ROYAL EXPEDITION.

The military strength of the expedition is supposed to consist of about 20,000 men. It is organized as follows:—

ACTING MAJOR GENERAL,
BRIGADIER GENERAL THOS. W. SHERMAN.

The division consists of three brigades, as follows:—

FIRST BRIGADE.
BRIGADIER GENERAL EGBERT L. VIELE.

New Hampshire Third . . . . . Col. E. W. Fellows.
Maine Eighth . . . . Col. Lee Strickland.
New York Forty-sixth . . . . . Col. Rudolph Rosa.
New York Forty-seventh . . . . Col. Henry Moore.
New York Forty-eighth . . . . Col. James H. Perry.

SECOND BRIGADE.
BRIGADIER GENERAL ISAAC INGALLS STEVENS.

Pennsylvania Fiftieth . . . . . Col. Benjamin C. Christ.
Pa. Roundhead Volunteers . . . Col. David Leasure.
Michigan Eighth . . . . Col. William M. Fenton.
New York Seventy-ninth . . . Lieut. Col. William H. Nobles.

THIRD BRIGADE.
BRIGADIER GENERAL HORATIO GATES WRIGHT.

New Hampshire Fourth . . . . Col. Thomas J. Whipple.
Connecticut Sixth . . . . Col. James L. Chatfield.
Connecticut Seventh . . . . . . Col. A. A. Terry.
Maine Ninth . . . . Col. Rishworth Rich.

There are various other regiments—as for instance the Third Rhode Island, Colonel Brown; the Engineer Volunteer battalion, Colonel E. W. Serrill, a corps of Sappers and Miners, which joined the expedition at Fortress Monroe, and which we cannot locate in any particular brigade; and there may be still others embarked at that and other points, of which we have as yet no definite information. In addition to the regular land force accompanying the expedition, there is also a battalion of United States Marines, under the command of Major Reynolds. The entire military arm of the expedition may safely be estimated, however, at not less than 20,000 men—for the most part picked troops detailed from General McClellan's command for this particular service.

THE NAVAL EXPEDITION.

	Commanders.	Guns.
1. Steam frigate Wabash, (flag ship,)	Captain Davis	50
2. Sloop Vandalia	S. F. Haggerty	20

Gunboats.	Commanders.	Guns.
1. Augusta	E. G. Parrot	9
2. Alabama	E. Lander	9
3. Curlew	P. G. Watmough	7
4. Florida	J. P. Goldsborough	9
5. Gem of the Seas	—— Baxter	4
6. Isaac M. Smith	J. W. A. Nicholson	6
7. Mohican	S. W. Godon	9
8. Ottawa	Thomas H. Stevens	4
9. Pawnee	R. H. Wyman	9
10. Pembina	J. P. Bankhead	4
11. Penguin	T. A. Budd	5
12. Pocahontas	P. Drayton	5
13. R. B. Forbes	H. S. Newcomb	2
14. Seminole	J. P. Gillies	5
15. Seneca	Daniel Ammen	4
16. Unadilla	N. Collins	4
17. Shawshene	E. Calhoun	2
18. Georgia	——	4

TRANSPORTS.

Steamers.	Commanders.	Tons.	Draft, ft.
1. Ariel	Terry	1296	14
2. Atlantic	Eldridge	2845	20½
3. Baltic	Comstock	2723	21
4. Ben Deford		1080	—
5. Cahawba	Baker	1643	11
6. Coatzacoalcos	Bocock	1500	8
7. Daniel Webster	Johnson	1035	11
8. Empire City	Baxter	1751	14
9. Ericsson	Cowles	1902	16
10. Locust Point	French	462	16
11. Marion	Phillips	800	13
12. Matanzas	Leesburg	875	—
13. Ocean Queen	Seabury	2802	16
14. Oriental	Tuzo	1000	—
15. Parkersburg	——	715	10
16. Philadelphia	Barton	1258	11
17. Potomac	Hilliard	448	—
18. Roanoke	Couch	1071	10
19. Star of the South	Kearney	960	—
20. Union	——	—	—
21. Vanderbilt	Lafevre	3360	20
22. Winfield Scott	Litchfield	—	16
23. Illinois	Rathbun	2122	—

STEAM-TUGS.

		Guns.
1. O. M. Petit	A. S. Gardner	2
2. Mercury	S. J. Mantou	2

FERRY BOATS.

1. Commodore Perry.   2. Ethan Allen.

STEAMBOATS.

1. May Flower.   4. Peerless.
2. Belvidere.   5. Osceola.
3. Governor.

SAILING VESSELS.

1. Ship Great Republic.
2. Ship Ocean Express.
3. Ship Golden Eagle.
4. Ship Zenas Coffin.
5. Bark J. A. Bishop.
6. Brig Belle of the Bay.
7. Brig Ellen P. Stewart.
8. Schr. S. F. Abbott.
9. Schr. E. F. Allen.
10. Schr. Aid.
11. Schr. J. M. Vance.
12. Schr. M. E. Clark.
13. Schr. Wm. G. Underwood.
14. Schr. E. English.
15. Schr. J. Frambes.
16. Schr. Effort.
17. Schr. Western Star.
18. Schr. Saratoga.
19. Schr. S. J. Bright.
20. Schr. Chas. McNeil.
21. Schr. David Faust.
22. Schr. R. S. Miller.
23. Schr. L. Chester.
24. Schr. J. Seatterthwaite.
25. Schr. Snowflake.
26. Schr. D. Molany.
27. Schr. Ariel.
28. Schr. Simms.
29. Schr. Hewitt.
30. Schr. Sarah.
31. Schr. Willard Saulsbury.
32. Schr. S. Collin.

RECAPITULATION OF VESSELS.

Naval vessels 20
Steam-tugs 2
Ferry boats 2
Steam transports 23
Sailing vessels 32
Steamboats 5

Total 84

This is exclusive of the Sabine, Susquehanna, St. Lawrence, Dale, Savannah, Flag, and other vessels of the blockading squadron, which joined the expedition as it passed the points off which they were stationed.

The Belvidere and Florida, the tug-boat O. M. Petit, and the two ferry boats, Ethan Allen and Commodore Perry, having returned, the fleet is now diminished to that extent.

THE RIVER NAVAL FLEET.

The Naval Expedition which sailed from Cairo for the South is as follows:—

The total number of boats is 78, of which 12 are gunboats, 38 mortar boats, and 28 are tugs and steamboats. The gunboats carry 15 guns of heavy caliber each, except the flag-ship of the expedition, the Benton, which has an armament of 18 guns. Seven of these boats cost $89,000 each to build. They are 175 feet in length, 51 feet 6 inches in breadth, and draw 5 feet when loaded. The bows and bow bulwarks consist of about three feet of oak timber, bolted together and sheathed with the best quality of wrought iron plates two and a half inches thick. The sides have the same sheathing, with less bulk of timber. The sides of the boats, both above and below the knee, incline at an angle of forty-five degrees, and nothing but a plunging shot from a high bluff could strike the surface at right angles. The boilers and machinery are so situated as to be perfectly protected, and may be considered quite out of danger. The iron plating has been severely tested by shots from rifled cannon at different distances, and has shown itself to be utterly impervious to any shots that have been sent against it, even at a range of 300 yards. The Benton is somewhat larger than the rest of the fleet, and has a double hull, with wheels working in the recess, near the stern. The hull is divided by five fore and aft bulkheads, and thirteen cross bulkheads, making forty-five water-tight compartments. Casemates extend around the whole boat, and are made of twelve-inch timber. At the knuckle on the main deck, the timber is from three to four feet in thickness, solid. The pilot and wheel houses are amply protected by timber and iron sheathing. The magazines, two in number, are each capable of carrying 100 rounds of ammunition for every gun, and afford ample room for the necessary evolutions within them. The magazines can be flooded with water in a moment from the main deck. The mortar boats are built of heavy timbers, the sides of boiler iron loopholed for musketry, and are so arranged that they can be used for bridges. They will each carry one 15-inch mortar. The mortar boats will be towed into position by tugs.

THE MANUFACTURE OF ORDNANCE.

Since the commencement of the war the three founderies at West Point, South Boston, and Pittsburg, Pa., have together manufactured for the government —

12-inch rifled cannon	1
11-inch	11
10-inch	10
9-inch	72
8-inch	67
7-inch	1
10-pounders	219
12-pounders	230
17-pounders	24
20-pounders	158
30-pounders	141
50-pounders	36
80-pounders	19
100-pounders	5
150-pounders	9
Rifle siege guns	20
Guns of small caliber	28
Total number of cannon	**1046**

Of mortars and howitzers they have made —

13-inch mortars	54
10-inch mortars	61
8-inch mortars	26
8-inch howitzers	10
Total	**151**

They have also turned out the following number of shot **and shell**: —

13-inch shells	6,000
11-inch shells	2,829
10-inch shells	2,050
9-inch shells	8,200
Shot and shell of smaller caliber	151,727
Total number of shot and shell	**178,226**

THE WESTERN RIVER FLOTILLA.

FLAG OFFICER, ANDREW H. FOOTE.

Fleet Captain	Com. A. M. Pennock.
Ordnance Officer	Lieut. J. P. Sanford.
Flag Lieutenant	J. M. Prickett.
Quartermaster	Lieut. Wise.

It was made evident at an early day, that an armed flotilla would be needed upon the western rivers. Secession held the Mississippi below Columbus; it held the Cumberland and Tennessee Rivers, and threatened the Ohio, interrupting trade and producing utter stagnation of business along its waters. Three gunboats were ordered to be built at Cincinnati,—Taylor, Lexington, and Conestoga, side-wheel steamers,—each carrying seven guns, which, so soon as they were put in commission, did excellent service, effectually awing secession aggressions, which at one time even threatened the city of Cincinnati! Subsequently it was decided to build eight floating batteries as gunboats, and to protect them in part with iron plates. A ferry boat, which had been employed at St. Louis, was reconstructed and christened the Essex. In addition, thirty-eight mortar rafts were ordered, and several steam tugs. The Essex was disabled in the Fort Henry fight, and is not yet repaired. The Cairo, one of the iron-clad boats, and the Taylor and Lexington are up the Tennessee River, leaving the following named boats to compose the expedition down the Mississippi:—

Gunboats.	Commanders.	Guns.
Benton (flag-ship)	Lieut. S. T Phelps	16
Mound City	A. H. Kilty	13
Cincinnati	R. N. Stembel	13
Louisville	Benj. M. Dove	13
Carondelet	Henry Walke	13
St. Louis	Lieut. Leonard Paulding	13
Pittsburg	Lieut. E. Thompson	13
Conestoga	Lieut. Blodgett	9

None of the guns are less than 32-pounders, some 42, and some 64-pounders. In addition, each boat carries a 12-pounder boat howitzer on the upper deck. Several of the guns are rifled. The Benton carries two 10-inch Dahlgren shell guns in her forward battery; the others, one each. The Benton is iron-clad every where; the others are iron-clad at the bows and over the wheel houses and engines, with the exception of the Conestoga, which, as before stated, is a side-wheel steamer, and has no plating.

All of these officers, with the exception of a portion of the fleet officers who have been detailed for duty at Cairo, have won the praises of the Flag Officer for their admirable bearing at Forts Henry and Donelson — with the exception also of Lieut. Blodgett, of the Conestoga, a native of Burlington, Vt., who on Wednesday last, assumed command, having been detailed from Boston for that purpose.

MORTAR FLEET.

The mortar fleet is commanded by Capt. Henry E. Maynadier, of the Tenth Infantry, an experienced ordnance officer, assisted by Capt. E. B. Pike, of the Engineer Corps. There are four masters, each of whom has the control of four mortars. The masters are,

H. A. Glassford, G. F. Johnson, G. B. Simon, and F. B. Gregory. Each mortar boat is manned by a crew of fifteen men, three of whom are flatboatmen, accustomed to navigating the river, who assist in bringing the boat into position, and maintaining it there.

Although there are thirty-eight mortar rafts, and although strenuous exertions have been made to bring all into service, yet the competent officers and complement of men needed could not be obtained, and a portion only is at present ready to accompany the gunboats. If others are needed, they will be sent for.

AMMUNITION BOATS.

Although the gunboats have their locker full of powder, shot, and shell, no prudent commander will attempt an expedition of this kind without a supply of ammunition. Accordingly, two large steamers have been converted into ammunition boats — the Great Western and Judge Torrence. They were fitted up at Cincinnati. There are twelve thousand rounds of naval ammunition of various kinds on board these boats; also rockets and signal fires. The boats are guarded against fire, so far as is possible, and are provided with water plugs, so that they may be scuttled in five minutes' time, if necessary, to prevent their falling into the hands of the enemy, or in case of fire or other contingency. Captain W. F. Hamilton commands the Great Western, and Captain J. F. Richardson the Judge Torrence.

In addition to these boats of the regular navy, numerous river steamers are in the employ of the government, used as tow boats and transports, to place mortars in position, and to supply the fleet with coal. Such is a brief notice of the naval portion of the expedition, which has been hurriedly improvised — if the word is allowable in this connection — brought together by the constant effort and energy of Commander Foote and his brother officers.

THE GREAT MORTAR FLOTILLA.
COMMANDER, DAVID D. PORTER, U. S. N.

FIRST DIVISION.

Schr. Norfolk Packet, Lieut. Watson Smith, U. S. N., commanding division.
    Acting Master, Edgar C. Merriam.
    Assistant Surgeon, A. B. Judson.
    Captain's Clerk, Wm. Ferguson.

Vessel.	Commander.
Schr. Olive H. Lee	Acting Master Washington Godfrey.
" Pera	" George H. Hood.
" C. P. Williams	" Amos R. Langthorn.
" Arletta	" Thomas E. Smith.
" Wm. Bacon	" William P. Rogers.
" Sophroula	" John A. Darling.

SECOND DIVISION.

Schr. T. A. Ward, Lieut. Walter W. Queen, U. S. N., commanding division.
    Acting Master, J. Duncan Graham.
    Assistant Surgeon, A. A. Hoehling.
    Captain's Clerk, Archer Tevio

Vessel.	Commander.
Schr. Sidney C. Jones	Acting Master Robert Adams.
" Matthew Vasser	" " Hugh H. Savage.
" Maria J. Carleton,	" " Charles E. Jack.
" Orvitta	" " Francis E. Blanchard.
" Adolph Hugel	" " Hollis B. Jenks.
" George Mangham,	" " John Collins, Jr.

THIRD DIVISION.

Barkintine Horace Beals, Lieut. K. Randolph Breeze, U. S. N., commanding division.
Acting Master, Geo. W. Sumner.
Assistant Surgeon, Robert T. Edes.
Captain's Clerk, Albert W. Bacon.

Vessel.	Commander.
Schr. John Griffiths	Acting Master Henry Brown.
" Sarah Bruin	" " Abraham Christian.
" Racer	" " Alvin Phinney.
Brig Sea Foam	" " Henry E. Williams.
Schr. Henry James	" " Lewis Pennington.
" Dan Smith	" " Geo. W. Brown.

RESERVE DIVISION.

Steamer Octorora, flag ship of Commander Porter, Lieut. George Brown commanding.

Vessel.	Commander.
Steamer Harriet Lane	Lieut. J. D. Wainwright.
" Owaska	Lieut. John Guest.
" Westfield	Wm. B. Renshaw.
" Clifton	Lieut. J. H. Baldwin.
" Miami	A. D. Harrall.
" Jackson	Lieut. Samuel Woodworth.
" R. B. Forbes	Acting Master —— Fly.

It is now about three months since the first steps were taken to form the fleet of bomb schooners, with which, from the first, the name of Commander David D. Porter has been inseparably connected. It is due to this gallant and experienced officer to say, that the fitting up and arming of this fleet has been done under his immediate supervision, and in many important details the government are indebted to his ingenuity and judgment. The plans of the undertaking were projected by him, and in the important matter of mounting and securing the immense mortars his skill is seen and acknowledged. The fleet consists of twenty-one mortar vessels, eight steamers, and one storeship.

The mortar vessels, which, with two exceptions, are schooner rigged, were purchased by the government expressly for the purpose. The vessels were fitted out with remarkable despatch, some having been ready for sea in ten days from the time the work was commenced, while the heavy mortars and shell were transported from Pittsburg, Pa., to New York, the beds built up, iron carriages constructed, the mortars mounted, and every vessel ready for sea in the short space of twenty-nine days. That Commander Porter intends to make his presence felt wherever he goes, is evident from the fact that the flotilla is provided with powder and bombshells enough to rain a shower of iron hail over half of rebeldom. The fleet is manned by two thousand officers and seamen, not one of whom is over thirty-five years of age, —strong, vigorous, and brave. Both officers and men were selected by Commander Porter for this special service, and, with the exceptions of the commanders of divisions, the officers all belong to the volunteer navy, than whom a more intelligent, brave, and experienced body of seamen cannot be found in the world. Their hearts are in the work, and all that men dare do will be attempted by these men,

The Harriet Lane is at present the flag ship of Commander Porter, the Octorora and the other steamers of the reserve division not having joined the flotilla. They are expected to proceed to Ship Island, where Commander Porter will transfer his flag to the Octorora, which has been fitted up especially for his accommodation.

THE 300-POUNDER GUN OF ENGLAND.

A preliminary trial of the immense three hundred-pounder gun, manufactured at the works of Sir W. Armstrong, Elswick, took place February 23d, at Shoeburyness, in the presence of the members of the Ordnance Select Committee, Sir W. Armstrong, and a number of scientific gentlemen. The tremendous weapon was worked with the utmost ease and facility by a small number of gunners, and the experiments were considered in every respect successful. The gun, not being yet rifled, was of course used as a smooth bore, and was repeatedly fired with a solid spherical shot weighing one hundred and fifty pounds, and a charge of forty pounds of powder. The experiments are preliminary to a trial of the power of the weapon when directed against armor plates, and after such trial the gun will be returned to the Royal Arsenal and rifled, so as to become adapted for projectile shot of three hundred pounds and upward.

RELATIVE VALUE OF PRISONERS OF WAR.

According to a general order issued by General Halleck, the following tariff of exchange of prisoners of war, which was adopted between the United States and Great Britain during the war of 1812, regulates the rate of exchange at the present time by order of General McClellan: —

General, Commander-in-Chief or Admiral — sixty men.
Lieutenant General or Vice Admiral — forty men.
Major General or Rear Admiral — thirty men.
Brigadier General or Commodore with a broad pennant and a Captain under him — twenty men.
Colonel or Captain of a line of battle ship — fifteen men.
Lieutenant Colonel or Captain of a frigate — ten men.
Major or Commander of a sloop of war, bomb ketch, fire ship or packet — eight men.
Captain or Lieutenant or Master — six men.
Lieutenant or Master's Mate — four men.
Sub-Lieutenant, or Ensign, or Midshipman, Warrant Officers, Masters of merchant vessels, and Captains of private-armed vessels — three men.
Non-commissioned officers, or Lieutenants, and Mates of private-armed vessels, Mates of merchant vessels, and all petty officers of ships of war — two men.
Private soldiers or seamen — one man.

STATISTICAL POCKET MANUAL. 47

STATISTICS OF THE ARMY.

States and Territories.	Enlisted for Three Months.	Enlisted for the War.	Aggregate.	Proportion of Population
California	...	4,638	4,638	1 to 82
Connecticut	2,236	12,400	14,636	1 to 31
Delaware	775	2,000	2,775	1 to 40
Illinois	4,941	80,000	84,941	1 to 20
Indiana	4,686	57,332	62,018	1 to 22
Iowa	908	19,800	20,708	1 to 33
Kentucky	...	15,000	15,000	1 to 77
Maine	768	14,239	15,007	1 to 41
Maryland	...	7,000	7,000	1 to 105
Massachusetts	3,435	26,760	30,195	1 to 41
Michigan	781	28,550	29,331	1 to 26
Minnesota	...	4,160	4,160	1 to 42
Missouri	9,356	22,130	31,486	1 to 38
New Hampshire	779	9,600	10,379	1 to 31
New Jersey	3,068	9,342	12,410	1 to 54
New York	10,188	110,390	120,578	1 to 32
Ohio	22,380	109,523	131,903	1 to 18
Pennsylvania	19,199	109,615	128,814	1 to 22
Rhode Island	1,285	5,898	7,183	1 to 24
Vermont	780	8,000	8,780	1 to 36
Virginia	779	12,000	12,779	1 to 125
Wisconsin	792	14,153	14,945	1 to 51
Kansas	...	5,000	5,000	1 to 23
Colorado	...	1,000	1,000	
Nebraska	...	2,500	2,500	1 to 11½
Nevada	...	1,000	1,000	
New Mexico	...	1,200	1,200	1 to 69
District of Columbia.	2,823	1,000	3,823	1 to 19
Totals	87,999	694,230	784,309	
Regular Army	...	20,334		
Total	...	714,564		

Arms of the Service.	Volunteers.	Regulars.	Aggregate
Infantry	577,208	11,379	588,587
Cavalry	68,654	4,748	73,402
Artillery	36,380	4,000	40,380
Rifles and Sharpshooters	11,395	...	11,395
Engineers	1,593	107	1,700
Totals	694,230	20,334	714,564

THE REBEL GENERALS OF THE SOUTH.

GENERALS IN THE REGULAR ARMY.

1. Samuel Cooper, Virginia, Adjutant General.
2. Albert S. Johnston, Texas.
3. Joseph E. Johnston, Va.
4. Robert E. Lee, Va.
5. P. G. T. Beauregard, La.

MAJOR GENERALS IN THE PROVISIONAL ARMY.

1. *D. E. Twiggs, Ga., resigned.
2. Leonidas Polk, La.
3. Braxton Bragg, La.
4. Earl Van Dorn, Miss.
5. Gustavus W. Smith, Ky.
6. Theopolis H. Holmes, N. C.
7. William J. Hardee, Ga.
8. Benjamin Huger, S. C.
9. James Longstreet, Ala.
10. John B. Magruder, Va.
11. Thomas J. Jackson, Va.
12. Mansfield Lovell, Va.
13. Edmund Kirby Smith, Fla.
14. George B. Crittenden, Ky.

BRIGADIER GENERALS IN THE PROVISIONAL ARMY.

1. Milledge L. Bonham, S. C.
2. John B. Floyd, Va.
3. Henry A. Wise, Va.
4. *Ben McCulloch, Texas.
5. *H.R. Jackson, Ga., resigned.
6. * R. S. Garnett, Va., killed.
7. * William H.T. Walker, Ga., resigned.
8. *Barnard E. Bee, S.C., killed.
9. Alexander R. Lawton, Ga.
10. *Gideon J. Pillow, Tenn.
11. Samuel R. Anderson, Tenn.
12. Daniel S. Donelson, Tenn.
13. David R. Jones, S. C.
14. Jones M. Withers, Ala.
15. John C. Pemberton, Va.
16. Richard S. Ewell, Va.
17. John H. Winder, Md.
18. Jubal A. Early, Va.
19. Thomas B. Flournoy, Ark., died in Arkansas.
20. Samuel Jones, Va.
21. Arnold Elzey, Md.
22. Daniel H. Hill, N. C.
23. Henry H. Sibley, La.
24. William H. C. Whiting, Ga.
25. William W. Loring, N. C.
26. Richard H. Anderson, S. C.
27. Albert Pike, Ark., Indian Commissioner.
28. *Thomas T. Fauntleroy, Va., resigned.
29. Robert Toombs, Ga.
30. Daniel Ruggles, Va.
31. Charles Clark, Miss.
32. Roswell S. Ripley, S. C.
33. Isaac R. Trimble, Md.
34. * John B. Grayson, Ky., died.
35. Paul O. Hebert, La.
36. Richard C. Gatlin, N. C.
37. * Felix K. Zollicoffer, Tenn., killed.
38. Benj. F. Cheatham, Tenn.
39. Joseph R. Anderson, Va.
40. *Simon B. Buckner, Ky., captured.
41. Leroy Pope Walker, Ala.
42. Albert G. Blanchard, La.
43. Gabriel J. Rains, N. C.
44. J. E. B. Stuart, Va.
45. Lafayette McLaws, Ga.
46. Thomas F. Drayton, S. C.
47. Thomas C. Hindman, Ark.
48. Adley H. Gladden, La.
49. John P. McCown, Tenn.
50. * Lloyd Tilghman, Ky., captured.
51. Nathan G. Evans, S. C.
52. Cadmus M. Wilcox, Tenn.
53. * Philip St. George Cocke, Va., died in Virginia.
54. R. E. Rhodes, Ala.
55. Richard Taylor, La.
56. Louis T. Wigfall, Texas.
57. James H. Trapier, S. C.
58. Samuel G. French, Miss.
59. William H. Carroll, Tenn.
60. Hugh W. Mercer, Ga.
61. Humphrey Marshall, Ky.
62. John C. Breckinridge, Ky
63. Richard Griffin, Miss.
64. Alexander P. Stewart, Ken.
65. William M. Gardner, Ga.
66. Richard B. Garnett, Va.
67. William Mahone, Va.
68. L. O'Brien Branch, N. C.
69. Maxey Gregg, S. C.
70. Edward Price, captured.
71. Bushrod Johnson, captured.

Those having a star affixed are dead, or have resigned or been captured since the commencement of the war.

GLOSSARY OF MILITARY TERMS.

ABATTIS. Felled trees, with their sharp branches placed outward, and so interlaced as to present an irregular and thick row of pointed stakes towards the enemy.

ACCOUTREMENTS. A word which comprises the belts, cartridge-box, bayonet-scabbard, &c., of a soldier. When besides these he has his arms, he is said to be armed and accoutred.

ADJUTANT. The regimental staff officer who assists the colonel or other commander in the details of regimental or garrison duty. When serving with a detachment of a regiment at a post, he is called a post adjutant. The adjutant is usually selected from the rank of lieutenants, and receives extra pay and allowances. He receives and issues orders, forms the daily parade, details and mounts the guards, &c.

ALIGNMENT. The straight line upon which troops are formed in battle order.

AMBULANCE. An easy carriage or litter for transporting one or more wounded men from the field to a hospital or other place, where their injuries may be attended to.

APPROACHES. The lines of intrenchment, ditches, &c., by which the besiegers approach a fortified place. The principal trenches are called the first, second, and third parallels.

APRON. A piece of sheet lead used to cover the vent of a cannon to protect it from the weather.

ARMSTRONG GUN. A rifle cannon loaded at the breech. Its projectile is made of cast iron, surrounded by two leaden rings placed at the extremity of the cylindrical part, for the purpose of fitting the grooves when it is forced through the bore.

ARSENAL. A place where arms are made and repaired, or deposited, and also where military stores are kept.

ARTILLERY. Troops whose duty it is to serve the cannon, either in the field or in fortifications. They are armed with swords. They are divided into light and heavy artillery. The former have light guns, and gun-carriages, which can be taken to pieces, and transported on the backs of horses and mules. The latter have charge of siege and other heavy guns. The artillery usually constitutes about one tenth of the force.

ASSEMBLY. An army-call beaten upon the drum, for assembling the troops by company.

BANQUETTE. A small elevation of earth inside of a fort, upon which the soldiers stand to fire over the parapet.

BARBETTE GUNS. Guns fired over a parapet with wide range, distinguished from guns in embrasure, which fire through a narrow cut in the embrasure, and with a limited field of range.

BASTION. In fortifications the advanced portion of a regular work, consisting of two faces, enclosing a salient angle and two flanks.

BATTALION. A body of infantry of two or more companies under one commander.

BAYONET. A sharp-pointed steel dagger, made to fit upon the end of a musket, as an additional weapon.

BOMB. A word formerly used to mean a shell, such as is thrown from a mortar. When mortars or Dahlgren guns are fired upon a place they are said to *bombard* it.

4

BREACH. An opening made by cannon in a wall or fort, by which infantry troops may attack it.

BREASTWORK. Any wall of defence breast-high, which shelters Infantry in loading and firing upon the enemy.

BREECH. The extremity of a gun near the vent.

BREVET. An honorary commission given to officers for meritorious service, but not affecting the lineal rank except under special circumstances.

BRIGADE. A body of troops consisting of two or three regiments.

BRIGADIER-GENERAL. An officer who commands a brigade. The second rank in our service, next below a major-general and above a colonel.

CADENCE. Exact time in marching and executing the manual of arms. It is indispensable to uniformity of motion.

CAISSON. The ammunition carriage accompanying a field piece.

CAMP. The ground upon which troops encamp, the form of the encampment, and the tents or temporary shelters of any kind which are used.

CANTEEN. A small flat bottle or runlet, in which a soldier carries water. Canteens are made of wood, tin, or india-rubber.

CARBINE. A small musket or rifle used by cavalry.

CARTRIDGE. A charge of powder for any kind of fire-arms. Those for muskets are rolled in paper; those for cannon are put up in flannel. A ball cartridge is one which has a ball inserted at the end of the powder, so that the piece is entirely loaded at once.

CARTRIDGE-BOX. The leather box worn on the right hip in which cartridges are kept.

CASEMATE. Casemates are bomb-proof chambers in fortifications, through holes in which, called embrasures, heavy guns are fired.

CASHIER. To dismiss an officer ignominiously from the army.

CAVALRY. This term includes all kinds of mounted troops, dragoons, hussars, light and heavy cavalry, &c.

CHAMBER. The cavity at the bottom of the bore of a mortar or howitzer into which the charge of gunpowder is put.

CHEVAUX-DE-FRISE. A square (or hexagonal) beam of timber or iron, from six to nine feet long, in each of which pointed stakes are placed at right angles to the sides.

CHEVRONS. The marks or bands on the sleeves of non-commissioned officers.

COLORS. The two silken flags belonging to a regiment.

COLUMBIAD. A gun of large caliber, for throwing solid shot or shells.

COMMISSARY. An officer who purchases and distributes provision.

COUNTER-MARCH. A change of the direction of a regiment or company from front to rear by a flank movement.

COUNTERSCARP. The outer wall or slope of the ditch of a fort.

COUNTERSIGN. A secret word of communication to the sentinels on post.

COURTS MARTIAL are divided into general courts to try important cases; garrison courts for lesser delinquencies; and drum-head courts for summary punishment.

COUP DE MAIN. A sudden attack connected with a surprise.

CRENELATED. Loop-holed.
CURTAIN. That part of a rampart which joins the **flanks of two bastions together.**
COLUMN. A body of troops so drawn up as to present a narrow front. A column is close or open, according to the distance between the companies.
DAHLGREN GUN. An improved gun, named after its inventor, very thick at the breech, and tapering down to less than the common size at the mouth.
DISPLAY. To open the order of troops from column into line of battle.
DRAGOONS. Cavalry who sometimes serve on foot.
DIVISION. Two or more brigades.
ECHELON. A formation of troops following each other on separate lines, like the steps of a ladder.
EMBRASURE. An opening cut in a parapet for cannon to fire through.
ENFILADE. To sweep with **a battery the whole length of a** work or line of troops.
ENGINEERS. Officers who build fortifications. Topographical engineers are those who make military surveys or reconnoissances.
ENTRENCH. To throw up a parapet with ditch in front.
EPROUVETTE. A small mortar for testing the strength and equality of gunpowder.
ESCALADE. An attack on a fort with scaling ladders.
ESCARP. The side of a ditch next to a parapet.
ESPLANADE. A level surface within a fortified place, for exercising, &c.
EVOLUTIONS OF THE LINE. Movements by which troops, consisting of more regiments than one, change their position with order and regularity upon the field of battle.
FASCINES. Brushwood, or long twigs, such as osier or willow, collected together and bound into bundles of convenient size. They are used to revet a parapet, or to make firm footing on marshy ground, and for other purposes.
FIELD OFFICERS. The colonel, lieutenant colonel, and major of a regiment are called field officers.
FILE. The front and rear rank man constitute a file.
FORAGE. The hay, straw, and oats required for the horses of an army.
FORLORN HOPE. A party of officers and men selected — generally volunteers — to attack a breach in storming a work. The duty is very dangerous, and the survivors receive promotion.
FORT. Any military work designed to strengthen a point against every attack is a fort. If it be an important and complete fort, it is called a fortress.
FORTIFICATIONS are works of strong character to defend a city or some extensive front. When they are made entirely of earth, they are called field fortifications; when of masonry, permanent fortifications.
FURLOUGH. Leave of absence granted to warrant and non commissioned officers and soldiers.
FUSE. A tube filled with combustible materials, which is fixed in a shell; it burns, when ignited, for a calculated time before it reaches the powder in the shell and explodes it.
GABIONS. Cylindrical baskets, without top or bottom, made

of pliant twigs, filled with earth, and placed to resist cannon-shot.

GLACIS. The declivity of ground running from beyond the counterscarp of the ditch to the open country, and swept by the fire of the parapet.

GRAPE. Large shot (usually nine) sewed together in cylindrical bags, which are made to fit like cartridges into cannon.

GRENADE. A small shell with a short fuse, which may be thrown into the enemy's works.

GRENADIERS. The infantry company on the right of the regiment is called the grenadier company, because they formerly carried hand grenades.

GUARD. A portion of troops regularly detailed, whose duty is to watch against surprise and disorder. The individual soldiers of the guard are called sentinels.

GUIDON. Small silken flags borne by cavalry and light artillery.

GUNPOWDER. A composition of saltpetre (76 parts), charcoal (14 parts), and sulphur (10 parts). The charcoal is the combustible part; the saltpetre furnishes the oxygen, and changes the mass into gas; the sulphur gives intensity of heat.

HAVERSACK. A coarse linen bag for carrying provisions on a march.

HAVELOCK. A cloth cap with large cape to protect the neck from the sun.

HOLSTERS. Cases fixed to the front of cavalry saddles to hold a pair of pistols.

HORS DU COMBAT. (French: literally, out of combat.) Not able to take part in immediate action. The term includes all dead, wounded, missing, or those who from any cause are thus disabled.

HOWITZER. A piece of artillery with a chamber at the bottom of the bore, in which the cartridge is placed; intended for firing shells.

INFANTRY. Foot troops, divided into infantry of the line and light infantry.

INVEST. To take measures for besieging a place.

INTERVAL. The distance between platoons, companies, or other divisions of troops. In manœuvring, it is very important to preserve the interval.

JUDGE ADVOCATE. A person who conducts the prosecution before courts martial.

KNAPSACK. A square satchel, usually covered with canvas or india-rubber, which contains the necessaries of an infantry soldier.

LADDERS, SCALING, are made of flat staves fastened in ropes, provided at the end with hooks for grappling.

LIGHT INFANTRY. Foot soldiers who act as skirmishers or sharpshooters.

LIMBER. A two-wheeled carriage fastened to the trail of a cannon when it is to be removed to a considerable distance.

LINSTOCK. A piece of wood shod with iron, and easily stuck in the ground, through a hole in the upper end of which a piece of prepared tow-rope is kept burning.

LODGMENT. A work thrown up by besiegers during their approaches.

LOGISTICS. That branch of "war art" which concerns the moving and supplying of armies.

LUNETTE. Small triangular field forts with the base angles cut away.

MALINGERER. A soldier who feigns ill health to avoid doing his duty. When discovered, his conduct is declared disgraceful, and he is tried.

MANŒUVRE. Any concerted movements of troops at drill.

MARTIAL LAW. A subordination of the civil law to the military, by which the *habeas corpus* act is suspended. Subjection to the articles of war.

MINE. A subterraneous passage dug under a work or glacis, and stocked with gunpowder, which may be exploded by a long train fired without danger.

MINIE. A kind of rifle invented by Captain Minié, of France, which carries a conical ball, hollow at the base.

MORTARS. Short pieces of ordnance, with large calibers and chambers, from which shells are fired at an elevated angle.

MUSTER ROLL. A roll, prepared at intervals of two months, containing all the details of company organization. At the same time the troops are mustered and inspected.

MUTINY. Seditious or refractory conduct among troops; the name is given to insubordination associated with violence.

MUZZLE. The extremity of a cannon, or any fire-arm, through which the ball makes its exit.

NON-COMMISSIONED OFFICERS are sergeants of various grades and corporals; they are appointed by authorities lower than the President — commissions issuing from him. As a punishment, non-commissioned officers may be reduced to the ranks.

ORDERLY. A soldier of any grade, appointed to wait officially upon a general or other officer, to carry orders or messages. The orderly sergeant is the first sergeant of the company. The officer of the day is sometimes called the orderly officer.

ORDNANCE CORPS. A corps of officers, with regimental grades, having charge of the making, keeping, and issuing of arms and ammunition. They are usually quartered at arsenals and armories.

OUTPOST. A body of troops — usually considered as guards, and relieved from time to time — posted beyond the lines, to guard against surprise of the main body.

OUTWORKS. The detailed works constructed outside the regular fortification, but connected with it according to the principles of defence.

PAIXHAN. A large howitzer, similar to a columbiad, and throwing very large shells and balls. It is named after the inventor.

PARADE. The assembling of troops in a prescribed manner. When equipped with arms, it is called a dress parade; when without, undress.

PARALLELS. The deep trenches parallel to the general direction of a fort, by means of which the besiegers approach it.

PARAPET. The mass of earth or masonry elevated so as to screen a place from a fire of the enemy. It is made so thick that shot cannot penetrate it.

PARK. A number of cannon arranged in close order; also, the place where they are.

PAROLE. The word of honor given by a prisoner to his captor.

PATROL. A small party, under a non-commissioned officer, which goes through or around an encampment at night, to keep order.

PICKET. A small out-post guard.
PIONEERS. Bodies of soldiery provided with suitable implements, who go in advance to clear the way.
PLATOON. One half a company. The two platoons are called respectively first and second platoons.
POINT BLANK. The point of distance at which, when a cannon or fire-arm is aimed, the axis of the piece is on a line with it.
PONTOONS. Boats, or inflated india-rubber bags, upon which planks are placed to form a bridge.
PORT-FIRE. A cylindrical case of paper, filled with a combustible material, and used sometimes in firing cannon.
QUARTERMASTER. The officer whose duty it is to provide the soldiers with quarters and clothing. The Quartermaster's department of the United States embraces officers of all grades, from the colonel commanding to captains.
RALLY. To re-form disordered troops; to bring skirmishers into close order; to collect retreating troops for a new attack.
RAMPART. A broad embankment surrounding a fortified place. It includes the parapet and other raised works.
RANK. The range or order of seniority in commission.
RANK AND FILE. The corporals and privates of an army, or those who parade in the ranks habitually. Lineal rank is the order of promotion by seniority. Brevet rank is honorary rank conferred for meritorious service.
RATIONS. The daily allowance of meat, bread, and other provisions to a soldier.
RECONNOISSANCE. The survey and examination of a portion of country, or any point, with a view to military movements.
RECRUIT. Literally, a soldier enlisted to take a vacant place in a company; commonly, any new soldier.
REDAN. A portion of fortification included in a single salient angle.
REDOUBT. Any small, isolated fort. It is usually defensible on all sides.
REGIMENT. A body of troops comprising ten companies, and commanded by a colonel.
REGULATIONS. A system of orders and instructions on all subjects connected with the management of the army. They are published together, and constitute "The Army Regulations."
RELIEF. A division of the guard—usually one third. These are called first, second, and third relief. The sentinels of each relief are on post for two hours, and off for four.
RESERVE. A select body of troops held back for a decisive moment. In light infantry, the compact nucleus upon which the skirmishers rally.
RETREAT. The parade at sunset, when the evening gun is fired, and the flag taken down for the night.
REVEILLE. The early morning drum-beat and roll-call, usually accompanied by the morning gun.
REVETMENT. Any wall or strengthening process of the earth-works of a fort. Sometimes a work is revetted with sand bags or fascines. Permanent forts are revetted with masonry.
RICOCHET. The rebounding of a shot, usually propelled by a small charge, and with the gun pointed at an elevation of less than ten degrees. By striking in more spots than one, it does greater damage.
RIFLE. Any fire-arm which has a curved groove running

down its length from the muzzle to the bottom of the bore. Cannon are rendered more effective by rifling.

ROLL-CALLS. Stated daily parades of the company, with or without arms, for calling the roll and seeing that every man is in his place.

ROSTER. A list of officers and men, from which details for guard and other duties are made,—on the principle that the longest off any duty shall be detailed for the next tour.

SABRETASCHE (German—*Sabel*, sabre, and *Tasche*, pocket). A leathern case, suspended at the left side of a mounted officer, in which papers are carried.

SAFEGUARD. A passport given by competent authority to a person passing through military lines. It is usually both for persons and property.

SALIENT. Any advanced point or angle in fortification.

SALLY-PORT. The chief entrance to a fort, to afford egress to bodies of troops, as in a sortie.

SALUTE. A discharge of artillery or musketry in honor of persons of rank. The rank is denoted by the number of guns fired.

SAND BAGS. Coarse bags filled with sand, for revetting earth-works and repairing breaches made in them by shot.

SAP. A ditch constructed rapidly by the besiegers in advancing upon a besieged place. According to the dimensions, it is called a full sap, a flying sap, or a double sap. Those who make them are called *sappers*.

SENTINEL. An individual of the guard who is posted to watch for the safety of the camp, and who paces on his post, always alert, and who holds no communication with any person unauthorized to approach him.

SERGEANT. The highest grade of non-commissioned officer. Besides the sergeants who form part of the company organization, in each regiment there is a sergeant-major, who assists the adjutant; a quartermaster-sergeant, who assists the quartermaster; and a color sergeant, who carries the colors; and, at military posts, an ordnance-sergeant, who has charge of the ammunition.

SHELLS. Hollow balls, filled with combustible matter, which is fired by a fuse. They are shot from guns and mortars, and explode when they reach the object aimed at.

SIEGE. The act of surrounding a fort or place with an army, with a view to reducing it by regular approaches.

SKIRMISH. A loose, desultory kind of engagement, generally between light troops thrown forward to test the strength and position of the enemy.

SORTIE. A secret movement, made by a strong detachment of troops in a besieged place, to destroy or retard the enemy's approaches.

STAFF. The officers connected with head-quarters.

STOCKADE. A line of stakes or posts fixed in the ground as a barrier to the advance of the enemy.

SPHERICAL CASE. A thin shell filled with musket balls and powder.

SPIKE. To close the vent of a gun with a nail forcibly driven in.

SHOT. The following are among the different kinds of shot: round, bar, canister or case, grape, and red-hot shot.

SECTIONS. Subdivisions of platoons.

TATTOO. The drum-beat just preceding the retirement of troops, usually at half-past nine o'clock.

TIME. The regular cadence in marching. Common time is ninety steps to the minute; quick time, one hundred and ten; double quick, one hundred and sixty-five.

TRAVERSES. Masses of earth thrown up at short distances in forts along the line of the work, to screen the troops from shot and shells fired in ricochet.

TERRE-PLAIN. The level terrace of a parapet on which the cannon are placed.

TETE-DU-PONT. Works thrown up at one end of a bridge to cover the communication across a river.

TRENCHES. The parallels dug by the besiegers in approaching a work.

TROOP. A company of cavalry.

TROUS DE LOUP. Conical holes dug in the earth, about six feet deep, and four and a half wide at the top. A sharp stake is fastened at the bottom, and the whole slightly covered, so as to conceal them from the enemy. Rows of *trous de loup* are very destructive to cavalry. (The name is French, and means wolf-holes.)

TRUNNION. A pivot projecting from the side of a piece of ordnance, by which it rests on the cheek of the carriage.

TUMBRELS. Covered carts used to convey tools, &c.

VANGUARD. The body of troops constituting a guard, detailed, from day to day, to march in advance of the army.

VIDETTE. Originally, sentinels on the farthest outposts. Now confined to mounted sentinels on outpost duty.

VOLLEY. The simultaneous discharge of a number of cannon, or muskets, or any fire-arms.

WINGS. The portion of an army on the right and left.

ZOUAVES. Light infantry troops, having a peculiar dress and drill, and trained to exercise quick and unusual movements with great rapidity and precision.

SIGNALS AND TELEGRAPHS,

INVENTED BY MAJOR MYERS.

Small flags by day and rockets and watch fires by night are the principal signals used by the Signal and Telegraph corps, and they are the occasion of many picturesque scenes.

Each army in the field has its corps in readiness with large coils of wire, portable apparatus, and every convenience. There are even reels, like hose carriages, on which is wound wire cased in cord, for communication with the aeronauts when these observers of the enemy's movements make their ascensions. One end of the wire is fixed to an apparatus taken up in the basket of the balloon, (which is held by a strong rope,) while the other end acts as an apparatus on the reel. An officer on the ground can thus direct the observations of those above him, and learn what they can see.

THE IRON-PLATED STEAM BATTERIES.

A proposition is now before Congress for the construction of twenty armor-clad gunboats, for which plans and specifications have been prepared by the Navy Department. The following description of these proposed vessels is from the New York Post:—

The length of the vessel on deck is to be two hundred and sixteen feet two inches; extreme breadth forty-eight feet; and depth of hold amidships thirteen feet eleven inches. The hull is to be built throughout of white oak, and copper-fastened to within five feet of the top of the deck. The deck planks are to be white oak, five and one half inches thick and nine inches wide. On this deck there will be deck lights, fitted with shutters to make them water-tight from below, and two conning houses, (for guiding the ship,) one at each end, which are to be of wrought iron plates, round in form, of two feet diameter in width, and forty-six inches high, the sides to be six inches thick, composed of one thickness of four-inch and one of two-inch iron. The lid of the box is to be four inches thick. At ten inches below the bottom of the cover the sides are to be pierced with four tapering peep-holes, two inches in diameter on the outside and six inches on the inside; while three inches lower down there will be, in intermediate spaces, four other peep-holes.

The armament of the vessel is to be contained in two revolving "Cole-towers," whose outside diameter is to be twenty-one and one half feet, and height somewhat over eight feet. The towers are to be composed of two thicknesses of wrought iron plates, securely bolted to a backing of oak ten inches thick, on vertical timbers. The outside plates to be three inches, and the inside two inches thick, and all plates and appendages to be of first quality wrought iron scrap, capable of sustaining a tensile strain of fifty-five thousand pounds per square inch.

Each tower will have one port-hole cut in its side for a gun; this hole to be twenty-four inches wide and forty-one inches extreme height, top and bottom to be semicircular. In the roof is to be a grating, composed of slabs of wrought iron six inches deep and one inch wide. Each tower rests on twelve wrought iron conical rollers, eighteen inches diameter, seven inches width of face, turned and polished, and with steel axles, to work in a wrought iron circular railway secured to the deck at every eighteen inches of its circumference.

On the outside of the tower, the base, to the height of twenty-six inches above the deck, is to be a glacis, or inclined plane, extending ten feet in every direction from the circumference of the tower itself, and composed of two plates, each one and a quarter inches thick, fastened on proper timbers. This glacis will protect the railway on which the tower revolves, with its machinery.

The sides of the vessel are to be plated with four and a quarter inch wrought iron plates, except for thirty feet from **the stern** and stern posts, where the plates are but three and three quarters, and nearer the bow three and a quarter inches thick. The deck is to be covered with ten thicknesses of rolled iron plates, each three quarters of an inch thick, and not less than fifteen feet long, and three feet wide.

The entire weight of iron plates needed for one of these vessels is thus estimated in the specifications:—

Plating on sides	221.0 tons.
Plating on deck	248.2 "
Plating for glacis of two towers	40.6 "
Plating for two towers	116.3 "
Roofs for two towers	17.3 "
Decks for two towers, &c.	48.2 "
Total	691.6 "

The motive power is to consist of two horizontal direct acting engines, to work two screw propellers, one under each counter of the vessel. The screw propellers are to be four-bladed, of ten feet diameter, with a mean pitch of twelve feet six inches.

The gun towers will each be worked by an oscillating engine. For ventilating the berth deck there are, besides these, to be four blowing engines and blowers.

STEEL-CLAD SHIPS.

QUALITIES OF STEEL-CLAD SHIPS.

Every one has read, for the last few years, of the progress of experiments in steel-plated men-of-war, and we have had detailed accounts of English and French ships, and elaborate discussions on their comparative merits. The testimony seems to be conclusive that this plating is to change the character of all navies; in fact, that a navy of wooden ships is no longer a navy worth having, if they are to be opposed to steel clad ships. It seems to be a settled thing that steel plates of four and one-half inches in thickness, and properly backed, will withstand the 100 pounder Armstrong gun at point-blank range. The vessels, plated on their sides, are generally protected on decks by a covering, which is intended to shed any shot which may strike. Besides these desirable qualities, the ships have protection for riflemen. In the great Stevens battery the men serving the guns are to accomplish their duty by the aid of mechanism, which allows them to remain in a place of perfect security. Assuming all this to be true,— and we believe it to be true,— it follows that, unless guns can be so improved as to advance in capability of destructiveness in proportion as material is combined to resist their power, all firing at a ship provided with the most approved armor would be a mere waste of ammunition. A ship so protected, and armed, as intended, with the heaviest cannon, is not only a fortification, but it is a line of forts; it is more— it is a perfect line of circumvallation. If such a ship, in action, should progress two miles, it would be equal, if not to a fortification of that length, at any rate it would be equal to a fortification not much less, and might be equal to much more, from capability of locomotion. Such a ship could destroy any number of wooden ships which might be opposed.

ENGAGEMENT BETWEEN TWO STEEL-CLAD SHIPS.

Another reflection is suggested by the adoption of armor for ships. How is a steel-plated ship to engage a steel-plated ship? Their guns can do no execution on each other, and sailors, marines, and every thing destructible are under cover. What is to be done when such ships, if hostile, meet? Are they to salute and retire in search of smaller fry, or are they to fight? If they fight, it would be the combat of two Achilles, without even vulnerable heels. If these ships are all that is claimed for them, there are but two ways for them to engage each other; either to sheer off, and, like two knights at tournament, charge each other, when the probability is that both would go down; or else to close and board, when victory would depend not upon the invulnerability of the ships, nor upon the caliber of their guns; and yet that is what these ships are built for. It follows that a steel-clad ship could not protect a convoy of ordinary transports against the attack of another steel-clad ship. The protector could do nothing but witness the destruction of his convoy. It results, then, that a steel-clad ship is useful only as opposed to wooden ones or fortifications.

STEEL-CLAD SHIPS FOR THE PROTECTION OF HARBORS.

It seems, then, that the peculiar province of steel-clad ships is the protection of harbors. The enemy could never make a landing in their presence, unless we suppose the whole of his forces to be embarked on similar vessels, which is impossible with the most wealthy nation, or unless we suppose the force to be a very small one. A single steel-clad ship issuing from a harbor and encountering a fleet of transports, however well protected, could destroy them. For the defence of a harbor, if a steel-clad ship encounters a similar one, the combatants who possess the shore would have an immense advantage, in the ability which they would have to put such masses of men on their ships as to overpower all resistance in an attempt to board the other. It is easily seen, then, that the protection of harbors and coasts is the true sphere for the action of steel-clad ships. We cannot be too eager to provide this protection. Government has so far had its attention entirely taken up with a pressing need for gunboats. It has done well — it has done wonders; but another need as pressing has arisen for steel-plated ships for our harbors. Let us have forts, but let us have floating steel forts, too. They are forts that do not require workmen to be sent to a certain point to erect them, but forts built wherever men and material are at hand, and to be stationed wherever needed. Such forts might sail soon enough to hold a southern harbor, when there would not have been time to gain a foothold to throw up more than a single breastwork. With such forts the harbor of Charleston can be taken, and only by such forts.

IRON PLATES FOR CASING WAR VESSELS.

A government agent lately left this country for Europe, for the purpose of obtaining some reliable data in regard to iron plates for casing war vessels. In this country, since the rebellion broke out, a number of inventions have been brought forward, both of improved armor plates, and of improved methods of securing them to the frame of the vessels. Some of them would seem to possess merit, and have been awarded patents. For instance, a patent has been secured for constructing armor plates, each having three or more ribs, which are afterwards cut by a lathe, so as to dovetail (by means of tongues and grooves) into each other. When placed upon the vessel's frame, they are wedged together with keys, driven between them from the inside.

A patent has also been granted for a plan of rolling the plates with flanges on their inner sides, so that they may be secured in position without the necessity of punching bolt holes through the plates. Their edges are so recessed that each fits into the edge of the plate immediately below it.

Letters patent have likewise been issued for a method of constructing and arranging the plates in such manner as to obtain the benefit of their maximum strength and resistance so as to render unnecessary the expense of a heavy wooden framework. The plates proposed are of the box form, and clasp the vessel's frame.

HARBOR DEFENCES.

The introduction of iron armor for ships of war necessitates the use of far heavier artillery than has hitherto been deemed sufficient for harbor defences. None but the most powerful guns possible of construction can be expected to cripple or sink such vessels. Fortunately for us — if the opinions of military authorities can be depended upon — we have a monster fire-arm, capable of crushing in the sides even of a Black Warrior or La Gloire. It is the Rodman gun, which throws a ball of 420 pounds, and which General Bernard says will smash in any steel-clad ship of war. He recommends this tremendous weapon for the defence of New York. It should be furnished for all our principal seaports. He also proposes to cut down and make shot-proof the old seventy-fours, no longer of any service, and use them as floating batteries. They would be towed to and from their moorings, and would need no intricate, heavy, and expensive machinery. They would need no store of provisions; no crew but the trained artillerists needed to serve the guns; none of the ponderous lashings needed to secure heavy ordnance in sea-going ships. Heavier guns could be used on such hulks than any ship will ever dare take to sea, except as cargo. Labor-saving machinery could be applied to the handling of the heavy shot and shell, which would not work in a sea-way.

The Rodman gun is cast hollow, a column of water being introduced into the core, which forms the mould of the bore. To insure that the cooling shall be exclusively internal, the exterior of the mould is kept heated during the whole process. By this means the inventor is enabled to cast a larger effective gun than is used by any other nation. They are cast as large as fifteen inches bore, and Mr. Rodman says they may be cast of thirty inches. A fifteen-inch gun is of the enormous weight of 49,100 pounds, and the solid shot thrown by it weighs 420 pounds. A thirty-inch gun would throw a projectile weighing 3300 pounds! The shells that would probably be used with these guns would weigh respectively about 800 and 2500 pounds. General Bernard says,—

"When these iron-clad ships come to engage at breaching distance our earth or stone forts, we do not try to punch holes in them, — we wish to stave in the whole side. For this purpose, masses of large diameter, moving with moderate velocity, are indispensable. The fifteen-inch shell would probably be effectual against the inclined-sided battery, and would be likely to convert Captain Cole's cupolas into shooting caps indeed. Penetrating and exploding in an iron-clad or wooden vessel, a single one would probably suffice. The inclined side of these newly-proposed ships would not, perhaps, be easily penetrated (though the side would doubtless be stove) even by such a shell. But it must be recollected that about one half of such a ship is not invulnerable — the citadel, or protected portion, occupying only the midships; and the effect of such an explosion in the bow or stern would tell fearfully upon the ship, and upon such of the crew as were not in the citadel. Fifteen inches is the caliber of the gun made as an experiment to test the practicability of casting guns of extraordinary caliber, and their efficiency. The result has convinced our ordnance officers that it is not an extreme limit. A twenty inch gun can probably be made, and not only made, but used with facility and efficiency. Enormous and expensive as they are, such guns may have their 'mission,' and a few of them in our important sea-coast batteries will probably be hereafter deemed an essential part of their armament."

THE MONITOR.
(See engraving, page 63.)

The iron-clad steam battery Monitor, which rendered such timely and efficient service in the naval engagement at the mouth of James River, is one of the steamers built under an act of Congress passed last summer, authorizing the Secretary of the Navy to advertise for proposals for the construction of iron-clad vessels of war, those making proposals in all cases to furnish their own plans. One of the designs accepted was from Captain Ericsson, the well-known engineer. The work on the battery assigned to him was rapidly completed, and she was launched at New York on the 30th of January last. The following description has been given of her, and we reproduce it as of interest at this time:—

The vessel is described as a broad, long, flat-bottomed vessel, with vertical sides and pointed ends, requiring but a very shallow depth of water to float in, though heavily loaded with an impregnable armor upon its sides, and a bomb-proof deck, on which is placed a shot-proof revolving turret, fitted to two very heavy guns. It is so low in the water as to afford no target for an enemy, and every thing and every body is below the water line, with the exception of the persons working the guns, who are protected by the shot-proof turret. The sides of the vessel are first formed of plate iron, half an inch thick, outside of which is attached solid white oak twenty-six inches thick; outside of this again is rolled iron armor five inches thick. The bomb-proof deck is supported by heavy braced oak beams, upon which is laid planking seven inches thick, covered with rolled plate iron one inch thick.

The turret consists of a rolled plate iron skeleton, one inch thick, to which are riveted seven thicknesses, of one inch each, of rolled iron, all firmly bolted together with nuts inside, so that if a plate is started it can be at once tightened again. Upon the sides of the turret that has the port holes through which the guns are discharged, the thickness is increased by an additional plating three inches in thickness, making the sides of the turret which will be presented to the enemy eleven inches. No cannon shot or bolt has ever yet been driven through such a mass of wrought iron. The turret is pierced in different places with four holes for the insertion of telescopes, and just outside of the holes reflectors are fixed to bend the ray of light which comes in a direction parallel with the guns through the axis of the telescope, which is crossed by a vertical thread of spider's web through the line of collimation. The sailing master takes his position in the turret, with his eye to the telescope and his hand upon the wheel that governs the motion of the small engine, and turns the turret so as to keep the guns always directed with absolute precision to the object against which the fire is directed. A scale is also arranged for adjusting the elevation of the guns with similar engineering precision, and it would seem that the firing should be directed with unprecedented accuracy. The top is covered with a bomb-proof roof perforated with holes. The lower part of the gun carriages consists of solid wrought iron beams. These are planed perfectly true, and are placed parallel in the turret — both of the guns pointing in the same direction. The ports through the side of the turret are only large enough to permit the muzzle of the gun to be thrust through. Inside of them are wrought iron pendulums, which close them against the enemy as soon as the gun recoils. Two of the largest Dahlgren guns are placed in this turret. The whole is made to revolve by a pair of steam engines placed beneath the deck.

To give the upper portion of the vessel the proper powers of locomotion, there is suspended beneath it another one of less strength, sufficiently narrow and sloping at the sides that if the enemy's balls should pass below the shot-proof upper vessel, these sides can only be hit at such an acute angle that no harm shall ensue, and in its length approaching the bow only so far that its raking stem may receive the shot fired from directly ahead in the same way, and at the stern giving sufficient space to permit the shot coming directly aft to pass under the shot-proof end without hitting the rudder, which is abaft the propeller. The lower vessel is of iron, one half inch thick, and made in the usual manner. It will carry the machinery, coal, &c., aft, and forward the officers' quarters, ammunition and stores. The two partitions of the vessel are separated by a wrought iron bulkhead. The machinery consists of two horizontal tubular boilers, and two horizontal condensing engines of forty inch diameter of cylinders and twenty-two inch stroke of piston.

The pilot house is only a few feet above the deck, the man standing on a platform below it. It and the turret are the only things above the surface of the deck. With all her armament, coals, and provisions on board, the Monitor draws 9 feet 9 inches, leaving 21 inches height above the water-line. On the trial trip in New York harbor, her speed, by the chip-log, was 6¼ knots an hour, with 65 revolutions of the engines. The boilers, being new could not be worked up to their maximum speed. The real speed of the Monitor is 7 knots, while that of the Merrimac is only 5. The Merrimac is five times as large, and carries four times the armament.

The dimensions of the upper vessel are, length, 174 feet; breadth of beam, 41½ feet; depth, 5 feet; and of the lower vessel, length, 124 feet; beam at top, 34 feet; at bottom, 18 feet; depth,

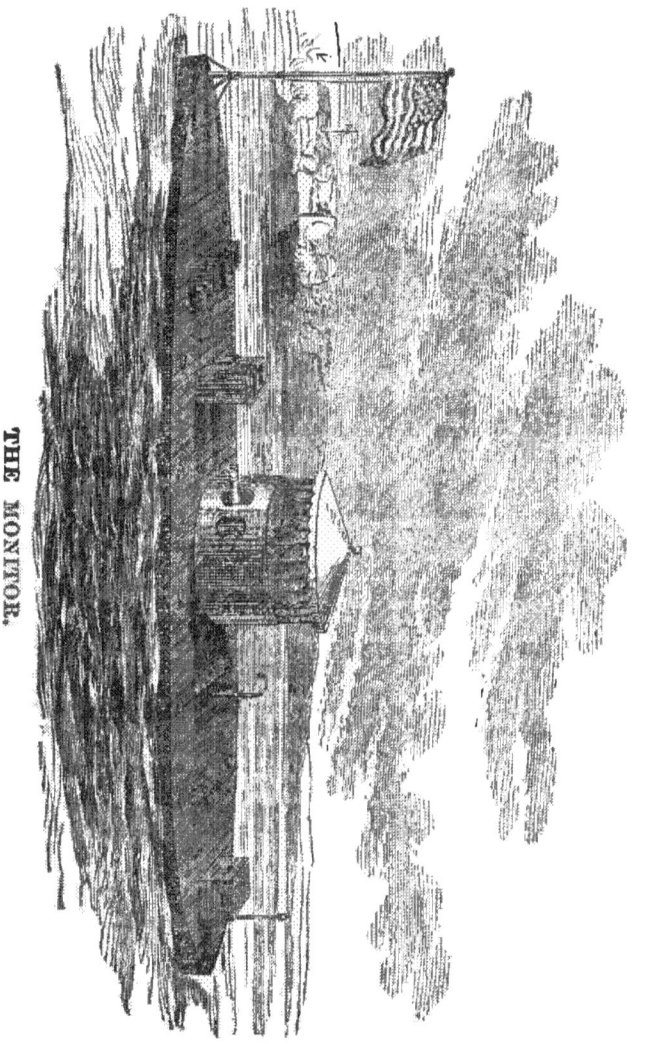

THE MONITOR.

6½ feet. Interior diameter of turret, 20 feet; and height 9 feet. The vessel was officered as follows: Lieutenant Commanding, John S. Worden; Lieutenant and Executive Officer, S. D. Green; Acting Masters, L. N. Stodder and J. W. Webber; Acting Assistant Paymaster, William F. Keeler; Acting Assistant Surgeon, D. C. Logue; Engineer, Alban C. Stimers; First Assistant Engineer, Isaac Newton; Second Assistant, Albert S. Campbell; Third Assistants, R. W. Sands and M. T. Sunstrou; Acting Master's Mate, George Frederickson.

Lieut. William M. Jeffers is now in command, Lieut. Worden having been seriously injured in the engagement with the Merrimac.

Our engraving represents the battery as ready for sea. In preparing for action, the awning over the turret is removed and the square smoke stacks, as well as the shorter pipes, through which air is drawn into the vessel, are taken down. The small square tower at the stern is the wheel house in which the steersman stands. It is made of bars or beams of iron 9 by 12 inches, interlocked at the corners.

STATEMENT OF THE PILOT OF THE CUMBERLAND.

The Cumberland and Congress were at anchor at some distance from each other at Newport News—about three hundred yards apart. This was on Saturday last. At about half past eleven, A. M., the rebel steamer Merrimac came in sight, and we were all on the alert, watching her movements. There was not very much surprise expressed, as she had been expected for some days. The men were beat to quarters almost immediately, and every preparation made for active resistance. The captain of the frigate, Commander Radford, was not on board, being then occupied on a Court of Inquiry on board the Roanoke. In his absence the command was assumed by First Lieutenant George U. Morris, Executive Officer. As soon as the Merrimac got within one mile of the Cumberland we opened fire upon her from our ten-inch pivot guns and our rifled cannon. Some of the shots struck her, and others passed and fell short. She paid no attention whatever to our firing until she got near up to the Congress, when she fired into her. The Congress immediately returned the compliment by discharging a whole broadside, followed by another. She continued on her course, still firing at the Congress, but seeming not to care much for her, and on coming much nearer passed by her and made direct for the Cumberland, under a full head of steam. On approaching sufficiently near she fired one shot at us, which killed five men, and cut away our main rigging, hammock netting, &c. The Cumberland at once replied by firing into her most vigorously. The Merrimac then drew off for a short distance, rounded to and ran into us, striking us on the port bow, backing off again and firing into us rapidly. We continued all the while pouring shot and shell against her from our nine-inch guns and ten-inch pivots, without producing any effect on her whatever. The Cumberland now began to sink. The iron monster had only run into us once, and still we knew that there was no chance at all of saving the vessel. Although in this dangerous and momently sinking condition, the men and officers nobly stood their ground. The Merrimac continued all this while firing occasional shots into us, killing four or five men at every shot. The cockpit was soon filled with wounded men, and poor fellows maimed for life were scattered over the upper, gun and berth decks. Still our men continued working and fighting their guns in the most gallant manner. Our forward magazine was soon filled with the water which was rushing into the ship, so that it became entirely useless. The best order, under the circumstances, prevailed, but the cries of the wounded were dreadful. At one time, a shell burst through the sick bay or hospital, killing four men who were on the sick list and unable to report for duty. At last the water rushed into the gun deck ports, and it was seen that the ship would not float much longer. She was now all down by the head, and going fast to the bottom. The boats were therefore ordered out, and with difficulty brought alongside. It was, however, almost impossible for the men to get from the gun deck to the spar deck; but some of them climbed into the rigging, and others sprang overboard as the ship was settling out of sight. Everybody was naturally endeavoring to reach the boats; some fifty or sixty men were seen floating and swimming about, catching at spars. The rule now was, every one for himself. Quite a number were crushed by the after pivot gun, which rolled about in a dangerous manner.

The Merrimac, seeing that she had finished up the Cumberland, then drew off finally and returned to the Congress, firing at her as she approached. The two other rebel steamers—the Jamestown and Yorktown—were now seen coming down the James River, and soon after opened fire on the fort and on the ships. The Congress had been fighting gallantly all the while, but now, having had about one hundred men killed, and being at the same time so riddled with shot that she was rapidly sinking, was taken in tow by the gunboat Zouave; but the firing still continuing, she hoisted the white flag and surrendered. A Confederate steamer then went alongside, and took off the officers as prisoners, allowing the men to leave in their boats. Lieutenant Smith, who commanded the Congress, was killed, with a number of other officers and men. Only officers were made prisoners.

The officers of the Cumberland suffered considerably. Among those killed was the Chaplain, J. L. Lenhart, who used to reside on Staten Island. He was not heard of after the fight, and is therefore supposed to have been drowned.

Master's Mate John M. Harrington, of Boston, had his head shot off.

All the poor fellows who were wounded went down with the ship, as they were totally unable to help themselves.

The fight between the Monitor or Ericsson battery and the Merrimac was very exciting. The former vessel was in no ways injured; but there is no doubt that the Merrimac had two or three holes put into her port side.

The men on the Cumberland (at least those who were unable to help themselves from their terrible wounds) all sank before any effort could be made to get them off. *But the good old frigate went down with the Union flag flying, as no man on board would haul it down, officers and men declaring that they would go down before they would surrender.* On the same night, the flag was nailed to her foretopmast, which remained above water after she sank, by some sailors who left specially to do so, and is still floating there, in defiance of the rebels.

During the whole engagement between the Cumberland and the Merrimac, there was but one man seen on the latter vessel. He came out of her hatch, and as soon as he was seen a shot was fired at him, which cut him completely in two, sending his head flying in one direction, and his legs and part of his body in another. When the Cumberland was going down the men on board cheered lustily, as they also did when the rebel flag and flagstaff were shot away from on board the Merrimac. There were no cheers nor shouts on board the Merrimac, which, it may be stated, is a screw steamer, completely covered. The other two Secesh steamers had French flags flying, which could be plainly seen at a great distance; but nobody can give any reason for this. To all appearances there were ten guns on board the Merrimac, four on each side, and one each at her bow and stern. They seemed to be nine and ten inch guns, although one or two might have been larger. She began to fire at about half past one o'clock, but we could only occasionally see the men who were working the guns. They were behind their ports, and we could only get a glimpse at them on the recoil of their pieces. Several attempts were made to pick them off with rifle shots, but with what success cannot be ascertained. Every shot fired by the Merrimac went through our ship, but we could make no impression at all upon her—although we gave her over twenty broadsides of solid shot and shell from our nine and ten inch guns.

Our officers behaved very bravely all through the action, losing every thing they had, and escaping only with their lives and the clothing they had on at the time.

The Cumberland sunk in water about fifty-four feet deep. The steamer Whilden saved a great number of those who fell into the water and were clinging to bits of spar and loose wood. The engagement lasted for about two hours, and the Cumberland finally went down with her flags flying.

It must be mentioned that the Congress was not destroyed by the rebels, but by two Union sailors, who were sent on board for that purpose, it is supposed by orders of General Mansfield.

DESCRIPTION OF THE MONITOR BY A VISITOR AFTER THE ACTION.

"I had the pleasure to-day of accompanying Lieut. William M. Jeffers when he proceeded, under orders from Commodore Goldsborough, to take command of the Monitor, and relieve Lieut. Selfridge, of the Cumberland, who had been appointed temporarily in the absence of Lieut. Worden. As we approached this novel naval wonder, I was struck with the pertinence of the Norfolk description of her as 'a Yankee cheese box on a raft.' It gives a better idea of her appearance than any of the engravings or descriptions in the New York papers.

"They all fail to afford a correct idea of the general appearance of the vessel, and especially when she is in action. She is oval shaped, one hundred and seventy-two feet long, and forty-one feet in width at the centre. Her hull rises perpendicularly out of the water, as straight all round as the sides of a stone wall, and as flat on top as a table, without any rail or guards around her. She has two square smoke stacks, about seven feet in height, but in time of action these are removed, and the smoke and steam come through grates in the deck, the iron of which is about eight inches thick. Nothing remains on her deck but the pilot house, which is a square iron statue, about three feet high, about the size of an ordinary dry goods box. When walking her deck, although anchored at the end of Hampton Bar, where the sea is quite rough, not the slightest motion of the waves could be felt. Her deck is as firm and steady as a rock. This position, half way between Newport News and Sewall's Point, has been chosen in order to keep watch and ward over the Merrimac, should she attempt to make another visit to the Roads. *Steam is all the time kept up, and a man on the lookout with a glass keeps a constant watch from the top of the tower.*"

The Monitor cost $275,000, and her first labor has been equivalent to saving many hundred times that sum. The original cost of such vessels is hardly one half that of common first class frigates, while they are not liable, as our frigates are, to decay, and consequently will cost little for repairs. It is held that, on the score of economy alone, keeping efficiency out of the question the best policy of our government will be to have a sufficient supply of iron-clad ships and floating batteries as soon as they can be constructed.

CAPTAIN ERICSSON'S DESCRIPTION OF THE MONITOR; HER CONSTRUCTION, WORKING, &C.

Before the Monitor left I charged the officer particularly to tell the men not to be frightened. I told him to tell the men, "Let every man go down on his knees, and don't be alarmed when the rebel shot strikes you, because it won't hurt you." They all put the question to him, "Won't the shot go through?" "No," says he, "it will stay out." "Then we don't care," they said. But for this precaution there would have been great consternation when the turret was struck. You may estimate the shock when a shot of 200 pounds weight, moving at the rate of 2000 feet in a second, strikes within a foot of a man's head.

I proposed to the captain to let the sailing-master turn the turret. On one side of the turret there is a telescope, a reflector, the image being bent by a prism. This sailing-master, who has nothing to do on the Monitor, I proposed should be stationed there. He not only looked through the telescope, but by means of a small wheel he turned the turret just exactly where he liked. He did that to admiration, pointing it exactly on the enemy. As the Monitor went round, the turret kept turning (it no doubt astonished Captain Buchanan) so that wherever the Monitor was, in whatever position it was placed, the two bulldogs kept looking at him all the time.

The men were new; their passage had been very rough, and the master had to put his vessel right under the heaviest guns that are ever worked on shipboard. It is evident that but for the presence of a master mind on board of that vessel success could not have been achieved. Captain Worden, no doubt, acquitted himself in the most masterly manner. But every thing was quite new. He felt very nervous before he went on board. The fact that the bulwark of the vessel was but one foot above the water line was enough to make him so. When I was before the Naval Committee, the grand objection was, that in sea way the vessel would not work. I gave it as my opinion that it would prove the most easy working in sea way, and it is an excellent sea-boat. The men are supplied with fresh air (though there is no opening except through the turret), by means of blowers worked by the engines, and they are perfectly comfortable. They can remain on the top of the turret in the sea way; it is 64 feet in circumference, quite a promenade. Though the deck is but a foot above the water line, the top of the turret is nine feet above; and here is the important point, that this vessel is in the sea way perhaps the safest vessel ever built. It takes 670,000 pounds to bring her down. There can be no danger of her swamping. It is very much like a bottle with a cork in it.

In relation to the point whether the Monitor is capable of taking care of the Merrimac, let me say that she would have sunk the Merrimac but for the fact of her having fired too high. If they had kept off at a distance of 200 yards, and held the gun exactly level, the shot would have gone clear through. But Mr. Stimers had the guns elevated a little, and the roof of the Merrimac is so strong that the balls rebounded. Next time they encounter the Merrimac they will leave the guns level, and they won't mind if the ball strikes the water, because the ricochet will take it where they want it. The next time they go out, I predict the third round will sink the Merrimac. There is another great point. They had 50 wrought iron shot which were not used. Captain Dahlgren issued peremptory orders that they should not be used, and they obeyed those orders. Now, wrought iron shot is one thing, and a cast iron shot is another. A wrought iron shot cannot break. The side armor of the Merrimac is insufficient to resist it. The channel is very narrow, and the Merrimac must follow it. But the Monitor can go any where and take the very best position.

A Member. How often can they fire?

Mr. Ericsson. In about one minute and a half. It is often said one gun would be sufficient, but it is not so. By having two guns you have time for one to cool. You may depend upon it, that if the Merrimac comes out again she will be sunk.

Mr. Wetmore. I should like to ask of Captain Ericsson whether he has heard that one of his shot entered the Merrimac, killed 17 men, and wounded Captain Buchanan, who has since died.

Mr. Ericsson. I have not.

Mr. Brown. It must have been a shell.

Mr. Ericsson. That is not possible; but if a solid shot goes through the Merrimac, the armor would be carried in in a great many splinters; the shot weighing 185 pounds, there would be a regular shower of wood and iron; but it is quite well ascertained that a shell cannot pass an iron plate two inches thick. You can hardly imagine what commotion would take place from such a shot. The decks would be almost literally covered.

A Member. I would like to ask Captain Ericsson whether his battery could not be erected on various points in our harbor for its defence?

Mr Ericsson. I imagine that the best kind of a harbor defence is a floating structure that can be removed from place to place.

The Member. You can move this turret in any direction, and save all the expense of your vessel; and you require only a small steam-engine.

Mr. Ericsson. This vessel is equal to twenty forts. It can move from place to place. In this battery you have a vessel that draws only twelve feet of water. The Warrior, drawing thirty-four feet of water, must come in the middle of the channel, and we could move along the shore. By means of one single floating battery you could defend the harbor better than by twenty forts. That is easily demonstrated.

In a letter replying to congratulations tendered him upon the success of the Monitor, Mr. Ericsson says,—

"Give me only the requisite means, and *in a very short time* we can say to those powers, now bent on destroying republican freedom, *Leave the Gulf with your frail craft or perish!* I have all my life asserted that mechanical science will put an end to the power of England over the seas.

"The ocean is nature's highway between the nations. It should be free, and surely nature's laws, when properly applied, will make it so."

The following letter from Captain Ericsson corrects the published statement that the ventilation of the Monitor is imperfect, and conveys some interesting information as to the capacity of the floating battery:—

New York, March 16, 1862.

MY DEAR SIR: It may safely be asserted that the Monitor is the best ventilated vessel afloat. The blowers draw in from the external atmosphere upwards of 4000 cubic feet of fresh air in every *minute*, part of which passes through the boiler furnaces, and part through the entire vessel. The trouble during the passage to Fortress Monroe was caused by the sea breaking over and passing into the ventilating trunks, these not being made high enough.

There appears to be a general misconception of nearly every important point relating to the impregnable battery. The most serious error is the assumption that its power was fully developed during the contest at Hampton Roads. The power of the guns alone was tested; with guns of such caliber as the structure *was made to bear*, the Monitor would sink the Merrimac or the Warrior in the first round. Yours very truly,

J. ERICSSON.

WHY SHE WAS NAMED THE MONITOR—LETTER FROM CAPTAIN ERICSSON.

The following letter from Captain Ericsson to Assistant Secretary Fox will now be read with interest:—

New York, Jan. 20, 1862.

SIR: In accordance with your request, I now submit for your approbation, a name for the floating battery at Greenpoint. The impregnable and aggressive character of this structure will admonish the leaders of the Southern rebellion that the batteries on the banks of their rivers will no longer present barriers to the entrance of the Union forces. The iron-clad intruder will thus prove a secure monitor to those leaders. But there are other leaders who will also be startled and admonished by the booming of the guns from the impregnable iron turret. Downing Street will hardly view with indifference this last Yankee notion—this monitor. To the Lords of the Admiralty the new craft will be a monitor, suggesting doubts as to the propriety of completing those four steel-clad ships at three and a half millions apiece. On these, and many similar grounds, I propose to name the new battery *Monitor*. I am, sir, respectfully,

Your obedient servant,

J. ERICSSON.

SKETCHES OF CAPT. ERICSSON, LIEUT. WORDEN, AND CHIEF ENGINEER STIMERS.

CAPTAIN JOHN ERICSSON

Was born in 1803, in the Province of Vermeland, among the iron mountains of Sweden. His father was a mining proprietor, so that in his youth he had ample opportunities to watch the operations of the various engines and machinery connected with the mines. At the age of ten years he constructed, with his own hands and after his own plans, a miniature saw-mill, and also made numerous drawings of complicated mechanical contrivances, with instruments of his own invention and manufacture.

In 1814 he attracted the attention of the celebrated Count Platen, who had heard of his boyish efforts, and desired an interview with him. After carefully examining the various plans and drawings which this youth exhibited on this occasion, the Count handed them back to him, simply observing, in an impressive manner, "Continue as you have commenced, and you will one day produce something extraordinary." These few words of kind encouragement from so distinguished a personage sunk deeply into the mind of the young mechanician, and confirmed him in the career on which he had entered. Immediately after this interview young Ericsson was appointed a cadet in the corps of engineers, and after six months' tuition, at the age of twelve years, was appointed *nivelleur* at the Grand Ship Canal of Sweden, which connects the North Sea with the Baltic, under Count Platen. In this capacity, in the year 1816, he was required to set out the work for more than six hundred men, and at that time he was not tall enough to look through the leveling instrument, and in using it he was obliged to mount upon a stool, carried by his attendants for that purpose. As the discipline in the Swedish army required that the soldier should always uncover his head in speaking to his superior, gray-headed men came, cap in hand, to receive their instructions from this mere child. There are now many important works on the canal constructed after drawings made by Ericsson at this early age. At the age of fifteen he was in possession of accurate plans of the whole work, drawn by his own hand. His associations with military men on the canal had given him a tendency for military life, and at the age of seventeen he entered the Swedish army as an ensign, without the knowledge of his friend and patron, Count Platen. This excited the indignation of the Count, who tried to prevail on him to change his resolution; but, finding all his arguments useless, he terminated an angry interview by bidding the young ensign to "go to the devil." The affectionate regard which he entertained for the Count caused the circumstances of this interview to make a deep impression upon young Ericsson. Soon after the young ensign had entered upon his regimental duties a matter occurred which threatened to obscure his hitherto bright prospects. His colonel, Baron Koskull, had been disgraced by the King about the time that he had recommended Ericsson for promotion. This circumstance induced the King to reject the recommendation. Prince Oscar, however, interceded for the young man with the King, who yielded to the persuasions of the Prince, and promoted Ericsson to the lieutenancy for which he had been recommended. About this time the government had ordered the northern part of Sweden to be surveyed, and that officers in the army should be employed in this service. Ericsson, whose regiment was stationed in the northern highland, proceeded to Stockholm, for the purpose of submitting himself to the severe examination then requisite to precede the appointment of government surveyor. The mathematical education which he had received under Count Platen now proved very serviceable. He passed the examination with great distinction, and in the course of it, to the surprise of the examiners, showed that he could repeat Euclid *verbatim*; not by the exercise of the memory, but from his perfect mastery of geometrical science. There are yet in the archives of Sweden detailed maps of upwards of fifty square miles made by his hand.

While thus variously occupied, being on a visit to the house of his colonel, Ericsson on one occasion showed his host how readily and by what simple means mechanical power may be produced, independently of steam, by condensing flame. On the 18th of May, 1826, he obtained permission from the King to visit England. He here proceeded to construct a number of engines of new inventions, which were attended with no trifling expenditure, and to meet the demands then made upon him, the young adventurer was compelled to draw on his mechanical resources.

Invention now followed invention in rapid succession, until the records of the Patent Office, in London, were enriched by the drawings of the remarkable steam boiler on the principle of artificial draught. In bringing this invention before the public, he thought it advisable to join some old and established mechanical house in London, and, accordingly, he associated himself with John Braithwaite. In the fall of 1829 the Liverpool and Manchester Railway Company offered a prize for the best locomotive engine, to be tested on the small portion of the railway then completed. Ericsson, not willing to allow this occasion to escape him, immediately set to work, planned the engine, executed the working drawings, and caused the patterns to be made, and the whole machine was completed within seven weeks. The day of trial arrived. The competing engines were on the ground, and the novelty of the race had attracted an immense concourse of people. Both sides of the railway, for more than a mile in length, were lined with thousands of spectators, and to the surprise and admiration of the crowd, the Novelty steam-carriage started, and, guided by its inventor, Ericsson, assisted by John Braithwaite, darted along the track at the rate of fifty miles an hour. In a short time afterwards he constructed a steam fire engine, which excited much interest in London at the time the Argyle Rooms were on fire. He subsequently constructed a similar engine for the King of Prussia, which was mainly instrumental in saving several valuable buildings at a great fire some years ago at Berlin. For this invention Ericsson received, in 1842, the large gold medal offered by the Mechanics' Institute of New York, for the best plan of a steam fire engine. Mr. Ericsson was the first to apply to marine engines centrifugal blowers, now so common in this country in all boilers using anthracite coal. In the year 1834 he applied such a blower, worked by a separate small steam engine, to the steam packet Corsair, of one hundred and twenty horse power, plying between Liverpool and Belfast.

Mr. Ericsson emigrated to this country in 1839, then being thirty-six years old. His first great achievement after his arrival was the building of the United States steam frigate Princeton, the first vessel that steam was ever introduced into with the works below the water line. She proved a complete success. About the same time he planned the French frigate Pomone, fifty guns, which is at present in our waters; she also proving a great success. Captain Ericsson, after the completion of these vessels, gave his whole time to his favorite work, the completion of the calorie engine, which he has since brought to great perfection, though on a small scale. His next undertaking was the planning and invention of the steamer Ericsson, which is familiar to all our readers. He did the whole work, from the time her keel was laid to the moment that her paddles were first turned, in the brief space of seven months. Although not answering all that was commercially expected of her, she was an entire mechanical success, speaking more than words of the great genius of the inventor, and as a marine structure she has never been equalled, much less surpassed. The name of Captain Ericsson has been comparatively unheard of for some time past, until the commencement of another new idea of his, as illustrated so satisfactorily in the now noble steam battery Monitor. He signed the contract for her construction on the 5th day of last October, and on the 31st of December — being a period of two months and eight days — her steam, machinery, and propeller were put into operation, and on the one hundred and first working day she was launched. This is a celerity which has never been equalled in this country or in England.

LIEUTENANT JOHN LORIMER WORDEN

Is a native and citizen of New York, from which state he was appointed to the navy. His original entry as a midshipman into the service bears date from the 10th of January, 1834, and he obtained his present commission on the 30th of November, 1846. His sea service under his present commission to the end of 1860, had been eight years and nine months; his total sea service being to that date nearly seventeen years. His shore or other duty amounted at that time to nearly seven years, and he was over three years unemployed. His total length of service up to the present time exceeds twenty-eight years. He was last at sea in November, 1860, on board the sloop Savannah, twenty-two guns, on the blockading squadron, and was granted a short leave of absence on his return, after which he was sent as a special messenger to Fort Pickens, with despatches to Captain Adams, of the Sabine, commanding the fleet off Pensacola, with notice that the fort would be reënforced by two companies of artillery, and instructions to Captain Adams and Colonel Brown as to their conduct in case of an attack by the rebels upon the fleet and fort. He went by the land route, and on the way he destroyed his despatches. As he anticipated, he was arrested at Montgomery, and as no papers were found on his person he was allowed to pass. On his arrival at Pensacola he obtained a pass from the rebel General Bragg, permitting him to carry a verbal message from Secretary Cameron to Captain Adams. He went to him and repeated from memory his despatches. The fort was reënforced, and as he was returning he was arrested by the rebel General Bragg, under the false pretence of having broken his parole; but the main object was to obtain his despatches to the government, if he should have had any in his possession. He was sent to Montgomery, where he was kept for some time as a prisoner of war. There was an intense excitement against him, as the rebel General Bragg had collected a force of 1000 men, and intended attack Fort Pickens the very night it was reënforced. Lieutenant Worden was kept in confinement until the middle of November last, when he was exchanged and went to Fortress Monroe, where he joined the Minnesota. He was afterwards detached from that vessel, and appointed to the command of the Monitor.

CHIEF ENGINEER ALBAN C. STIMERS

Is a native and citizen of the State of New York, and was appointed to the navy from this state. He first entered the service on the 11th of January, 1849, and gradually worked himself up to the position of Chief Engineer, which rank he obtained on the 21st of July, 1858. Up to the 1st of January, 1861, his register of services stood as follows: His sea service, under the present commission to that date, was thirteen months; his total sea service has been six years and six months; he was on shore and other duty for three years and three months, and has been unemployed for three years and a quarter, making his total service under the government up to that date twelve years, or over thirteen years to the present time. Since then he has been Chief Engineer of the steam frigate Roanoke, from which he was detached to superintend the construction of the Monitor, or Ericsson battery. He was also one of the committee of three to examine into the merits of the Stevens battery. At the commencement of the year 1860 he was in a situation entirely opposite to his present one, for he was then *the Chief Engineer of the steam frigate Merrimac*. Twelve months afterwards he was on special duty at Erie, in Pennsylvania, and when the Roanoke went into commission was attached to her in the capacity before mentioned. He is a man of a little over thirty years of age, and is well esteemed in both a professional and social capacity by those with whom he is connected. He now stands No. 14 on the list of Chief Engineers, and his future prospects are very good.

THE REBEL IRON-CLAD GUNBOAT MERRIMAC.
(See engraving, page 75.)

The Merrimac, the iron-plated rebel steamer, was formerly the United States frigate of the same name, which was scuttled and sunk at the Norfolk Navy Yard, at the commencement of the rebellion, by the officers of the Union government, to prevent her falling into the hands of the rebels. She was built at Charlestown, in 1855, and was pierced for forty guns. Her last service had been in the Pacific squadron. After the rebels took possession of the yard she was raised, and converted into a man-of-war, for their own use. Her hull was cut down to within three feet of her water-mark, and a bomb-proof house built on her gun-deck. She was also iron-plated, and her bow and stern steel-clad, with a projecting angle of iron, for the purpose of piercing vessels. She has no masts, and there is nothing to be seen over her gun-deck, with the exception of her pilot house and smoke stack. Her bomb-proof is three inches thick, and is made of wrought iron. Her armament consists of four eleven-inch navy guns on each side, and two one hundred-pounder Armstrong guns at the bow and stern. Last November she made a trial trip from Norfolk, running down so close to Fortress Monroe as to be seen by the naked eye, but ventured no nearer. Although she was looked upon by the rebels as a very tough customer for a vessel or vessels not protected as she is, she remained inactive, anchored off Norfolk, until her present engagement. The next engagement will be terrific, as orders have been given to capture or sink her at whatever cost.

The Merrimac was commanded by Franklin Buchanan, formerly of the Union navy.

SKETCH OF FRANKLIN BUCHANAN, COMMANDER OF THE MERRIMAC.

This rebel officer was formerly in the service of the United States, and while in the navy filled the post of Captain, and afterwards was Commandant of the Washington Navy Yard, continuing in that position up to the period of his resignation. Some time after he expressed a desire to withdraw his resignation, but was not permitted to do so. He is a native of Maryland, and entered the federal service on the 28th of January, 1815, and had seen some forty-five years service in the federal navy, twenty-one years of which were at sea. On joining the rebels he was appointed to the command of the Merrimac. His brother was an officer on board the Congress, and was in the action of Saturday last.

In addition to the Merrimac, the rebels are now completing two other mail-clad vessels, at the Gosport Navy Yard. One of these is the sunken Delaware, which shared the fate of the Merrimac at the commencement of this rebellion — a very large vessel, which, if ever launched, will be a great acquisition to the secession navy. The history of the other is not known, but it is doubtless some old hulk which has been brought from the watery sepulchre to new and diabolic life. At Richmond, also, two iron-clad vessels are being built, and the utmost activity in this direction characterizes the rebels since their partial success with the Merrimac.

SIX NEW MONITORS TO BE BUILT.

The Secretary of the Navy has determined upon the immediate construction of six floating batteries, exactly or nearly like the Monitor, and the preliminary arrangements to that end have been made with Captain Ericsson. The batteries are to be built with all possible despatch. No better illustration can be given of the remarkable inventive genius of Captain Ericsson than the fact, that after the severe and complete test to which his battery has been subjected, only one improvement, and that a trifling one, can be pointed out. It is the substitution of a cylindrical, instead of a square form in the little pilot house. In the engagement at Hampton Roads, the only injury sustained by the Monitor was the slight springing of one of the "logs" in this square pilot house. Had the shape of the house been round, like that of the turret, it is supposed that the balls would have glanced from the former harmlessly, as from the latter. This change will, therefore, be made in the Monitor, if it has not been already made, and will be introduced into models of the four new batteries. Another alteration of doubtful expediency has been suggested, viz., the transfer of the pilot house from its place, about a rod from the turret, to the top of the turret, giving to that "Yankee cheese box" the appearance of a telescope with one joint drawn out. The only obvious advantage in this change is the elevation of the lookout to a higher range of vision.

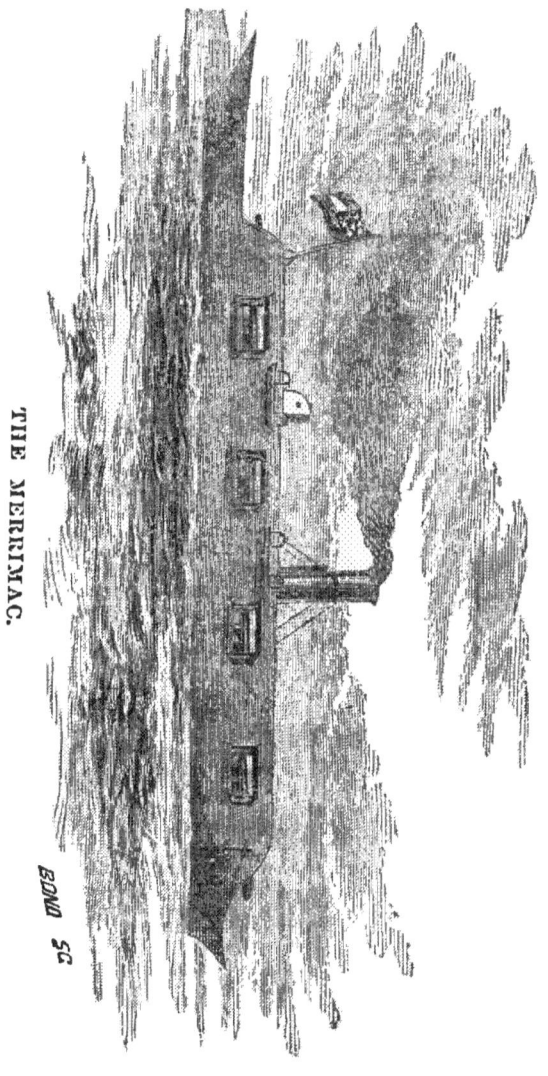

THE MERRIMAC.

Improving the experience gained by the first fight, the Monitor has been strengthened in important parts, and it is believed will go into the next fight perfectly impervious to the heaviest missiles that can be sent against her. The appearance of her pilothouse is altogether altered, and now presents no salient point against which a ball can strike. Such an accident as occurred to Captain Worden will now be rendered impossible.

These alterations and improvements are made under the direction of Mr. Stimers, the government engineer, who superintended the building of the Monitor, and directed her machinery and the revolving of her tower during the fight. His whole energies are enlisted in the success of the battery, and in desiring another opportunity to prove its power against the Merrimac.

The navy officers who have tested the Monitor are willing to go to sea in her; and Mr. Ericsson is so confident of the sea-going abilities of his description of vessels that he is now preparing specifications for an iron-clad ship-of-war more than 300 feet in length.

Assistant Secretary Fox has quite a collection of relics, which afford practical hints upon gunnery and iron-clad ships. Among them are specimens of plates from the armor of Commodore Foote's gunboats, which were damaged in the attack on Fort Donelson. One of the plates, three quarters of an inch thick, was struck, apparently at an angle of forty-five degrees, and the ball glanced off, making an indentation corresponding to one third the thickness of the ball, and about fifteen inches lo g. The plate was partially fractured, but the iron was tough enough to ward off the missile. The most interesting object in the collection is a portion of the shell fired from the Merrimac into the tower of the Monitor. The head of the shell was imbedded in the iron armor of the Monitor, the remainder having been scattered by the explosion. Secretary Fox says it is useless to make any more guns of the caliber now used, but that some 15 inch columbiads, that will smash through any thing that floats, must be provided for naval warfare.

OUR NEW IRON-CLAD NAVY.

Senator Hale, as Chairman of the Senate Committee on Naval Affairs, has reported a bill providing for the construction of a steam ram of five or six thousand tons burden, at the cost of a million of dollars, and also appropriating $13,000,000 for the construction of iron-clad gunboats; $783,000 for the completion of Stevens's battery, and $500,000 for extending the facilities of the Washington Navy Yard, so as to roll and forge plates for the armored ships.

There is one grand, practical result from the present war which could not have been attained for the republic under any other circumstances, and that is an iron-clad, invincible navy, the greatest in the world. Hitherto such vessels had been little more than a theory — an experiment in the course of development. The first practical test is in American waters, and by American vessels, constructed by the genius of American mechanics. Their immense success will startle all Europe, add vastly to their public burdens, for it involves not only the construction of new navies, but an entirely different system of fortifications.

It is a grand point to have the start in these engines of destruction, and America will have gained that point over every power of Europe. In the event of a war between two maritime powers, that nation which has the most and best iron-clad vessels first at sea will be able to maintain the superiority to the end. No coast fortifications now built can keep such vessels out of an enemy's harbors. Seaboard cities, with their navy yards and ships on the stocks, will be at the mercy of iron-clad frigates. How do the powers of Europe and the United States relatively stand in regard to such vessels? The following table will show what has been done and is now in progress in Europe:—

England is building	15
France	14
Spain	5
Austria	2
Total	36

Of the English, acording to the recent statement of Lord Paget, six are to be of the same model as the Monitor, having a turret and two guns. The Warrior and Black Prince, already completed, are each upwards of 5000 tons burden. In addition to her other guns, the Warrior carries one which throws a projectile of 450 pounds weight. This vessel is shown, by her trial trip to Lisbon, in smooth water, to be in some respects a failure. The iron-clad ram, the Defence, appears to be more seaworthy, but a clumsy structure, though it is stated she made eleven knots an hour. Her burden is 3660 tons. The French iron-plated frigate Gloire is the first ever built, and a few others have been finished by order of Napoleon, which are regarded as an improvement on her; but what is done in this respect is kept as secret as possible.

The United States have the following already built, contracted for, and proposed:—

The Monitor	1
The Galena, built at Mystic	1
The powerful vessel at Philadelphia	1
The Adirondack	1
The Stevens battery	1
The Naugatuck, built by Stevens	1
Iron-clad gunboats ordered by Congress	20
Iron-clad frigates recommended by Senate Naval Committee	20
The iron ram do.	1
Gunboats ordered by Massachusetts	2
Total	49

New York State will probably add one or two more; thus making a naval force of fifty iron-clad gunboats — greatly exceeding the combined iron-plated vessels of all Europe, and able to whip the navies of the world. In the foregoing list we have not included our iron-plated gunboats on the inland waters of the West. As yet we have only one — the Monitor — ready for action. The Galena and the formidable boat at the Philadelphia Navy Yard will also soon be ready, and it will not take very long to clothe with iron armor the new sloop-of-war Adirondack, now at the Brooklyn Navy Yard. The Naugatuck — a present to the government by Mr. Stevens — is not completed. She is a small but stanch iron gunboat — a miniature of Mr. Stevens's leviathan floating battery. Her speed is ten knots an hour. She can carry coal for twelve days, and her armament is a single one hundred-pounder Parrott gun — the most formidable rifled cannon in the world. Like the Monitor, she can be sunk at will nearly to the top of her deck. The Stevens large battery can throw a greater weight of metal than any thing afloat, and she can outsail any war vessel in the world. It will only take two or three months to finish her.

When to these is added the swift ram of far greater weight and power than the English Defence, and the forty gunboats and frigates, all iron-clad, no navy in the world can resist such a force. Not a moment ought to be lost in preparing them for action. The experience of each vessel engaged in actual battle will be sufficient for the improvement of those not yet finished. Soon shall we have an armada which will sweep the seas and be able to lay in ruins all the sea coast fortresses known to modern science.

NEW PLAN FOR IRON-CLAD SHIPS.

Mr. William N. Van Wagenen, of Newark, has a model of an entirely new plan of a shot-proof hull, and iron fort on deck, for an armored gunboat. This plan is fitted, not only for a gunboat, but also for a marine ram. Mr. Van Wagenen proposes an iron-clad boat, entirely shot-proof, thoroughly stanch and seaworthy, with a stationary iron fort, within which shall revolve on a turn-table three or four of the heaviest cannon made. The peculiarity of the form of the hull is, that it presents absolutely no mark for the enemy. The side consists, in fact, of two disks joined together at the outer edge, which is sharp, and in practice would be of solid oak, ten feet through, armed on the outside with a band of eight-inch iron. The deck slants upward at an angle of about ten degrees, is sufficiently protected by two-inch and inch iron plates, and it is impossible to fire a shot straight at it.

Every thing which hits must glance off. The bow and stern are of solid oak for twenty to twenty-five feet, and as the ship has no cutwater, the sharp, angular prow makes an excellent ram. The water-line of the vessel is a little below the sharp edge, and the bottom is therefore armored for one or two feet down. The stern projects far beyond the rudder and propeller, and gives important protection to these vital parts, which are altogether submerged and out of the reach of shot.

The tower or fort Mr. Van Wagenen purposes to fasten to the deck, believing it much safer to make the guns revolve within, and present themselves accurately to numerous portholes made in the tower. This he proposes to make of fifteen layers of inch boiler plates, laid over each other in a very ingenious way.

He proposes the following dimensions for a sea-going and perfectly sea-worthy iron-clad boat, which will show the novel proportions he brings into use. The hull to be two hundred feet long, sixty-five feet extreme beam, tapering to a sharp point at bow and stern. The lines are alike, stem and stern. Ship builders will see some novel advantages in her form. The ribs and deck beams are nearly alike in shape, and scarcely any crooked timber need be used in the construction. The tower is to be forty feet in outside diameter, thirty-seven inside, eight feet high on the outboard edges, five feet high amidships. It sets in the vessel, instead of on its deck. She is to be moved by one propeller, and her lines admit of almost any speed, twelve knots easily. She will be of very light draught, as is evident from her shape, and would draw about twenty feet when in running trim. The cost of a vessel of the dimensions above mentioned, built on Mr. Van Wagenen's plan, he estimates at $250,000.

IRON-CLAD FRIGATE.

The iron-clad frigate now building at Kensington will be ready for launching by the first of May, and handed over to the government in July, according to the terms of the contract.

The vessel, when finished, will be one of the finest of the kind in the world, and will be far superior in many respects to the British frigate Warrior. The new frigate is to be 3500 tons burden. Her armament has not yet been fully determined, but she will carry at least sixteen guns, of eleven-inch bore, and will, doubtless, have several deck pivot guns. Notwithstanding her immense weight, she has been so modelled as to draw but fifteen feet of water, besides having the additional advantage of greater steadiness in a heavy sea. She is two hundred and thirty feet long, sixty feet beam, twenty-five feet hold, and will have three full decks. The greatest feature about the new frigate will be the exceedingly small quantity of water which she will be made to draw. She will be the lightest draught of over five hundred tons, except the Pawnee, in our navy.

In this respect the vessel will be superior to the much-talked of Warrior, the weight of both being taken into consideration. The latter draws twenty-seven feet of water, or more than the whole depth of the Kensington frigate—twenty-five feet. Owing to the declivity in the sides of the new frigate, it will almost be a work of impossibility for an enemy to board her. The declivity of the sides commences at the water's edge. The bulwarks are exposed eleven feet above water mark, and the tops of the bulwarks are situated ten feet from a vertical line that joins the foot of the bulwarks and the water mark. Besides this, the iron plates will be so constructed as to project six feet beyond the stem below water, which will enable them to act as a battering ram, by which vessels may be run down and swamped.

The iron for this purpose has already been prepared, and is now ready for use. Her boilers, engines, rudder, and steering apparatus will all be below water mark and out of harm's reach in case of action. The deck will also be covered with iron. The iron plates below the water mark will all be fastened on before launching, while those on the sides will be put in place afterwards. The iron plates on the sides will be hammered smooth, and owing to the declivity, balls will glance from the vessel. Behind the iron plates the wooden hull will be twenty-three inches thick, in addition to the knees and waterways. The wood used in the construction of this vessel is principally oak, of the best quality. At the present time about 400 men, of which 100 are laborers, and the balance borers and ship carpenters are employed on the new frigate. As soon as she gets more fully under way this force will be greatly increased. The total cost to the government for the construction of this vessel will be about $900,000.

THE TWENTY-INCH GUNS.

Many objections are raised to the plan proposed by the War Department of casting twenty-inch guns, besides the danger of bursting. The Philadelphia U. S. Gazette says, this gun is twenty feet long — too long to be handled on board a vessel, as it must be run in and out to load. The gun carries a solid shot weighing one thousand pounds, or a shell weighing nine hundred and **twenty-five pounds. It must, therefore, be loaded by machinery.**

SUBMARINE ARTILLERY BATTERIES.

Another project, supposed by many to be new at the present day, is that of submarine artillery batteries — firing guns under water. This invention engaged Fulton's attention. He several times fired a four-pounder, submerged three feet in the waters of the Hudson, and on one occasion he also fired a one hundred-pounder situated at the same depth. With such a battery he proposed to fire into the hulls of enemies' war vessels under their water lines, and thus sink them. Such submarine batteries were designed to be carried in war vessels, and when required they were to be hung and slung over their sides, and submerged.

The advantage that the invention recently brought forward probably has, is in the method of mounting and regulating the guns beneath the water line.

REBEL OFFICIAL STATEMENT OF THE BULL RUN BATTLE.

The rebel force actually engaged in that battle, as appears from the official return, was only fourteen regiments of infantry, five batteries of artillery, and twelve companies of cavalry. The plan of the battle was drawn by Beauregard, and approved by Gen. Joseph E. Johnston on the 20th, the day before the battle; so that Johnston was first and Beauregard, second in command. Beauregard commanded the reserve in person.

Just 1421 of our soldiers were captured by the enemy. Of this number, 871 were sent to Richmond, and 550 wounded men were sent to the rebel hospitals. Our losses of cannon and ordnance stores, which have never been accurately estimated by the Federal officers, are summed up in an official return from Capt. Alexander, of the rebel engineer service, as follows:—

"One 30-pounder Parrott gun, with 300 rounds of ammunition; nine 10-pounder Parrott guns, with 100 rounds each; three 6-pounder brass guns, with 100 rounds each; three 12-pounder brass howitzers, with 100 rounds each; two 12-pounder boat howitzers, with 100 rounds each; nine James's rifled field pieces, with 100 rounds each; 37 caissons; 6 travelling forges; 4 battery wagons, splendidly equipped; 64 artillery horses, with harness, &c.; 500,000 rounds small arms ammunition; 4500 sets of accoutrements, cartridge boxes, &c.; 4000 muskets. Total number of cannon taken, twenty-seven; muskets, four thousand."

In the panic of our troops they threw away great quantities of tools and equipments, the most important of which were 1650 camp cooking utensils, 2700 mess utensils, 700 blankets, 23 horses, 21 wagons, and a large quantity of miscellaneous articles.

MILITARY EDUCATION.

We are glad to see that this is already receiving the careful attention of practical minds. It is not too early to begin the discussion that must lay the foundation for a system of military education adapted to our wants and peculiarities as a nation. We have received a pamphlet entitled "A Plan for Military Education in Massachusetts," written by Edmund Dwight, which is worthy of attention, not only on account of the plan proposed, but for the information it gives on the general subject, some of which we condense. France, Prussia, Switzerland, Austria, and other European nations require a certain amount of military service from the whole male population, in order that the material for efficient armies may always be at hand and ready for any emergency. Had we been thus prepared, how much of blood and treasure might have been saved to us! War has been with us a slow, expensive process, and fruitful of disastrous blunders. Mr. Dwight cites the example of Switzerland, our sister republic, to show what the history of the present rebellion might have been had we been prepared for such a crisis. In 1847, seven of the Swiss cantons seceded from the Confederation. They held the strongest military position in Europe, but the loyal cantons put on foot an army of 100,000 men, well armed, drilled and officered, and in thirty days from the first proclamation of the commanding general the war was ended and order restored. Had we been able to do the like, how quickly the days of the present unholy rebellion would have been numbered! In 1856, a quarrel having arisen with Prussia, Switzerland raised an army of 200,000 men, well provided with artillery. Switzerland has no standing army, and as the state is a confederacy of cantons under democratic forms of government, we may find something in her system applicable to our own case. The constitution of Switzerland declares that every citizen is a soldier. Military service is required between the ages of twenty and forty-four. The substitution of one man for another is forbidden, but exemption from service is allowed to certain persons, such as officers of the government and of public institutions, clergymen, students of theology, and others. The militia is divided into the federal contingent and the landwehr. The former consists first of the *elite*, which includes three per cent. of the whole male population between the ages of twenty and thirty-four. The time of service is eight years. Second, the *reserve*, being one and a half per cent. of the population not above the age of forty. The landwehr includes men up to the age of forty-four. The landstrum, or *levy en masse*, comprises the whole population capable of bearing arms, between the ages of twenty and fifty, and not included in the classes before described. The male population of Switzerland is 1,140,000, and under this system the little republic has always at her service 275,000 effective men, well armed, drilled, and officered. This force is not a mere conglomeration of militia, but suitably divided into artillery, cavalry, light and heavy infantry, engineers, sappers and pontoniers, &c. The men are put through courses of instruction which last from twenty-eight to fifty-six days, according to the arm of the service, in the first year, and for shorter periods in the subsequent years. To complete their instruction the cantons send their men yearly to federal camps of three or four thousand troops each, where they are kept under canvas for two weeks. A close inspection of the condition and arms of the men is constantly maintained by officers appointed by the federal government. Great care is taken in the instruction and selection of the officers. Each one must go through a course of instruction at a military school appropriate to each arm. There is no higher rank than that of colonel, but when a colonel is appointed commander-in-chief of the army he receives for the time being the title of General, which he afterwards retains by courtesy

The system proposed by Mr. Dwight for Massachusetts is that every man be required to perform a certain amount of drill before he is allowed to vote. Young men between the ages of eighteen and twenty-one should be placed in camps of instruction for six weeks during each of these three years. About 12,500 young men arrive every year at the age of eighteen in this State. Deducting 2500 for exempts, we should have 10,000 fresh recruits offering themselves for instruction every year, and as the instruction would extend through three years, a body of 30,000 young men would be in camp every year, who should be formed into infantry, cavalry, and rifle regiments, besides a proper proportion of the special arms of artillery, engineers, and cavalry. The headquarters of these regiments and their camps might be distributed in districts corresponding to the present congressional districts. It should be provided that the youths should be well instructed in the school of the soldier before joining the camps, and this could easily be done at the public schools.

To provide competent officers we should establish a State Military School, whose standard should be at least as high as that of West Point Academy. Mr. Dwight suggests the plan of the Polytechnic School at Paris for a model. It should combine a scientific with a military education. The course of instruction should be such that the best engineers, architects, chemists, mechanicians, and constructors would be graduates of this school, as our best engineers have been from West Point. The cost of establishing the school should be defrayed partly by the State and partly by individuals; and its current expenses should be met partly by the State and partly by the pupils. Pupils from other States to pay a double rate. From the pupils of such a school would be drawn the officers and instructors of the militia. In case of war, officers holding commissions in the militia should have a claim to a similar rank in the volunteer service. By such a system, an effective corps of educated officers would be kept up without expense in time of peace, and in time of war the skeleton of an army would exist, needing only those supplies which a patriotic people, trained to the use of arms, would promptly furnish.

Mr. Dwight thinks the cost of such a system would not exceed $350,000 annually.

STEVENS'S BATTERY, &c.

The Senate Naval Committee has formally voted in favor of an appropriation sufficient to complete the Stevens battery, and fifteen millions for the construction of iron clad steamers.

THE NATIONAL TAX.

The Taxes imposed by the Tax Bill, as passed by Congress, Monday, June 23, 1862.

Advertisements inserted in newspapers, magazines, reviews, or any other publication, on gross receipts, 3 per cent.
do., all receipts for, to the amount of $1,000, exempt.
do., do., by newspapers denied the use of the mails, 10 per cent.
do., do., by papers whose circulation does not exceed 2,000 copies, exempt.
Agreements, for each sheet or piece of paper on which written, stamp duty, 5 cents.
Agreements for the hire, use, or rent of any land, tenement, or portion thereof, if for a period of time not exceeding three years, stamp duty, 50 cents.
do., do., if for a period of time exceeding three years, stamp duty, $1.
Ale, per barrel of thirty-one gallons, fractional parts of a barrel to pay proportionally, $1.
Alteratives, each package of, the retail price or value of which does not exceed 25 cents, stamp duty, 1 cent.
do., each package of, the retail price or value of which exceeds 25 cents and does not exceed 50 cents. stamp duty, 2 cents.
do., each package of, the retail price or value of which exceeds 50 cents and does not exceed 75 cents, stamp duty, 3 cents.
do., each package of, the value of which exceeds 75 cents, and does not exceed one dollar, 4 cents.
do., each package of, the retail price or value of which exceeds one dollar, for each and every fifty cents, or fractional part thereof, over and above $1, an additional stamp duty of 2 cents.
Animal Oils per gallon, 2 cents.
Anodynes, each package of, the retail price or value of which does not exceed 25 cents, stamp duty, 1 cent.
do., each package of, the retail price or value of which exceeds 25 cents and does not exceed 50 cents, stamp duty, 2 cents.
do., each package of, the retail price or value of which exceeds 50 cents and does not exceed 75 cents, stamp duty, 3 cents.
do., do., exceeding 75 cents and not exceeding one dollar, 4 cents.
do., each package of, the retail price or value of which exceeds one dollar, for each and every 50 cents, or fractional part thereof over and above $1, an additional stamp duty of 2 cents.
Apothecaries, when a license as wholesale or retail dealer has not been taken out, for license, $10.
Appraisements of value or damage, on each a stamp duty of 5 cents.
Aromatic snuff, on each package of, the retail price or value of which does not exceed 25 cents, a stamp duty of 1 cent.
do., do., on each package of, the retail price or value of which exceeds 25 cents and does not exceed 50 cents, a stamp duty of 2 cents.
do., do., on each package of, the retail price or value of which exceeds 50 cents and does not exceed 75 cents, a stamp duty of 3 cents.
do., do., exceeding 75 cents and not exceeding one dollar, 4 cts.
do., do., on each package of, the retail price or value of which exceeds one dollar, for each and every fifty cents, or fractional

part thereof, over and above one dollar, an additional stamp duty of 2 cents.

Auctioneers, under which term is included every person whose business it is to offer property for sale to the highest or best bidder, for license, $20.

Auction sales of goods, merchandise, articles, and things on gross amount of sales, ⅒ of 1 per cent.

Badger's cod-liver oil, on each package of, the retail price or value of which does not exceed 25 cents, a stamp duty of 1 cent.
  do., on each package of, the retail price or value of which exceeds 25 cents and does not exceed 50 cents, a stamp duty of 2 cents.
  do., on each package of, the retail price or value of which exceeds 25 cents, but does not exceed 75 cents, a stamp duty of 3 cents.
  do., do., exceeding 75 cents and not exceeding $1, 4 cents.
  do., do., on each package, of the retail price or value of which exceeds $1, for each and every 50 cents, or fractional part thereof over and above $1, an additional stamp duty of 2 cents.

Balm of a Thousand Flowers, each package of, the retail price of which does not exceed 25 cents, a stamp duty of 1 cent.
  do., each package of, the retail price or value of which exceeds 25 cents and does not exceed 50 cents, a stamp duty of 2 cents.
  do., each package of, the retail price or value of which exceeds 50 cents and does not exceed 75 cents, a stamp duty of 3 cents.
  do., each package of, the value of which shall exceed 75 cents and shall not exceed $1, 4 cents.
  do., each package of, the retail price or value of which exceeds one dollar, for each and every 50 cents, or fractional part thereof over and above one dollar, an additional stamp duty of 2 cents.

Balm of Life, same as "Balm of a Thousand Flowers."

Balsam of Liverwort, same as "Balm of a Thousand Flowers."

Balsam of Wild Cherry and Iceland Moss, same as "Balm of a Thousand Flowers."

Band Iron, see "Iron."

Banks, on all dividends, 3 per cent.

Bankers, under which term is included every person who keeps a place of business where credits are opened in favor of any person, firm, or corporation, by the deposit or collection of money or currency, on the same, or any part thereof, shall be paid or remitted upon the draft, check, or order of such creditor, but which does not include incorporated banks or other banks legally authorized to issue notes as circulation, for license, $100.

Bar Iron, see "Iron."

Barytes, sulphate of, per 100 pounds, 10 cents.

Beer, per barrel of 31 gallons, fractional parts of a barrel to pay proportionally, $1.

Bend leather, per pound, 1 cent and 5 mills.

Benzine, per gallon, 10 cents.

Bi Carb. Soda, per lb., 5 mills.

Billiard tables, for each table, $5.

Bills of exchange (inland) for the payment of any sum of money not exceeding $100 on sight or demand, stamp duty of 5 cents.
  do., do., exceeding $100 and not exceeding $200, 10 cents.
  do., do., exceeding $200 and not exceeding $350, 15 cents.
  do., do., exceeding $350 and not exceeding $500, 20 cents.
  do., do., exceeding $500 and not exceeding $750, 30 cents.

Bills of exchange, &c., exceeding $750 and not exceeding $1,000, 40 cents.
  do., do., exceeding $1,000 and not exceeding $1,500, 60 cents.
  do., do., exceeding $1,500 and not exceeding $2,500, $1.
  do., do., exceeding $2,500 and not exceeding $3,750, $1.50.
  do., do., exceeding $3,750 and not exceeding $5,000, $1.85.
  do., do., for every $2,500, or part of $2,500, in excess of $5,000, $1.
  do., for the payment in any other manner than at sight or on demand, same as above.
Bills of exchange (foreign) drawn in, but payable out of the United States, if drawn singly or if drawn otherwise than in sets of more than one, according to the custom of merchants and bankers, same as bill of exchange (inland).
  do., do., if drawn in sets of three or more, for every bill of each set, where the sum made payable shall not exceed $150, or the equivalent thereof in any foreign currency, 3 cents.
  do., do., above $150 and not above $250, 5 cents.
  do., do., above $250 and not above $500, 10 cents.
  do., do., above $500 and not above $1,000, 15 cents.
  do., do., above $1,000 and not above $1,500, 20 cents.
  do., do., above $1,500 and not above $2,250, 30 cents.
  do., do., above $2,250 and not above $3,500, 50 cents.
  do., do., above $3,500 and not above $5,000, 70 cents.
  do., do., above $5,000 and not above $7,500, $1.
  do., do., for every $2,500, or part thereof, in excess of $7,500, 30 c.
Bills of lading for any goods, merchandise, or effects to be exported from a port or place in the United States to any foreign port or place, a stamp duty of 10 cents.
  do., for any goods, merchandise, or effects to be carried from one port or place in the United States to any other port or place in the United States, either by land or water, except when carried by any express company or carrier, a stamp duty of 5 cents.
Bitters, same as "Balm of a Thousand Flowers."
Boards are not to be considered as manufactures.
Bonds, auction sales of, on gross amounts of sales, 1-10 of 1 pr. ct.
Bonds for indemnifying any person who shall have become bound or engaged as surety for the payment of any sum of money, or for the execution or performance of the duties of any office, and to account for money received by virtue thereof, a stamp duty of 50 cents.
  do., of any description, other than such as are required in legal proceedings, not otherwise charged, a stamp duty of 25 cents.
Bone, manufactures of, wholly or in part, if not otherwise specified, ad valorem, 3 per cent.
Books are not to be regarded as a manufacture, or submitted to a rate of duty as a manufacture.
Bottles, containing medicine, &c., the retail price or value of which, contents included, does not exceed 25 cents, a stamp duty of 1 cent.
  do., containing medicines, &c., the retail price or value of which, contents included, exceeds 25 cents, but does not exceed 50 cents, a stamp duty of 2 cents.
  do., containing medicines, &c., the retail price or value of which, contents included, exceeds 50 cents, but does not exceed 75 cents, 3 cents.
  do., containing medicines, &c., the value of which, contents included, shall exceed 75 cents, and shall not exceed $1, 4 cts.

Bottles, containing medicines, &c., the value of which, contents included, exceeds $1, for each and every 50 cents, or fractional part thereof, over and above $1, an additional stamp duty of 2 cents.
Bowling alleys, for each alley, duty for license, $5.
Boxes, containing medicines, &c., same as "Bottles," which see.
Brandreth's Pills, same as "Balm of a Thousand Flowers," which see.
Brass, manufactures of, if not otherwise specified, 3 per cent.
Bricks are not to be considered as a manufacture.
Bridges, toll on gross receipts, 3 per cent.
Brewers, under which term is included every person who manufactures fermented liquor of any name or description for sale, from malt, wholly or in part, for license, $50.
  do., who manufacture less than 500 bbls. per year, for license, $25.
Bristles, manufactures of, not otherwise specified, 3 per cent.
British Oil, same as "Balm of a Thousand Flowers."
Brokers, auction sales by, of goods, wares, merchandise, articles or things, on gross amount of sale, ¼ of 1 per cent.
Brokers, under which term is included every person whose business is to purchase or sell stocks, coin, money, bank-notes, drafts, promissory notes, or other securities for the payment of money, for themselves or others, or who deals in exchanges relating to money, for license, $50.
Brokers, commercial, under which term is included every person who purchases or sells goods or produce, or seeks orders therefor, in original or unbroken packages, or manages business matters for the owners of vessels, or the shippers or consignors of freight carried by vessels, or purchases or sells real estate for others, for license, $50.
Brokers, land warrant (see Land Warrant Brokers), $25.
Bull's Sarsaparilla, same as "Balm of a Thousand Flowers," which see.
Bullion, in the manufacture of silver ware is not to be considered a manufacture.
Burnett's Cocaine, same as "Balm of a Thousand Flowers," which see.
Burning Fluid is not to be considered a manufacture.

Calf Skins tanned, each 6 cents.
  do., American patent, 5 per cent.
Candles, tallow, 3 per cent.
  do., lard, 3 per cent.
  do., of whatever material made, 3 per cent.
Cards, playing, per pack, of whatever number, when the price per pack does not exceed 18 cents, 1 cent.
  do., do., over 18 and not over 25 cents per pack, 2 cts.
  do., over 25 and not over 30 cents per pack, 3 cents.
  do., over 30 and not over 36 cents, 4 cents.
  do., over 36 cents, 5 cents.
Calves, slaughtered, per head, 5 cents.
Carriages, &c., valued at $75 or over, drawn by one horse, $1.
  do., drawn by two horses, valued at $75 and not exceeding $200, $2.
  do., exceeding in value $200 and not exceeding $600, $5.
  do., exceeding $600, $10.
Cassia, ground, and all imitations of per lb., 1 cent.

Castile Soap, see Soap.
Catarrh Snuff, each package of, the retail price or value of which does not exceed 25 cents, a stamp duty of 1 cent.
do., each package of, the retail price or value of which exceeds 25 cents and does not exceed 50 cents, a stamp duty of 2 cents.
do., each package of, the retail price of which exceeds 50 cents and does not exceed 75 cents, a stamp duty of 3 cents.
do., each package of, the value of which exceeds 75 cents and does not exceed $1, 4 cents.
do., each package of, the retail price or value of which exceeds $1, for each and every additional 50 cents or fractional part thereof, over and above $1, an additional stamp duty of 2 cents.
Cathartic Pills, same as "Catarrh Snuff."
Cattle, horned, exceeding eighteen months old, slaughtered for sale, each 30 cents.
do., under eighteen months old, per head, 5 cents.
do., do., slaughtered by any person for his own consumption, free.
Cattle Brokers, including every person whose business it is to buy and sell and deal in cattle, hogs, and sheep, for license, $10.
Cavendish Tobacco, valued at more than 30 cents per pound, per pound, 15 cents.
do., do., valued at any sum not exceeding 30 cents per pound, per pound, 10 cents.
Cement, made wholly, or in part, of glue, to be sold in a liquid state, per gallon, 25 cents.
Certificates of stock in any incorporated company, stamp duty on each, 25 cents.
Certificates of profits, or any certificate or memorandum showing an interest in the property or accumulation of any incorporated company, if for not less than $10, and not exceeding $50, stamp duty, 10 cents.
do., do., for a sum exceeding $50, 25 cents.
Certificate. — Any certificate of damage, and all other certificates or documents issued by any port warden, marine surveyor, or other person acting as such, stamp duty, 25 cents.
Certificates of deposits of any sum of money in any bank or trust company, or with any banker or person acting as such, if for a sum not exceeding one hundred dollars, stamp duty, 2 cents.
do., if for a sum exceeding $100, stamp duty, 5 cents.
Certificate of any other description than those specified, a stamp duty of 10 cents.
Charter Party. — Contract or agreement for the charter of any ship or vessel, or steamer, or any letter, memorandum, or other writing between the captain, master, or owner, or person acting as agent of any ship or vessel, or steamer, and any other person or persons for or relating to the freight or charter of such ship, or vessel, or steamer, if the registered tonnage of such ship, or vessel, or steamer does not exceed three hundred tons, stamp duty, $3.
do., do., exceeding three hundred tons and not exceeding six hundred tons, stamp duty, $5.
do., do., exceeding six hundred tons, stamp duty, $10.
Checks drawn upon any bank, trust company, or any person or persons, companies or corporations, for the payment of money at sight or on demand, see "Bill of Exchange."

Cheese is not to be considered a manufacture.
Chemical preparations, same as "Catarrh Snuff."
Chocolate, prepared, per lb., 1 cent.
Circuses, under which term is included every building, tent, space, or area, where feats of horsemanship, or acrobatic sports, are exhibited for license, $50.
Claim agents, under which term is included every person whose business it is to prosecute claims in any of the executive departments of the federal government, for each yearly license, $10.
Clearance, stamp duty, 25 cents.
Clock movements, made to run one day, each, 5 cents.
  do., made to run over one day, 10 cents.
Cloth, before it has been dyed, printed, bleached, or prepared in any other manner, 3 per cent.
Cloves, ground, and all imitations of, per lb., 1 cent.
Coal, all mineral, except pea coal and dust coal, per ton, 3½ cents.
Coal Gas, see "Gas."
Coal Oil, refined, per gallon, 10 cents.
Coal oil distillers, under which term is included any person who shall refine, produce, or distil crude petroleum or rock oil, or crude oil, made of asphaltum, shale, peat, or other bituminous substances, for each license, $50.
Coal Tar produced in the manufacture of gas, exempt.
Coffee, ground, per lb., 3 mills.
Cocoa, prepared, per lb., 1 cent.
Commercial Brokers, see "Brokers."
Concentrated milk is not to be considered a manufacture.
Confectioners, under which term is included every person who sells at retail confectionery, sweetmeats, comfits, or other confects, in any building (confectioners who have taken out a license as wholesale or retail dealers are not required to take a separate license), for each license, $10.
Confectionery, made wholly or in part of sugar, per pound, 1 cent.
Consumption entry at any custom house, not exceeding $100 in value, stamp duty, 25 cents.
  do., do., exceeding $100, and not exceeding $500, 50 cents.
  do., do., exceeding $500 in value, $1.
Contracts, for each sheet or piece of paper on which written, stamp duty, 5 cents.
  do., for the hire, use, or rent of any land, tenement, or portion thereof, if for a period of time not exceeding three years, stamp duty, 50 cents.
  do., do., for a period of time exceeding three years, $1.
Contracts, brokers' note, or memorandum of sale of any goods or merchandise, stocks, bonds, exchange, notes of hand, real estate, or property of any kind or description issued by brokers, or persons acting as such, stamp duty, 10 cents.
Conveyance, deed, instrument, or writing, whereby any lands, tenements, or other realty sold, shall be granted, leased, assigned, transferred, or otherwise conveyed to or vested in the purchaser or purchasers, or to any person or persons, by his, her, or their direction, when the value exceeds $100 and does not exceed $1,000, stamp duty, $1.
  do., do., when the value exceeds $1,000 and does not exceed $2,500, $2.
  do., do., exceeding $2,500 and not exceeding $5,000, $10.
  do., exceeding $5,000 and not exceeding $10,000, $20.

Conveyance, &c., exceeding $10,000 and not exceeding $20,000, $30.
do., exceeding 20,000 and not exceeding $35,000, $60.
do., exceeding 35,000 and not exceeding $50,000, $100.
do., for every additional $10,000, or fractional part in excess of $50,000, $20.
Copper, manufactures of, not otherwise provided for, ad valorem, 3 per cent.
Cordials, medical, same as "Catarrh Snuff."
Cosmetics, same as "Dentifrice."
Cotton, raw, per pound, ½ cent.
Cotton, manufactures of, wholly or in part, not otherwise provided for, 3 per cent.
Cotton umbrellas, 5 per cent.
Cough syrup, same as "Catarrh Snuff."
Coupons, railroad, 3 per cent.
Croup remedy, same as "Catarrh Snuff."
Croup syrup, do. do.

Deeds, whereby any lands, tenements, or other things sold, shall be granted, leased, assigned, transferred, or otherwise conveyed to or vested in the purchaser or purchasers, or to any person or persons by his, her, or their direction, st. duty, $1.
Deerskins, dressed and smoked, per pound, 2 cents.
Dentifrice, each package of, the retail price or value of which does not exceed 25 cents, stamp duty, 1 cent.
do., do., exceeding 25 cents, but not exceeding 50 cents, stamp duty, 2 cents.
do., do., exceeding 50 cents, but not exceeding 75 cents, 3 cents.
do., do., each package of, the value of which shall exceed 75 cents and shall not exceed $1, 4 cents.
do., exceeding $1 for each and every 50 cents, or fractional part thereof, over and above $1, an additional stamp duty of 2 cents.
Dentists, for license, $10.
Despatch, telegraphic, when the charge for the first ten words does not exceed 20 cents, stamp duty, 1 cent.
do., when it exceeds 20 cents, 3 cents.
Diamonds, 3 per cent.
Distilled spirits, first proof, per gallon, 20 cents.
Distilled Spirits. — The duty on spirituous liquors and all other spirituous beverages enumerated in the Tax Bill, is to be collected at no lower rate than the basis of first proof, and shall be increased in proportion for any greater strength than the strength of proof.
Distilled Spirits. — The term "first proof" is declared to mean that proof of a liquor which corresponds to fifty degrees of Tralles' centesimal hydrometer, at the temperature of sixty degrees of Fahrenheit's thermometer; and in reducing the temperatures to the standard of sixty, and in levying duties on liquors above and below proof, the table of commercial values contained in the Manual for Inspectors of Spirits, prepared by Prof. McCulloch, under the superintendence of Prof. Bache, and adopted by the Treasury Department, is to be used and taken as giving the proportions of absolute alcohol in the liquid ganged and proved, according to which duties shall be levied.
Distillers, under which term is included every person or copartnership who distils or manufactures spirituous liquors for sale, for license, $50.

Distillers, making less than 300 barrels per year, $25.
  do., of apples and peaches, making less than 150 bbls. p. yr, $12.
Dividends— Annual income from, when exceeding $600 and not exceeding $10,000, on excess over $600, 3 per cent.
  do., exceeding $10,000, and not exceeding $50,000, on excess over $600, 5 per cent.
  do., exceeding $50,000, 7½ per cent.
Dividends, annual income from, when realized by any citizen of the United States, residing abroad, and not in the employ of the United States, otherwise provided for, when exceeding $600, on the excess over $600, 5 per cent.
Drafts, drawn upon any bank, trust company, or any person or persons, companies, or corporations, for the payment of money at sight or on demand, same as "Bills of Exchange."
Draining Tiles are not considered as a manufacture.
Drops, medicinal, same as "Dentifrice."

Eating houses, under which term is included every place where food or refreshments of any kind are provided for casual visitors and sold for consumption therein; but the keeper of an eating house, having taken out a license therefor, is not required to take out a license as confectioner; for license, $10.
Electuaries, same as "Dentifrice."
Emeralds, 3 per cent.
Embrocations, same as "Dentifrice."
Enamelled leather, per square foot, 5 mills.
Enamelled skirting leather, per square foot, 1¼ cents.
Entry of any goods, wares, or merchandise at any custom house, for consumption, see "Consumption Entry."
Entry of any goods, wares, and merchandise, at any custom house, for warehousing, see "Warehousing Entry."
Entry for the withdrawal of any goods, wares, or merchandise from bonded warehouse, stamp duty, 50 cents.
Epileptic pills, same as "Dentifrice."
Erasive soap, see "Soap."
"Essence of Life," same as "Dentifrice."
Express.— For every receipt issued by any express company or carrier, or person whose occupation it is to act as such, for every single box, bale, package, or bundle, when the fee for transportation does not exceed 25 cents, 1 cent.
  do., when it exceeds 25 cents, but does not exceed one dollar, 2 cents.
  do., when one or more packages are sent to the same address, and the compensation exceeds one dollar, 5 cents.
Eye water, same as "Dentifrice."

Family pills, same as "Dentifrice."
Female pills,   do   do.
Ferryboats, propelled by steam or horse power, on gross receipts, 1½ per cent.
Fine cut tobacco, see "Tobacco."
Fire insurance companies, on all dividends, 3 per cent.
Fish, preserved, ad valorem, 5 per cent.
Fish Oil, exempt.
Flax, manufactures of, not otherwise specified, 3 per cent.
  do., prepared for textile or felting purposes, is not to be considered a manufacture until actually woven or felted into fabric for consumption.

Flour, made from grain, is not to be considered a manufacture.
Fruits, preserved, 5 per cent.

Gains, annual, of every person, when exceeding 600, and do not exceed 10,000, on the excess of gain over 600, 3 per cent.
  do., exceeding 10,000 and not exceeding 50,000, on excess over 10,000, 5 per cent.
  do., from property of any kind in the United States, realized by any citizen of the United States residing abroad, and not in the employ of the United States, not otherwise provided for, 5 per cent.
Gas, coal, when the product shall not be above 500,000 cubic feet per month, per 1,000 cubic feet, 5 per cent.
  do., do., when the product shall be above 500,000 and not exceeding 5,000,000 cubic feet per month, per 1,000 cubic feet, 10 cents.
  do., do., when the product shall be above 5,000,000, per 1,000 cubic feet, 15 cents.
Gas, all illuminating, same as "Coal Gas."
Gelatine, of all descriptions, in solid state, per pound, 5 mills.
Ginger, ground, and all imitations, per pound, 1 cent.
Glass, manufactures of, not otherwise specified, 3 per cent.
Glue, in a liquid form, per gallon, — cents.
  do., in a solid state, per pound, 5 mills.
Glycerine lotion, same as "Dentifrice."
Goat skins, curried, manufactured or finished, 5 per cent.
Gold, manufactures of, not otherwise provided for, 3 per cent.
Goods, made for the use or consumption of the maker, free.
  do., except spirituous and malt liquors, and leaf, stem, or manufactured tobacco, where the annual product does not exceed $600, provided that this shall not apply to any business or transaction where one party furnishes the materials, or any part thereof, and employs another party to manufacture, make, or finish the goods, wares, or merchandise, or articles paying or promising to pay therefor, and receiving the goods, wares, and merchandise, or articles; but, in all such cases, the party furnishing the materials and receiving the goods, wares, and merchandise, or articles, shall be liable to and charged with all accruing duties thereon, free.
Gunpowder, and all explosive substances used for mining, artillery, or sporting purposes, when valued at 18 cents per pound or less, per pound, 5 mills.
  do., when valued above 18 cents per pound and not exceeding 30 cents, per pound, 1 cent.
  do., when valued above 30 cents per pound, per pound, 6 cents.
Gutta percha, manufactures of, not otherwise provided for, 3 per cent.
Gypsum is not to be considered a manufacture.

Hair dye, same as "Dentifrice."
Hair restorative, same as "Dentifrice."
Harness leather, per pound, 7 mills.
Harness leather, made of hides imported east of the Cape of Good Hope, per pound, 5 mills.
Headings are not to be considered as a manufacture.
Hemp, manufactures of, when not otherwise specified, 3 per cent.
Hog skins, tanned or dressed, 4 per cent.

Hogs, exceeding six months old, slaughtered, when the number thus slaughtered exceeds 20 in any year, for sale, 10 cents.
do., slaughtered by any person for his own consumption, free.
Hollow ware, iron, per ton 2,000 pounds, $1.50.
Hoop Iron, see "Iron."
Horn, manufactures of, not otherwise provided for, 3 per cent.
Horned cattle, exceeding eighteen months old, slaughtered for sale, each 30 cents.
do., under eighteen months old, per head, 5 cents.
Horse skins, tanned and dressed, 4 per cent.
Horse dealers, under which term is included every person whose business it is to buy and sell horses and mules, for each license, $10.
do., when they shall take out a license as livery stable keepers, are not required to take out an additional one.
Hostetter's bitters, same as "Dentifrice."
Hotels, under which term is included every place where food and lodgings are provided for and furnished to travellers and sojourners in view of payment therefor, where the rent or the valuation of the yearly rental of the house and property occupied shall be $10,000 or more, for each yearly license, $200.
do., do., where the rent or the valuation of the yearly rental shall be $5,000 and less than $10,000, for each yearly license, $100.
do., do., where the rent or the valuation of the yearly rental shall be $2,500 and less than $5,000, for each yearly license, $75.
do., do., where the rent or the valuation of the rental shall be $1,000 and less than $2,500, for each yearly license, $50.
do., do., where the rent or the valuation of the yearly rental shall be $500 and less than $1,000, for each yearly license, $25.
do., do., where the rent or the valuation of the yearly rental shall be $300 and less than $500, for each yearly license, $15.
do., do., where the rent or the valuation of the yearly rental shall be $100 and less than $300, for each yearly license, $10.
do., do., where the rent or the valuation of the yearly rental shall be less than $100, for each yearly license, $5.
Hyperion fluid, same as "Dentifrice."

Income, annual, of every person, when exceeding $600, and not exceeding $10,000, on the excess over $600, 3 per cent.
do., exceeding $10,000, and not exceeding $50,000, on excess over $600, 5 per cent.
do., exceeding $50,000, do., 7½ per cent.
do., annual, from property of any kind in the United States realized by any citizen of the United States residing abroad, and not in the employ of the United States government, not otherwise provided for, 5 per cent.
India rubber, manufactures of, not otherwise specified, 3 per cent.
Inns, same as "Hotels."
Insurance companies, all, on dividends, 3 per cent.
Insurance companies, inland or marine, upon gross receipts for premiums and assessments, 1 per cent.
Insurance companies, foreign, doing business in the United States, 3 per cent.
Insurance, life.—Policy of insurance, or other instrument, by whatever name the same shall be called, whereby any insurance shall be made or renewed, marine or inland, upon property of any description, whether against perils by the sea or

STATISTICAL POCKET MANUAL. 93

by fire, or other peril of any kind made by any insurance company or its agents, or by any other company or person, 25 cts.
Interest, income from, when exceeding the sum of $600 per annum, and not exceeding $10,000 on the excess of income over $600, 3 per cent.
do., exceeding $10,000 and not exceeding $50,000, on the excess over $600, 5 per cent.
do., income from, when realized by any citizen of the United States residing abroad, and not in the employ of the United States government, not otherwise provided for, 5 per cent.
Iron, manufactures of, if not otherwise specified, 3 per cent.
do., railroad, per ton, $1.50.
do., re-rolled, per ton, 75 cents.
do., advanced beyond slabs, blooms, or loops, and **not advanced beyond bars or rods, per ton, $1.50.**
do., band, hoop, and sheet, not thinner than No. 18 wire gauge, per ton, $1.50.
do., plate, not less than one eighth of an inch in thickness, per ton, $1.50.
do., band, hoop, or sheet, thinner than No. 18 wire gauge, per ton, $2.
do., plate, less than one eighth of an inch in thickness, per ton, $2.
do., nails, cut, and spikes, per ton, $2.
do., bars, rods, bands, hoops, sheets, plates, spikes, and nails, upon which the duty of $1.50 has been levied and paid, are only subject to an additional duty of, per ton, 50 cents.
Iron, pig, is not to be considered a manufacture.
Ivory, manufactures of, if not otherwise specified, 3 per cent.

Jewelry, 3 per cent.
Jute, manufactures of, if not otherwise specified, 3 per cent.
Jugglers, including every person who performs by sleight of hand, $20.

Kid skins, curried, manufactured, or finished, 5 per cent.

Lager bier, per barrel containing 31 gallons (fractional parts of a barrel to pay proportionately), $1.
Land warrant brokers, under which term is included every person who makes a business of buying and selling land warrants, and furnishing them to settlers or other persons, under contracts that the land procured by means of them shall be bound for the prices agreed on for the warrants, for each license, $25.
Lard oil, per gallon, 2 cents.
Lawyers, under which term is included every person whose business it is, for fee or reward, to prosecute or defend any cause in any court of record or other judicial tribunal of the United States, or of any of the States, or give advice in relation to any cause or matter pending therein (lawyers refusing to pay for this license shall not be allowed to practise in any such court or tribunal), for each license, $10.
Lead, manufactures of, if not otherwise specified, 3 per cent.
Lead, white, per hundred, 25 cents.
Lease, for the hire, use, or rent of any land, tenement, or portion thereof, if for a period of time not exceeding three years, a stamp duty of 50 cents.
do., do., for a period of time exceeding three years, a stamp duty of $1.

Leather, bend, per pound, 1¼ cents.
do., butt, per pound, 1¼ cents.
do., damaged, per pound, 5 mills.
do., enamelled, per square foot, 5 mills.
do., enamelled skirting, per square foot, 1¼ cents.
do., harness, per pound, 7 mills.
do., harness made from hides imported east of the Cape of Good Hope, per pound, 5 mills.
do., offal, per pound, 5 mills.
do., oil dressed, per pound, 2 cents.
do., patent, per square foot, 5 mills.
do., patent, japanned splits, used for dasher leather, square foot, 4 mills.
do., patent or enamelled skirting, per square foot, 1¼ cents.
do., rough, made from hides imported east of the Cape of Good Hope, per pound, 5 mills.
do., rough, all other, hemlock-tanned, per pound, 8 mills.
do., rough, tanned in whole or in part with oak, per pound, 1 ct.
do., sole, made from hides imported east of the Cape of Good Hope, per pound, 5 mills.
do., sole, all other, hemlock-tanned, per pound, 8 mills.
do., sole, tanned in whole or in part with oak, per pound, 1 cent.
do., tanned calf skins, each, 6 cents.
do., upper, finished or curried, except calf skins made from leather tanned in the interest of the parties finishing or carrying such leather, not previously taxed in the rough, per pound, 1 cent.
do., manufactures of, when not otherwise specified, 3 per cent.

Legacies.—Any person having in charge or trust as administrators, executors, or trustees of any legacies or distributive shares arising from personal property, of any kind whatsoever, where the whole amount of such personal property, as aforesaid, shall exceed the sum of one thousand dollars in actual value, passing from any person who may die after the passage of this act, possessed of such property, either by will or by the intestate law of any State or Territory, or any part of such property or interest therein, transferred by deed, grant, bargain, sale, or gift, made or intended to take effect in possession or enjoyment after the death of the grantor or bargainer, to any person or persons, or to any body or bodies, politic or corporate, in trust or otherwise, are subject to the following taxes: Where the person or persons entitled to any beneficial interest in such property, shall be the lineal issue or lineal ancestor, brother or sister, to the person who died possessed of such property, for each and every hundred dollars of the clear value of such interest in such property, 75 cts.

do., do., where the person or persons entitled to any beneficial interest in such property shall be a descendant of a brother or sister of the person who died possessed of such property, for each and every hundred dollars of the clear value of such interest, $1.50.

do., do., where the person or persons entitled to any beneficial interest in such property shall be a brother or sister of the father or mother, or a descendant of a brother or sister of the father or mother of the person who died possessed of such property, for each and every hundred dollars of the clear value of such interest, $3.

Legacies. — Where the person or persons entitled to any beneficial interest in such property shall be a brother or sister of the grandfather or grandmother, or a descendant of the brother or sister of the grandfather or grandmother of the person who died possessed of such property, for each and every hundred dollars of clear value of such interest, $4.

do., do., where the person or persons entitled to any beneficial interest in such property shall be in any other degree of collateral consanguinity than is stated above, or shall be a stranger in blood to the person who died possessed, as aforesaid, or shall be a body politic or corporate, for each and every hundred dollars of the clear value of such interest, $5.

do., passing, by will or by the laws of any State or Territory, to husband or wife of the person who died possessed of such property, free.

Legal documents, writs, summons, or other original process commenced in any court or law of equity, stamp duty, 50 cents.

Letters of Credit, see " Bills of Exchange, foreign."

Letters of Administration. — Where the estate and effects for or in respect of which such letters of administration applied for shall be sworn or declared not to exceed the value of $2,500 stamp duty, 50 cts.

do., do., to exceed $2,500 and not exceeding $5,000, $1.

do., to exceed $5,000 and not exceeding $20,000, $2.

do., do., to exceed $20,000 and not exceeding $50,000, $5.

do., do., to exceed $50,000 and not exceeding $100,000, $10.

do., do., exceeding $100,000 and not exceeding $150,000, $20.

do., for every additional $50,000 or part thereof, $10.

Licenses must be taken out each year by the following named persons, for which they are to pay the sum placed opposite their names, viz. : —

Apothecaries, $10.
Auctioneers, $20.
Bankers, $100.
Billiard Tables, each $5. [& $50.
Brewers, see " Brewers," $25
Brokers, $50.
Bowling alleys, each alley, $5.
Cattle brokers, $10.
Claim agents, $10.
Coal oil distillers, $50.
Commercial brokers, $50.
Confectioners, $10.
Circuses, $50.
Dentists, $10.
Distillers, see " Distillers."
Eating houses, $10.
Horse dealers, $10.
Hotels, see "Hotels," $5 to $200.

Jugglers, $20.
Lawyers, $10.
Livery stable keepers, $10.
Manufacturers, $10.
Pedlers, see "Pedlers," $5 to $20.
Photographers, $10.
Pawnbrokers, $50.
Physicians, $10.
Retail dealers, $10.
Retail dealers in liquors, $20.
Rectifiers, see " Rectifiers."
Surgeons, $10.
Tobacconists, $10.
Theatres, $100.
Tallow chandlers, $10.
Soap makers, $10.
Wholesale dealers, $50.
Wholesale deal. in liquors, $100.

Life Insurance companies, see " Insurance."
Lime is not to be regarded as a manufacture.
Liniments, same as " Dentifrice."
Linseed oil, per gallon, 2 cents.
Livery stable keepers, under which term is included every person whose occupation is to keep horses for hire or to let, for license, $10.
Lotions, same as " Dentifrice."

Lozenges, medicinal, same as "Dentifrice."
Lumber is not to be considered a manufacture.

Magazines are not to be regarded as a manufacture of paper or submitted to a rate of duty as a manufacture.
do., for all advertisements, on gross receipts, 3 per cent.
Magic liniment, same as "Dentifrice."
Malt is not to be considered a manufacture.
Manifest of the cargo of any ship, vessel, or steamer, for a foreign port, if the registered tonnage of such ship, vessel, or steamer does not exceed three hundred tons, stamp duty, $1.
do., exceeding three hundred tons, and not exceeding six hundred tons, $3.
do., do., exceeding six hundred tons, $5.
Manufacturers, for license, $10.
Manufacturers not otherwise specified as bone, brass, bristles, copper, cotton, flax, glass, gold, gutta percha, hemp, india rubber, horn, iron, ivory, jute, lead, leather, paper, pottery, silk, silver, steel, tin, willow, wood, worsted, wool, and other materials, 3 per cent.
Marine insurance companies, see "Insurance."
Marine protest, 25 cents.
Meats, preserved, 5 per cent.
Medicated herbs, same as "Dentifrice."
Medicated water, do. do.
Medicines, see "Dentifrice."
Merchandise, see "Goods."
Mineral coal, except pea coal, per ton, 3½ cents.
Morocco skins, curried, manufactured, or finished, 5 per cent.
Mortgage of lands, estate, or property, real or personal, heritable or movable, whatsoever, where the same shall be made as a security for the payment of any definite and certain sum of money lent at the time or previously due and owing or forborne to be paid, being payable; also any conveyance of any lands, estate, or property whatsoever, in trust to be sold or otherwise converted into money, which shall be intended only as security, and shall be redeemable before the sale or other disposal thereof, either by express stipulation or otherwise, or any personal bond given as security for the payment of any definite or certain sum of money exceeding $100 and not exceeding $500, 50 cents.
do., exceeding $500 and not exceeding $1,000, $1.
do., do. 1,000 do. 2,500, 2.
do., do. 2,500 do. 5,000, 5.
do., do. 5,000 do. 10,000, 10.
do., do. 10,000 do. 20,000, 15.
do., do. 20,000 do. 35,000, 30.
do., do. 35,000 do. 50,000, 50.
do., for every additional $10,000, or fractional part thereof, in excess of $50,000, $10.
Movements, clock, made to run one day, each 5 cents.
do., do., made to run over one day, each 10 cents.
Mustard, ground, per pound, 1 cent.
Mustard seed oil, per gallon, 2 cents.
Mutual insurance companies, see "Insurance."

Nails, cut, per ton, $2.
Naphtha, per gallon, 10 cents.
Newspapers are not to be regarded as a manufacture, or submitted to a rate of duty as a manufacture.
Newspapers, for all advertisements, on gross receipts, see "Advertisements," 3 per cent.
Notarial act, see "Protest."
Note, promissory, for the payment of any sum of money at sight or on demand, stamp duty, 2 cents.
   do., do., for the payment in any other manner than at sight or on demand of any sum of money not exceeding $500, stamp duty, 5 cents.
   do., do., do., exceeding $500 and not exceeding $2,500, stamp duty of 10 cents.
   do., do., do., exceeding $2,500, stamp duty, 25 cents.

Officinal preparations, same as "Dentifrice."
Oils, animal, all, pure or adulterated, if not otherwise provided for, per gallon, 2 cents.
   do., illuminating, refined, produced by the distillation of coal, asphaltum, shale, peet, petroleum, or rock oil, and other bituminous substances used for like purposes, per gallon, 10 cents.
   do., lard, pure or unadulterated, if not otherwise provided for, per gallon, 2 cents.
   do., linseed, do., per gallon, 2 cents.
   do., mustard seed, do., per gallon, 2 cents.
   do., all vegetable, per gallon, 2 cents.
   do., medical, same as "Dentifrice."
Oil, refined, produced by distillation of coal exclusively, per gallon, 8 cents.
Oleic acid, produced in the manufacture of candles and used in the manufacture of soap, free.
Order for the payment of any sum of money drawn upon any bank, trust company, or any person or persons, companies or corporations, at sight or on demand, stamp duty same as bill of exchange.
Oxide of zinc, per 100 pounds, 25 cents.
Oxygenated bitters, same as "Dentifrice."

Packet, containing medicines, &c., same as bottles containing the same, see "Bottles."
Pain-killer, same as "Dentifrice."
Paints, dry or ground in oil, or in paste with water, not otherwise provided for, 5 per cent.
Painters' colors, do., 5 per cent.
Palm oil, see "Soap."
Pamphlets are not to be regarded as a manufacture, or submitted to a rate of duty as a manufacture.
   do., on gross receipts for advertisements, 3 per cent.
Panaceas, same as "Dentifrice."
Paper, manufactures of, unless otherwise specified, 3 per cent.
   do., account book, 3 per cent.
   do., bank note, 3 per cent.
   do., binders' board, 3 per cent.
   do., card, 3 per cent.
   do., hanging, 3 per cent.

Paper, letter, 3 per cent.
do., map, 3 per cent.
do., note, 3 per cent.
do., printing, sized and colored, 3 per cent.
do., printing, unsized, 3 per cent.
do., pasteboard, 3 per cent.
do., plate, 3 per cent.
do., uncolored calendered, 3 per cent.
do., wrapping, made of Manilla hemp, or made in imitation thereof, 3 per cent.
do., writing, 3 per cent.
do., all other descriptions of, 3 per cent.
Paraffine oil, exempt.
Parasols, of any material, 5 per cent.
Passport, on each issued from the office of Secretary of State, $3.
do., on each issued by ministers or consuls of the U. States, $3.
Passage ticket, by any vessel from a port in the United States to a foreign port, of less than $30, 50 cents.
do., do., exceeding $30, $1.
Pasteboard, made of junk, straw, or other material, 3 per cent.
Patent leather (see "Leather"), per square foot, 5 mills.
Pawnbrokers, under which term is included every person whose business or occupation is to take or receive, by way of pledge, pawn, or exchange, any goods, wares, or merchandise, or any kind of personal property whatever, for the repayment or security of money lent thereon, for license, $50.
Pearl barley is not to be considered a manufacture.
Pectoral balsam, same as "Dentifrice."
Pedlers, under which term is included every person who sells, or offers to sell, at retail, goods, wares, or other commodities, travelling from place to place, in the street, or through different parts of the country, when travelling with more than two horses, for each license, $20.
do., do., when travelling with two horses, for each license, $15.
do., do., when travelling with one horse, for each license, $10.
do., do., when travelling on foot, for each license, $5.
do., who sell newspapers, Bibles, or religious tracts, exempt.
do., who sell, or offer to sell, dry goods, foreign or domestic, by one or more original packages or pieces at one time to the same person, for each license, $50.
Pepper, ground, and all imitations of, per pound, 1 cent.
Perfumery, same as "Dentifrice."
Petroleum, refined, per gallon, 10 cents.
Phial, containing medicine, &c., same as "Bottle," which see.
Photographers, under which term is included every person who makes for sale photographs, ambrotypes, or pictures on glass, metal, or paper, by the action of light, for each license, when the receipts do not exceed $500, $10.
do., do., when the receipts are over $500 and under $1,000, for license, $15.
do., do., when the receipts are over $1000, for license, $25.
Physicians, under which term is included every person (except apothecaries) whose business it is to, for fee or reward, prescribe medicine or perform any surgical operation for the cure of any bodily disease or ailing, dentists included, for each license, $10.
Pickles, 5 per cent.

Pig iron is not to be considered a manufacture.
Pills, same as "Dentifrice."
Pimento, ground, and all imitation of, per pound, 1 cent.
Pins, solid head or other, 5 per cent.
  do., solid head or other, in boxes, packets, bundles, or other form, 5 per cent.
Plaster is not to be considered a manufacture.
Plasters, same as "Dentifrice."
Plate iron, see "Iron."
Plate of gold, kept for use, per ounce troy, 50 cents.
Plate of silver, per ounce troy, 3 cents.
  do., as above, to the extent of forty ounces, free.
Playing cards, see "Cards."
Plug tobacco, see "Tobacco."
Policy of Insurance (life), see "Insurance."
  do. (marine or inland), see "Insurance."
  do. (fire), see "Insurance."
Pomades, same as "Dentifrice."
Porter, per barrel of 31 gallons, fractional parts in proportion, $1
Pot, containing medicine, &c., same as "Bottles."
Potions, same as "Dentifrice."
Pottery ware, if not otherwise specified, 3 per cent.
Powders, medicinal, same as "Dentifrice."
Power of attorney for the sale or transfer of any stock, bonds, or scrip, or for the collection of any dividends, or interest thereon, stamp duty, 25 cents.
Power of attorney, or proxy voting at any election for officers of any incorporated company or society, except charitable, religious, literary, and cemetery societies, stamp duty, 10 cents.
Power of attorney to sell and convey real estate, or to rent or lease the same, or to perform any and all other acts not specified, stamp duty, $1.
Power of attorney to receive or collect rent, stamp duty, 25 cents.
Preparations, medical, same as "Dentifrice."
Preparations of which coffee forms a part, or which are prepared for sale as a substitute for coffee, per pound, 3 mills.
Preserved fish, 5 per cent.
Preserved fruit, 5 per cent.
Preserved meats, 5 per cent.
Printed books are not to be considered as a manufacture, or submitted to a rate of duty as a manufacture.
  do., on all advertisements, on gross receipts for, 3 per cent.
Printers' ink is not to be considered a manufacture.
Probate of will, where the estate and effects for or in respect of which such probate applied for shall be sworn or declared not to exceed the value of $2,500, stamp duty, 50 cents.
  do., do., to exceed $2,500 and not exceeding $5,000, $1
  do., do., to exceed $5,000 and not exceeding $20,000, $2.
  do., do., to exceed $20,000 and not exceeding $50,000, $5.
  do., do., to exceed $50,000 and not exceeding $100,000, $10.
  do., do., exceeding $100,000 and not exceeding $150,000, $20.
  do., for every additional $50,000, or fractional part thereof, $10.
Profits, annual, of every person, when exceeding $600, and not exceeding $10,000, on the excess over $600, 3 per cent.
  do., annual, when realized by any citizen of the United States residing abroad, and not in employ of the United States, not otherwise provided for, 5 per cent.

Promissory notes, see "Notes."
Property, annual income from, same as "Profits."
Property left by legacy, see "Legacies."
Protest of every note, bill of exchange, acceptance, check, or draft, 25 cents.
Publications, same as "Printed books."
Pulmonary balsam, same as "Dentifrice."
do. syrup,   do.   do.
Pulmonic syrup,   do.   do.
do. wafers,   do.   do.

Railroads.—On gross receipts from carrying passengers, 3 per ct.
do., the motive power of which is not steam, on gross receipts from carrying passengers, 1½ per cent.
Railroads.—On bonds or other evidences of indebtedness upon which interest is stipulated to be paid, on the amount of interest, 3 per cent.
Railroad iron, per ton, $1.50.
do., re-rolled, per ton, 75 cents.
Railroad pills, same as "Dentifrice."
Ready Relief,   do.   do.
Receipt, warehouse, stamp duty, 25 cents.
Receipt (other than charter party) for any goods, merchandise, or effects to be exported from a port or place in the United States to any foreign port or place, stamp duty, 10 cents.
do., for any goods, merchandise, or effects to be carried from one port or place in the United States to any other port or place in the United States, either by land or water, except when carried by any express company or carrier, stamp duty, 5 cents.
Rectifiers, under which term is included every person who rectifies, purifies, or refines spirituous liquors or wines by any process, or mixes distilled spirits, whiskey, brandy, gin, or wine, with any other material for sale under the name of rum, whiskey, brandy, gin, wine, or any other name or names, for each license to rectify any quantity of spirituous liquors not exceeding 500 barrels, containing not more than forty gallons to each, $25.
do., for each additional 500 barrels, or any fraction thereof, $25.
Red oil, used as a material in the manufacture of soap, free.
Rents, annual income from, when exceeding $600, on the excess over $600, 3 per cent.
do., annual income from, when realized by a citizen of the United States residing in a foreign country, and not in the employ of the United States, 5 per cent.
Retail dealers, under which term is included every person whose business or occupation is to sell or offer to sell groceries, or any goods, wares, or merchandise, of foreign or domestic production, in less quantities than a whole original piece or package at one time, to the same person (not including wines, spirituous or malt liquors, but not excluding stationery, drugs, medicines, segars, snuff, or tobacco), for each license, $10.
Retail dealers in liquors, under which term is included every person who shall sell or offer for sale distilled spirits, fermented liquors, and wines of every description, in less quantities than three gallons at one time, to the same purchaser—(this does not authorize any spirits, liquors, wines, or malt liquors, to be drunk on the premises)—for each license, $20.
Reviews, same as "Pamphlets."

Richardson's bitters, same as "Dentifrice."
Rock oil, refined, see "Oils."
Russia salve, same as "Dentifrice."
Roman Cement is not to be regarded as a manufacture.

Salaries, annual income from, when exceeding $600, on the excess
    over $600, 3 per cent.
do., of all persons in employ of the United States, when exceed-
    ing the rate of $600 per year, on the excess above $600, 3 per ct.
Saleratus, per pound, 5 mills.
Sales, auction, of goods, &c., on gross amount of sale, ⅛ of 1 per ct.
    do., of Stocks, &c., 1-10 of 1 per cent.
Sales, made by public officers, &c., exempt.
Salt, per hundred pounds, 4 cts.
Salves, same as "Dentifrice."
Sarsaparilla, Bull's, same as "Dentifrice."
    do., Townsend's, same as "Dentifrice."
Savings institutions, on all dividends, 3 per cent.
Scheidam Schnapps, same as "Dentifrice."
Screws, called wood screws, per pound, 1¼ cents.
Segars, valued at not over $5 per thousand, per thousand, $1.50.
    do., valued at over $5 per thousand and not over $10, per thou
    sand, $2.
    do., valued at over $10 and not over $20, per thousand, $2.50.
    do., valued at over $20 per 1000, per thousand, $3.50.
Shell fish, in cans or air-tight packages, 5 per cent.
Sheep, slaughtered for sale, per head, 5 cents.
    do., slaughtered by any person for his own consumption, free.
Sheep skins, tanned, curried, or finished, 5 per cent.
Sheet iron, see "Iron."
Sherry wine bitters, same as "Dentifrice."
Shingles are not to be considered a manufacture.
Silk parasols, 5 per cent.
Silk umbrellas, 5 per cent.
Silk, manufactures of, not otherwise specified, 3 per cent.
Silver, manufactures of, when not otherwise specified, 3 per cent.
Skins, calf, tanned, each, 6 cents.
Skins, goat, curried, manufactured or finished, 5 per cent.
    do., kid, do., 5 per cent.
    do., morocco, do., 5 per cent.
    do., sheep, tanned, curried, or finished, 5 per cent.
    do., deer, dressed and smoked, per pound, 2 cents.
    do., hog, tanned and dressed, 4 per cent.
    do., horses, do., 4 per cent.
Slates are not to be considered a manufacture.
Slaughtered cattle, see "Cattle."
Snuff, aromatic, same as "Dentifrice."
    do., catarrh,   do.   do.
Snuff, per pound. 12 cents.
Soap, Castile, valued not above 3¼ cents per pound, per pound, 1
    mill.
    do., Castile, valued above 3¼ cents per pound, per pound, 5 mills.
    do., cream, per pound, 2 cents.
    do., erasive, not valued above 3¼ cts. per pound, per pound, 1 mill.
    do., erasive, valued above 3¼ cents per pound, per pound, 5 mills.
    do., fancy, per pound, 2 cents.
    do., honey, per pound, 2 cents.

Soap, palm oil, not valued above 3½ cents per pound, per pound, 1 mill.
  do., do., valued above 3½ cents per pound, per pound, 5 mills.
  do., scented, per pound, 2 cents.
  do., shaving, per pound, 2 cents.
  do., toilet, of all descriptions, per pound, 2 **cents**.
  do., transparent, per pound, 2 cents.
  do., of all other descriptions, white or colored, except soft soap and soap otherwise provided for, valued not above 3½ cents per pound, per pound, 1 mill.
  do., do., valued above 3½ cents per pound, per pound, 5 mills.
Soapmakers, under which head is included every person whose business is to make or manufacture soap, for each license, $10.
Soda, Bi-Carbonate of, per pound, 5 mills.
Sole leather, see "Leather."
Spikes, per ton, $2.
Spirits, distilled, per gallon, 20 cents.
  do., rectified and mixed, per gallon, 10 cents.
  do., medical, same as "Dentifrice."
Split peas are not to be considered a manufacture.
Starch, made of corn, per pound, 1½ mills.
  do., made of potatoes, per pound, 1 mill.
  do., made of rice, per pound, 4 mills.
  do., made of any other material, per pound, 6 mills.
Stoves are not to be considered a manufacture.
Steamboats, except ferry boats, on gross receipts, 3 per cent.
Steel, manufactures of, when not otherwise specified, 3 per cent.
Steel, in ingots, bars, sheets, or wire, not less than one quarter of an inch in thickness, valued at 7 cents per pound or less, per ton, $4.
  do., do., valued **above 7 cents, and** not above 11 cents per pound, per ton, $8.
  do., do., valued above 11 cents per pound, per ton, $10.
Stills used in distilling spirituous liquors, for each yearly license, $50.
  do., used in **distilling** spirituous liquors, for each half-yearly license, $25.
  do., used by distillers of apples and peaches, may be licensed for the space of three months, upon payment for each license for such time, $1.50.
Stock Insurance Companies, see "Insurance."
Stoves, per ton of 2,000 pounds, $1.50.
Sugar, brown or muscovado, not advanced above No. 12, Dutch standard, produced from cane (excepting sorghum and imphee cane), per pound, 1 cent.
  do., all domestic, advanced above No. 12, by whatsoever process and not refined, per pound, 1½ cents.
  do., granulated, per pound, 2 mills.
  do., loaf, per pound, 2 mills.
  do., lump, per pound, 2 mills.
  do., pulverized, per pound, 2 **mills**.
  do., refined, per pound, 2 mills.
  do., refined or made from molasses, syrup of molasses, melado or concentrated melado, per pound, 2 mills.
Sugar candy, made wholly or in part of sugar, per pound, 1 cent.
Sugar-coated pills, same as "Dentifrice."
Sulphate of Barytes, per 100 pounds, 10 cents.

Tallow chandlers, under which term is included every person whose business it is to make or manufacture candles, for each license, $10.
Tar, coal, produced in the manufacture of gas, exempt.
Taverns, same as "Hotels."
Telegraphic Despatches, see "Despatch."
Theatres, under which term is included every place or edifice erected for the purpose of dramatic or operatic representations, plays, or performances, and not including halls rented or used occasionally for concerts or theatrical representations, for each license, $100.
Ticket, passage, by any vessel from a port in the United States to a foreign port, if less than thirty dollars, 50 cents.
do., do., exceeding thirty dollars, $1.
Timber is not to be considered a manufacture.
Tin, manufactures of, when not otherwise specified, 3 per cent.
Tinctures, same as "Dentifrice."
Tobacconists, under which term is included every person who shall offer for sale, at retail, segars, snuff, or tobacco in any form (wholesale and retail dealers, keepers of hotels, inns, and taverns, having taken out a license are not required to take out a license as tobacconists), for each license, $10.
Tobacco, cavendish, valued at more than 30 cts. per pound, 15 cts.
do., do., valued at any sum not exceeding 50 cts. per pound, 10 cts.
do., fine cut, valued at more than 30 cents per pound, 15 cents.
do., do., valued at any sum not exceeding 30 cts. per pound, 10 cts.
do., ground, dry or damp of all descriptions (except aromatic or medicinal snuff in phials, pot, boxes, or packets), per pound, 8 cents.
do., manufactured, of all kinds, not including snuff or segars, or tobacco prepared with stems in, valued at over 30 cents, per pound, 15 cents.
do., do., valued at less than 30 cents per pound, 10 cents.
do., smoking tobacco, prepared with stems in, per pound, 5 cents.
do., plug, same as "Tobacco, cavendish."
do., twist, do. do.
Tonic mixtures, same as "Dentifrice."
Tooth powder, do. do.
Trust companies, on dividends, &c., 3 per cent.

Umbrellas, made of cotton, 5 per cent.
do., made of any other material, 5 per cent.
Umbrella stretchers are not to be considered a manufacture.
Unguents, same as "Dentifrice."

Varnish, made wholly or in part of gum copal, 5 per cent.
do., made of other gums or substances, 5 per cent.
Vegetable oils, per gallon, 2 per cent.
Vegetable pulmonary balsam, same as "Dentifrice."
Vermifuge, same as "Dentifrice."

Warehouse entry, at custom houses, not exceeding $1 in value, stamp duty, 25 cents.
do., do., exceeding $1 and not exceeding $5, 50 cents.
do., do., exceeding $5 in value, $1.
Warehouse receipts, stamp duty, 25 cents.
Whiskey, per gallon, 20 cents.

Whiskey, rectified, is not to pay an additional duty.
White lead, per 100 pounds, 25 cents.
Wholesale dealers, under which term is included every person whose business or occupation is to sell or offer to sell groceries or any goods, wares, or merchandise, of foreign or domestic production, by more than one original package or piece at one time to the same purchaser, not including wines, spirituous or malt liquors, for each license, $50.
Wholesale dealers in liquors of every description, including distilled spirits, fermented liquors and wines of all kinds (persons other than distillers, who sell or offer for sale any such liquors in quantities of more than three gallons at one time to the same purchaser are included), for each license, $100.
Willow, manufactures of, 3 per cent.
Wine made of grapes, per gallon, 5 cents.
Withdrawal entry, at custom house, stamp duty, 50 cents.
Wood, manufactures of, if not otherwise provided for, 3 per cent.
Wood screws, 1½ per cent.
Wool, manufactures of, not otherwise specified, 3 per cent.
Worsted, manufactures of, not otherwise specified, 3 per cent.
Worm lozenges, same as "Dentifrice."
Writ, stamp duty, 50 cents.

Zinc, manufactures of, not otherwise specified, 3 per cent.
  do., oxide of, per 100 pounds, 25 cents.

The following amendments were made by the Conference Committee:—

CHECKS, DRAFTS, ETC.

Sight checks, drafts, &c., for any sum exceeding twenty dollars, two cents stamp duty.

BILLS OF EXCHANGE.

Bills of exchange, inland draft or order, otherwise than at sight or demand, or any promissory note, except bank note, issued for circulation, for any sum exceeding twenty and not exceeding one hundred dollars, five cents each; exceeding twenty-five hundred and not exceeding five thousand dollars, one dollar and fifty cents each.

CONVEYANCES.

Conveyances for property, to the value exceeding twenty-five hundred and not exceeding five thousand, five dollars each; exceeding five thousand and not exceeding one hundred thousand, ten dollars each; exceeding one hundred thousand and not exceeding two hundred thousand, twenty dollars; and for each and every additional ten thousand dollars, or fractional part thereof, twenty dollars.

INSURANCE POLICIES.

All insurance policies of every description, or renewals of the same, twenty-five cents each.

MORTGAGES.

On mortgages, for every additional ten thousand dollars, or fractional part thereof, exceeding twenty thousand dollars, ten dollars.

SEC. 9. *And be it further enacted,* That if any such person shall deliver or disclose to any assessor or assistant assessor appointed in pursuance of this act, and requiring a list or lists, as aforesaid, any false or fraudulent list or statement, with intent to defeat **or** evade the valuations or enumeration hereby intended to be made, such person so offending, and being thereof convicted on indictment found thereof in any circuit or district court of the United States, held in the district in which such offence may be committed, shall be fined in a sum not exceeding five hundred dollars, at the discretion of the court, and shall pay all costs and charges of prosecution; and the valuation and enumeration required by this act shall, in all such cases, and in all cases of under valuation, **or** under statement in such lists or statements, be made, as aforesaid, upon lists, according to the form prescribed, to be made out by the assessors and assistant assessors, respectively; which lists the said assessors and assistant assessors are hereby authorized and required to make according to the best information they can obtain, and for the purpose of making which they are hereby authorized to enter into and upon all and singular the premises, respectively; and from the valuation and enumeration so made there shall be no appeal.

SEC. 10. *And be it further enacted,* That in case any person shall be absent from his or her place of residence at the time an assistant assessor shall call to receive the list of such person, it shall be the duty of such assistant assessor to leave at the place of residence of such person, with some person of suitable age and discretion, if such be present, otherwise to deposit in the nearest post office, a written note or memorandum, addressed to such person, requiring him or her to present to such assessor the list or lists required by this act within ten days from the date of such note or memorandum.

SEC. 26. *And be it further enacted,* That each and every collector, or his deputy, who shall exercise or be guilty of any extortion, or wilful oppression, under color of this act, or shall knowingly demand other or greater sums than shall be authorized by this act, shall be liable to pay a sum not exceeding double the amount of damages accruing to the party injured, to be recovered by and for the use of the party injured, with costs of suit, and shall be dismissed from office, and be disqualified from holding such office thereafter; and each and every collector, or his deputies, shall give receipts **for all** sums by them collected and retained in pursuance of this act.

SEC. 27. *And be it further enacted,* That a collector or deputy collector, assessor or assistant assessor, shall be authorized to enter, in the daytime, any brewery, distillery, manufactory, building, or place where any property, articles, or objects subject to duty or taxation under the provisions of this act, are made, produced, or kept, within his district, so far as it may be necessary for the purpose of examining said property, articles, or objects, or inspecting the accounts required by this act from time to time to be made. And every owner of such brewery, distillery, manufactory, building, or place, or persons having the agency or superintendence of the same, who shall refuse to admit such officer, or to suffer him to examine said property, articles, or objects, or to inspect said accounts, shall, for every such refusal, forfeit and pay the sum of five hundred dollars.

SEC. 28. *And be it further enacted,* That if any person shall forcibly obstruct or hinder a collector or deputy collector in the execution of this act, or of any power and authority hereby vested in him, or shall forcibly rescue, or cause to be rescued, any property, articles, or objects, after the same shall have been seized by him, or shall attempt or endeavor so to do, the person so offending shall, for every such offence, forfeit and pay the sum of five hundred dollars.

SEC. 92. *And be it further enacted,* That it shall be the duty of all persons of lawful age, and all guardians and trustees, whether such trustees are so by the virtue of their office as executors, administrators, or other fiduciary capacity, to make return in the list or schedule, as provided in this act, to the proper officer of internal revenue, of the amount of his or her income, or the income of such minors or persons as may be held in trust as aforesaid, according to the requirements hereinbefore stated, and in case of neglect or refusal to make such return, the assessor or assistant assessor shall assess the amount of his or her income, and proceed thereafter to collect the duty thereon in the same manner as is provided for in other cases of neglect and refusal to furnish lists or schedules in the general provisions of this act, where not otherwise incompatible, and the assistant assessor may increase the amount of the list or return of any party making such return, if he shall be satisfied that the same is understated: *Provided,* That any party, in his or her own behalf, or as guardian or trustee, as aforesaid, shall be permitted to declare, under oath or affirmation, the form and manner of which shall be prescribed by the Commissioner of Internal Revenue, that he or she was not possessed of an income of six hundred dollars, liable to be assessed according to the provisions of this act, or that he or she has been assessed elsewhere and the same year for an income duty, under authority of the United States, and shall thereupon be exempt from an income duty; or, if the list or return of any party shall have been increased by the assistant assessor, in manner as aforesaid, he or she may be permitted to declare, as aforesaid, the amount of his or her annual income, or the amount held in trust, as aforesaid, liable to be assessed, as aforesaid, and the same so declared shall be received as the sum upon which duties are to be assessed and collected.

STAMP DUTIES
IMPOSED BY THE ACT OF 1862.
To go into effect on and after October 1st, 1862.

No stamp appropriated to denote the duty charged on any particular instrument, and bearing the name of such instrument on its face, shall be used for denoting any other duty of the same amount, or if so used, the same shall be of no avail.

No vellum, parchment, or paper bearing a stamp appropriated by name to any particular instrument, shall be used for any other purpose, or if so used, the same shall be of no avail.

In all cases where an adhesive stamp shall be used for denoting any duty imposed by this Act, the person using or affixing the same, shall write upon it the initials of his name, or deface the same in such a manner as to show distinctly that such stamp has been used, under a penalty of $50.

Any person may present to the Commissioner of Internal Revenue any instrument, and require his opinion whether the same is chargeable with any duty; and if the said Commissioner shall be of opinion that it is not chargeable with any stamp duty, he is required to impress on it a particular stamp, with words to signify that it is not chargeable with stamp duty; and every instrument on which said stamp is impressed, shall be received in evidence in all courts, notwithstanding objections on the ground of such instrument being without the proper stamp.

Bank Check, or Draft at Sight.
For amount exceeding $20, . .02

Promissory Note or Draft,
Other than at sight, or on demand, of
From $ 20 to $ 100 . . . $ .05
"   100 "   100 10
"   200 "   350 15
"   350 "   500 20
"   500 "   750 30
"   750 "   1,000 40
"   1,000 "   1,500 60
"   1,500 "   2,500 . . . 1.00
"   2,500 "   5,000 . . . 1.50
Every additional $2,500 or fraction thereof 1.00

Certificate of Stock
In Incorporated Company . .25

Certificate of Profits
In Incorporated Company, for an amount not less than $10, nor exceeding $50 10
Exceeding $50 25

Power of Attorney
To transfer stock, bonds, or scrip 25
To receive dividends or interest 25
To vote by proxy 10

Broker's Note,
Or Memorandum of Sale . . .10

Passage Ticket
To a foreign port, if of less price than $30 50
If exceeding $30 . . . . . . 1.00

Bill of Lading
For goods and merchandise exported to foreign port, each 10

Manifest for Entry or Clear'ce
Of cargo of vessel for foreign port, if tonnage does not exceed 300 tons   1.00
From 300 to 600   . 3.00
Exceeding 600   5.00

Protest of Note, &c., or
Marine Protest, &c. 25

Certificate of Deposit
For a sum not exceeding
$100 02
Exceeding $100 05

Bill of Exchange, (foreign,)
In sets of 3 or more, not exceeding $150 03
From $ 150 to $ 250 05
" 250 " 500 10
" 500 " 1,000 15
" 1,000 " 1,500 20
" 1,500 " 2,250 30
" 2,250 " 3,500 50
" 3,500 " 5,000 70
" 5,000 " 7,500 . . . . 1.00
On every additional $2,500, or fraction thereof . . .30
Bill of Exchange, (foreign,) or Letter of Credit, drawn simply, or other than in a set of three or more, the same as Promissory Note or Draft at Sight.

Warehouse Receipt
For goods on storage 25

Express Company's or Common Carrier's Receipt,
Where compensation is .25 or less 01
From .25 to $1.00 02
Exceeding $1.00 05

Telegraphic Despatch,
The charge for which does not exceed 20 cts. for the first ten words 01
When it does exceed 20 cts. for the first ten words . . .03

Mortgage or Bond,
To secure a debt of
From $ 100 to $ 500 . . $ .50
" 500 " 1,000 . 1.00
" 1,000 " 2,500 . 2.00

From 2,500 to 5,000 . . . 5.00
" 5,000 " 10,000 . . . 10.00
" 10,000 " 20,000 . . . 15.00
Every additional $10,000, or fraction thereof 10.00

Bond
To indemnify a surety . . .50

Bond,
Other than those required in legal proceedings, and such as are not otherwise charged herein 25

Probate of Will, or Letter of Administration,
Where the estate does not exceed $2,500 . . . . . . $ .50
From $ 2,500 to $ 5,000 . . 1.00
" 5,000 " 20,000 . . 2.00
" 20,000 " 50,000 . . 5.00
" 50,000 " 100,000 . . 10.00
" 100,000 " 150,000 . . 20.00
For every additional $50,000, or fraction thereof . . . 10.00

Original Writ,
Except those issued by a Justice of the Peace, and those issued in criminal prosecutions by the United States, or any State . .50

Deed of Grant,
Where the consideration is more than $100, and not exceeding $500 . . . . $ .50
From $ 500 to $ 1,000 . . 1.00
" 1,000 " 2,500 . . . 2.00
" 2,500 " 5,000 . . . 5.00
" 5,000 " 10,000 . . . 10.00
" 10,000 " 20,000 . . . 20.00
Every additional $10,000, or fraction thereof 10.00

Power of Attorney
To sell or lease Real Estate 1.00
To receive rent 25

Lease,
For three years, or less . . .50
For more than three years 1.00

Policy of Insurance

On any life or lives, where the amount insured does not exceed $1,000 25
From $1,000 to $5,000 50
Exceeding $5,000 . . . . . 1.00
Fire and Marine Risks 25

Certificate of Damage, &c.
And all other documents issued by any Port Warden or Marine Surveyor 25

Charter Party,
Or any Letter or Memorandum relating to the charter of any vessel,
If the registered tonnage does not exceed 300 tons 3.00
From 300 to 600 tons 5.00
Over 600 tons 10.00

Entry of Goods

At Custom House, not exceeding in value $100 25
From $100 to $500 50
Exceeding $500 . . . . . . 1.00

Entry
For withdrawal of goods from bonded warehouse . .50

Certificate,
Other than those mentioned above 10

Agreement,
Other than those mentioned above, (or any appraisement,) for every sheet or piece of paper on which it is written 05

PENALTIES.

Penalty for making, signing, or issuing any instrument, document, or paper of any kind whatsoever, without the same being duly stamped, for denoting the duty hereby imposed thereon — $50; and the instrument shall be deemed invalid and of no effect.

Penalty for making, signing, issuing, accepting, or paying any Bill of Exchange, Draft, Order, or Promissory Note without stamp — $200.

Penalty for accepting or paying a foreign Bill of Exchange without first affixing a stamp — $100.

Penalty recoverable from any Telegraph Company for receiving or transmitting any message without the proper adhesive stamp being affixed to a written copy thereof — $10.

Penalty recoverable from any Express Company, for receiving for transportation any package or article of any description, without giving therefor a receipt properly stamped, so as to denote the duty imposed by this act — $10.

EXEMPTIONS.

The stamp duties on Express Companies' receipts do not extend to receipts for articles or packages transported for the Government, nor to receipts for articles or packages transported by such companies without charge thereon.

The stamp duties on Passage Tickets, Bills of Lading, and Manifests, do not extend to vessels plying between ports or places in the United States and ports or places in British North America.

STABILITY AND RESOURCES OF THE U. S.

Supposing the war debt on July 1, 1863, should amount to twelve hundred millions ($1,200,000,000), the annual interest at six per cent. would be only $72,000,000, and the annual sum necessary for the sinking fund would be $60,000,000 — in all $132,000,000. Now, this is only about one third the annual taxation of Great Britain; and who will pretend that the United States cannot bear taxation better than the British empire? The relative stability of our government and its resources may be estimated by comparing the prices of its securities in time of peace with those of the principal nations of Europe. United States stocks have been as high as 125, and immediately before the commencement of our national troubles they ranged as high as 114 and 118. Even now, in the midst of the most gigantic rebellion in modern times, they are now above par. The following table will show at what prices the national stocks of other governments are selling for in time of peace: —

English consols 92
English 3 per cents 91
French rentes, 4½ per cent 96
French rentes, 3½ per cent 67
Russian 5 per cents 98
Russian 4½ per cents 91
Russian 3 per cents 58
Austrian 5 per cent metalliques 66
Austrian national loan 81
Prussian national loan 57
Spanish 3 per cents 50
Spanish new deferred account 41
Dutch 4 per cents 98
Dutch 2½ per cents 63
Turkish 6 per cents 78
Turkish now 70
Mexican 3 per cents 28

BANKS:

Their Capital, Specie, and Circulation.

The following table shows the per cent. of bank capital, specie, and circulation in each state, to the whole, on January 1, 1862, or according to the latest previous returns: —

	Capital. $426,008,032.	Specie. $103,501,336.	Circulation. $182,857,346.
Massachusetts	15.81	10.33	11.49
New York	25.81	36.81	15.42
Rhode Island	4.98	0.57	1.85
Connecticut	5.15	0.97	3.66
Pennsylvania	6.12	9.54	8.78
Illinois	0.17	0.00¼	0.27
New Jersey	1.96	0.90	2.38
Ohio	1.37	2.11	4.48
California			

STATISTICAL POCKET MANUAL. 111

	Capital.	Specie.	Circulation.
Maine	1.89	0.59	2.18
Indiana	1.04	3.01	2.97
Missouri	3.26	4.02	4.38
Kentucky	3.59	4.83	7.45
Minnesota	0.05	0.04	0.11
Iowa	0.17	0.36	0.34
Maryland	2.94	2.41	2.59
Michigan	0.18	0.05	0.12
Wisconsin	1.03	0.37	2.54
Vermont	0.92	0.18	2.02
New Hampshire	1.18	0.24	1.82
Delaware	0.45	0.24	0.55
Georgia	2.51	1.93	2.75
Louisiana	5.79	10.63	4.39
Kansas			
North Carolina	1.87	1.45	2.47
Virginia	4.42	2.90	6.57
Texas			
Tennessee	2.38	1.93	1.92
Oregon			
Arkansas			
Alabama	1.15	1.93	2.18
South Carolina	3.50	1.45	4.00
Florida	0.12	0.07	0.16
Mississippi	0.19	0.05	0.16
	100.00	100.00	100.00

NEW CONGRESSIONAL APPORTIONMENT.

The following table shows the number of members assigned to each state, under the census of 1850 and 1860:

	1850.	1860.		1850.	1860.
Alabama	7	6	Michigan	4	6
Arkansas	2	3	Minnesota	2	2
California	2	3	New Hampshire	3	3
Connecticut	4	4	New Jersey	5	5
Delaware	1	1	New York	33	31
Florida	1	1	North Carolina	8	7
Georgia	8	7	Ohio	21	19
Illinois	9	14	Oregon	1	1
Indiana	11	11	Pennsylvania	25	24
Iowa	2	6	Rhode Island	2	2
Kansas	1	1	South Carolina	6	4
Kentucky	10	9	Tennessee	10	8
Louisiana	4	5	Texas	2	4
Maine	6	5	Vermont	3	3
Maryland	6	5	Virginia	13	11
Massachusetts	11	10	Wisconsin	3	6
Mississippi	5	5			
Missouri	7	9	Total	238	241

TABLE

Showing the Federal Population, and the Assessed Value of Real and Personal Property of the Several States of the Union.—Census 1860.

States.	Federal Population.	Value of Real Estate.	Value of Personal Property.
Alabama	700,243	$155,034,089	$277,164,073
Arkansas	390,985	63,254,740	116,950,590
California	380,016	66,906,631	72,748,036
Connecticut	460,151	191,478,842	149,778,131
Delaware	111,408	26,273,803	13,493,439
Florida	115,737	21,722,810	47,206,875
Georgia	872,436	179,301,441	438,430,946
Illinois	1,711,753	287,219,940	101,987,483
Indiana	1,350,941	201,829,902	119,212,432
Iowa	674,948	149,433,423	55,733,560
Kansas	107,110	16,088,602	6,429,630
Kentucky	1,065,517	277,925,054	250,287,039
Louisiana	576,086	280,704,988	155,082,277
Maine	628,276	86,717,710	67,062,672
Maryland	652,158	65,441,538	231,793,806
Massachusetts	1,231,065	475,413,165	301,744,651
Michigan	749,112	123,605,084	39,927,921
Minnesota	172,022	25,301,771	6,727,002
Mississippi	616,717	157,836,737	351,636,175
Missouri	1,136,331	153,450,577	113,485,274
New Hampshire	326,072	59,638,346	64,171,743
New Jersey	672,031	151,161,942	145,520,550
New York	3,880,727	1,069,638,080	320,806,568
North Carolina	860,234	116,366,573	175,931,029
Ohio	2,339,599	687,518,121	272,348,980
Oregon	52,464	6,279,602	12,745,313
Pennsylvania	2,906,370	561,192,980	158,060,355
Rhode Island	174,621	83,778,204	41,320,101
South Carolina	542,795	129,772,684	359,546,444
Tennessee	909,533	210,991,180	162,504,020
Texas	530,159	112,476,013	155,316,322
Vermont	315,116	65,639,973	19,118,646
Virginia	1,399,731	417,952,228	239,069,108
Wisconsin	775,873	148,238,766	37,706,723
Total	29,568,427	$12,006,756,585	$5,081,661,000

THE RAILWAYS OF THE WORLD.

It is estimated that there are now completed and in operation throughout the world 70,000 miles of railway, which cost the sum of $5,850,000,000. The extent of railway known to be in operation, from actual returns, according to the London Engineer, is as follows:—

	Miles open.		Miles open.
England and Wales	7583	New Brunswick	175
Scotland	1486	Nova Scotia	99
Ireland	1364	Victoria	183
India	1408	New South Wales	125
Canada	1826	Cape of Good Hope	28

Total, Great Britain and Colonies 14,277

Continental Railways.

France	6147	Norway	63
Prussia	3162	Sweden	288
Austria	3165	Belgium	955
Other German States	3239	Holland	308
Spain	1450	Switzerland	600
Italy	1350	Portugal	80
Rome	50	Turkey	80
Russia	1289½	Egypt	204
Denmark	262		

Total 22,692½

North and South America.

Exclusive of British America, the railways of which are included with Great Britain and Colonies —

United States	22,384½	Brazil	111¼
Confederate States	8784	Paraguay	8
Mexico	20	Chili	195
Cuba	500	Peru	50
New Granada	49½		

Total 32,102¼

Grand total of all the railways in the world 69,072

It will be seen that the United States possess the most extensive system of railways of any country in the world. This method of intercommunication has been developed with extraordinary rapidity in the United States, and although temporarily checked by the civil war, will, when the rebellion is crushed, be even more rapidly extended than in the past.

NATIONAL TELEGRAPH ROUND THE WORLD.

An appropriation of $100,000, and two small vessels, will be asked for in Congress for the purpose of instituting a survey, in conjunction with other nations, of a telegraph line from San Francisco to the north-west coast, overland, via Behring's Straits and Asiatic Russia, to the mouth of the Amoor River, as proposed by McDonald Collins. The scheme is to connect the American system of telegraphs, from a point in Missouri, with the line now being constructed from Kanzan to the Amoor. When finished, the line will bring in telegraphic union the whole European and American systems, and belt the world.

PACIFIC TELEGRAPH — TABLE OF DISTANCES

The following table of distances will be found of permanent interest, sufficient to warrant its preservation. It gives the distance, from station to station, throughout the entire line traversed by the *Pacific Telegraph* and by the Overland Stage Company; and also the distances from New York to Omaha by two routes, viz.: by way of Chicago, and also by way of St. Louis. The Pacific Telegraph Company's connection with the East was first established via St. Louis. But the war in Missouri caused such frequent interruptions to telegraph communication through that state, as to threaten the most serious consequences. The Company accordingly took early and prompt measures to secure the construction of a new line through Iowa, which, with lines already existing, would give them a connection with Chicago by a more direct route, and so far north as to be safe from rebel incursions. That line is now finished. The two lines — one from St. Louis, and another from Chicago — meet at Omaha.

The names of places set in *italics* (as also Great Salt Lake and San Francisco, which are set in SMALL CAPITALS) are Telegraph Stations. Those set in Roman are Stations of the Overland Stage Company —

FROM NEW YORK TO		
Chicago		982
Omaha	511	1493
FROM NEW YORK TO		
St. Louis		1140
St. Joseph	407	1547
Brownsville	75	1622
Nebraska City	25	1647
Omaha	50	1697
Elkhorn City	22	1719
Fremont	15	1734
North Bend	23	1757
Columbus	26	1783
Prairie Creek	12	1795
Cedar Island	20	1815
Grand Island	30	1845
Wolf River	20	1865
Fort Kearney	22	1887
Platt Station	7	1894
Gardner's	14	1908
Plum Creek	15	1923
Willow Island	15	1938
Midway	14	1952
Gilman's Ranche	15	1967
Cottonwood Springs	16	1983
Cold Springs	15	1998
Fremont Springs	14	2012
Dorsey's	11	2023
Alkali	14	2037
Gills	12	2049
Diamond Springs	11	2060
South Platte	15	2075
Overland City	13	2088
Hugh's Ranche	10	2098
Texas	10	2108
Pole Creek	14	2122
Deep Well	12	2134
Mud Springs	13	2147
Court-house Rock	13	2160
Chimney Rock	14	2174
Ficklin's Ranche	11	2185
Scott's Bluffs	12	2197
Horse Creek	16	2213
Cold Springs	11	2224
Laramie City	14	2238
Fort Laramie	9	2247
Centre Star	10	2257
Bitter Cottonwood	12	2269
Horse Shoe	15	2284
Elk Horn	10	2294
Laboute	15	2309
Clute's Ranche	11	2320
La Prelle	9	2329
Box Elder	9	2338
Deer Creek	10	2348
Platte Station	14	2362
Platte Bridge	14	2376
Red Buttes	10	2386
Willow Springs	15	2401
Horse Creek	14	2415
Sweet Water Bridge	10	2425
Plant's Station	14	2439
Split Rock	14	2453
Three Crossings	10	2463
Ice Springs	13	2476
Warm Springs	9	2485
Rocky Bridge	12	2497
Dry Sandy	10	2543

STATISTICAL POCKET MANUAL. 115

Strawberry		12	2509	Bate's		15.3001
Sweet Water		12	2521	Mountain Springs		11.3012
Pacific Springs		12	2333	*Ruby Valley*		9.3021
Little Sandy		15	2558	Jacob's Well		12.3033
Big Sandy		12	2570	Diamond Springs		12.3035
Big Timbers		14	2584	Sulphur Springs		12.3057
Green River		12	2596	Roberts' Creek		13.3070
Ham's Fork		20	2616	Camp Station		13.3083
Church Buttes		10	2626	Dry Creek		15.3098
Millersville		10	2636	Simpson's Park		21.3119
Fort Bridger		12	2648	*Reese River*		15.3134
Muddy		12	2660	Dry Wells		14.3148
Quaking Asp Springs		10	2670	Smith's Creek		14.3162
Bear River		10	2680	Edwards' Creek		8.3170
Needle Rocks		10	2690	Cold Springs		14.3184
Head Echo Canon		10	2700	*Middle Gate*		10.3194
Hanging Rock		10	2710	Sandy Springs		24.3228
Weber River		10	2720	Sandy Hill		9.3237
Dixie		11	2731	Carson Sink		14.3251
East Canon		10	2741	Desert Station		15.3266
Mountain Dell		12	2753	*Fort Churchill*		10.3276
GREAT SALT LAKE CITY		13	2766	Clugagis		11.3287
				Nevada		11.3298
Traders' Rest		9	2775	*Carson City*		13.3311
Rockwell's		10	2785	*Genoa*		14.3325
Dug Out		10	2795	Friday's		11.3336
Fort Crittenden		10	2805	Yanks		10.3346
Rush Valley		17	2822	*Strawberry*		12.3358
Point Lookout		10	2832	Webster's		12.3370
Simpson's Springs		14	2846	Moss		12.3382
Deep Creek		18	2864	Sportsman's Hall		11.3393
Fish Springs		11	2875	*Placerville*		12.3405
Willow Springs		21	2896	Duroc		14.3419
Deep Creek		26	2822	*Fulsom*		14.3433
Antelope Springs		25	2857	*Sacramento*		22.3455
Shell Creek		24	2881	SAN FRANCISCO		140.3595
Egan Canon		15	2896			

WEIGHT OF CANNON BALLS.

Assuming the specific gravity of cast iron to be seven and one fifth (7.207) times that of distilled water, and that the balls are perfect spheres,—their weight will be as follows in pounds and tenths:—

Inches.	Weight.	Inches.	Weight.
3	3.7 pounds.	9	99.4 pounds.
4	8.7 "	10	130.3 "
5	17.0 "	11	181.4 "
6	29.4 "	12	235.2 "
7	46.7 "	15	460.0 "
8	69.8 "	20	1090.3 "

TOTAL OF THE ARMIES AND NAVIES OF THE PRINCIPAL POWERS.

UNITED STATES.
Army, number of Men 670,000
Navy, number of Vessels 264
"   "   Guns 2,557
"   "   Tons 218,016
"   "   Seamen 22,000

GREAT BRITAIN.
Army, number of Men 213,778
"   "   Horses 21,904
Navy, number of Vessels 893
"   "   Guns 16,411
"   "   Seamen 51,650
"   "   Marines 18,000
"   "   Coast Guard 8,550

FRANCE.
Army, number of Men 767,770
"   "   Horses 130,000
Navy, number of Vessels 600
"   "   Guns 13,358
"   "   Seamen 60,000
"   "   Marines 26,878
"   "   Coast Guard 25,501

The Army of France in times of peace is reduced to 414,864 men; 72,850 horses; her seamen to 38,375; and marines to 22,400.

RUSSIA.
Army, number of Men 577,855
Navy, number of Vessels 313
"   "   Guns 3,854

Russia has, in addition to her Army, 136 regiments of Cavalry, 31 battalions and 31 batteries of Irregulars. She has 474 Guard and Transport ships not mentioned above.

AUSTRIA.
Army, number of Men 587,695
Navy, number of Vessels 197
"   "   Guns 895

PRUSSIA.
Army, number of Men 622,366
Navy, number of Vessels 34

The Prussian Army in times of peace numbers 212,649 men.

ITALY.
Army, number of Men 327,290
Navy, number of Vessels 106
"   "   Guns 1,036
"   "   Men 18,000

POPULATION OF GREAT BRITAIN.
FROM THE CENSUS OF 1861.

England	19,647,057	Channel Isles		143,770
Scotland	3,061,329			
Wales	1,111,795	Total		29,756,015
Ireland	5,792,055			

PRINCIPAL CITIES.

London, England	2,803,034	Nottingham	74,531
Tower Hamlets	647,585	Leicester	68,052
Liverpool	443,874	Plymouth	62,823
Marylebone	436,298	Southampton	46,970
Manchester	357,604	Glasgow, Scotland	394,857
Finsbury	386,844	Edinburgh	168,098
Birmingham	295,955	Dundee	90,425
Lambeth	298,032	Aberdeen	73,794
Leeds	207,153	Greenock	42,100
Westminster	253,985	Leith	33,530
Sheffield	185,157	Perth	25,251
Southwark	193,443	Dublin, Ireland	258,328
Bristol	154,093	Belfast	76,491
Greenwich	139,286	Cork	101,534
Newcastle-on-Tyne	109,291	Limerick	55,234
Bradford	106,218	Waterford	29,160
Salford	102,114	Galway	24,990
Hull	98,994	Kilkenny	17,441
Portsmouth	94,546	Londonderry	20,493

POPULATION OF PRINCIPAL EUROPEAN CITIES.

Paris, France	1,621,530	Prague, Austria	128,965
Lyons, "	302,092	Trieste, "	75,000
Marseilles, "	173,377	Berlin, Prussia	491,334
Bordeaux, "	146,303	Cologne, "	85,529
Rouen, "	115,000	Dantzic "	60,725
Nantes, "	85,063	Munich, Ger. Conf.	129,893
Toulouse, "	79,940	Dresden, "	124,500
Lisle, "	70,648	Leipsic, "	68,950
Strasburg, "	60,052	Hamburg, F. City	180,927
Orleans, "	56,380	Frankfort, "	68,417
Madrid, Spain,	378,642	Bremen, "	81,405
Barcelona, "	134,060	Rome, S. of Church	213,000
Seville, "	89,206	Bologne, "	79,500
Valencia, "	76,321	Naples, Naples	500,000
Granada, "	74,180	Palermo, "	200,674
Cadiz, "	64,098	Messina, "	91,979
Cordova, "	56,380	Athens, Greece	33,900
Lisbon, Portugal	310,971	Constantinople, Turkey	600,050
Oporto, "	105,690	Adrianople "	107,811
Vienna, Austria	576,946	Solonica, "	79,473
Pesth, "	130,422		

MILITARY UNION VICTORIES

GAINED BY THE ARMY SINCE THE COMMENCEMENT OF THE REBELLION.

Philippi, Va.	June 3, 1861.
Romney, Va.	June 12 "
Booneville	June 18 "
Patterson's Creek	June 26 "
Bealington, Va	July 8 "
Laurel Hill, Va.	July 10 "
Rich Mountain	July 11 "
Beverly (General Pegram's surrender)	July 12 "
Carrick's Ford (General Garnett killed)	July 13 "
Forsyth	July 26 "
Dog Springs	Aug. 2 "
Wilson Creek, (Gen. Lyon killed,)	Aug. 10 "
Boone Court House	Sept. 1 "
Gauley Bridge	Sept. 10 "
Lewinsville	Sept. 11 "
Elk Water	Sept. 11 "
Cheat Mountain, Va.	Sept. 12 "
Papinsville	Sept. 21 "
Santa Rosa Island	Oct. 9 "
Lebanon	Oct. 13 "
Linn Creek	Oct. 13 "
Pilot Knob	Oct. 16 "
Bolivar	Oct. 16 "
Fredericktown	Oct. 21 "
Camp Wild Cat	Oct. 21 "
Charge of General Fremont's Body Guard	Oct. 25 "
Romney (General Kelly)	Oct. 29 "
Woodbury	Oct. 29 "
Platte City	Nov. 2 "
Belmont, Mo.	Nov. 6 "
Piketon	Nov. 11 "
Eastern Virginia	Nov. 19 "
Camp Alleghany	Dec. 13 "
General Pope's victories in Missouri	Dec. 18 "
Dranesville	Dec. 20 "
Capture of Port Royal	Jan. 1, 1862.
Bombardment of Barrancas and Warrenton	Jan. 1 "
Huttonville	Jan. 4 "
Defeat of Poindexter	Jan. 6 "
Defeat of Humphrey Marshall at Paintville, Ky.	Jan. 7 "
Romney	Jan. 7 "
Blue's Gap	Jan. 8 "
Rout of Marshall's army	Jan. 10 "
Mill Springs, Ky., (Zollicoffer killed)	Jan. 19 "
Occoquan	Jan. 29 "
Romney, Va., (General Lander)	Feb. 6 "
Roanoke Island, N. C.	Feb. 7-8 "
Springfield, Mo., (General Curtis)	Feb. 13 "
Surrender of Fort Donelson, Tenn.	Feb. 16 "
Sugar Creek (defeat of Price)	Feb. 18 "
Bentonville, Ark	Feb. 19 "

STATISTICAL POCKET MANUAL. 119

Valverde, New Mexico, (Col. Canby) . . . . Feb. 21,1862.
Pea Ridge, Ark., (Gen. Curtis) . . . . Mar. 6-8 "
Newbern, N. C., (Gen. Burnside) . . . . Mar. 14 "
Winchester, Va., (Gen. Shields) . . . . Mar. 23 "

NAVAL VICTORIES.

Hatteras Inlet . . . . Aug. 28,1861.
Lucas Bend . . . . Sept. 10 "
Destroying the privateer Judith . . . . Sept. 14 "
Chicamacomico . . . . Oct. 5 "
Repulse of the rebels at mouth of the Mississippi . Oct. 11 "
Port Royal . . . . Nov. 7 "
Destruction of rebel lightships in Wilmington harbor, N. C . . . . Jan. 15, 1862.
Fort Henry . . . . Feb. 6 "
Trip up the Tennessee . . . . Feb. 9 "
Roanoke Island . . . . Feb.7-8 "
Capture of Elizabeth City, Edenton, &c . . . . . . Feb. 10 "
Clarksville . . . . Feb. 19 "
Fort Donelson, Tenn. . . . . Feb13-16 "

REBEL VICTORIES.

Sumpter, S. C. . . . . Ap'l 12,1861.
Big Bethel, Va. . . . . June 10 "
Bull Run . . . . July 21 "
Lexington . . . . Sept.20 "
Massacre of Ball's Bluff. . . . . Oct. 25 "
Belmont . . . . Nov. 7 "
Wilson's Creek . . . .
Hampton Roads, Va. . . . . Feb.21, 1862.

RECAPITULATION.

Union victories, 68 ; Rebel victories, 7 ; ratio, nearly ten to one.

Federal killed . . . . 2484 | Rebel killed and wounded 12,429
Federal wounded . . . . . 4192 | Rebel prisoners 18,707
Federal prisoners . . . . . 1440 | Rebel losses — 220 cannon.
Federal killed and wounded 8216
Federal losses — 33 cannon, 4 ships, 1000 muskets.

By statement of Surgeon General, 3990 have died of disease up to Dec. 31, 1861, which, added to the 2484 killed, will make our loss 6474, besides those who have fallen in minor engagements, of which there are 77.

Federal Generals Killed — Lyon and Baker.
Rebel Generals Killed — Bee, Bartow, Garnett Herbert, McCulloch, McIntosh, Slack, and Zollicoffer.

CONTENTS OF PART I.

	PAGE
Pay of Commissioned Army Officers	3
Pay of Non-commissioned Officers, Privates, &c.	14
Rank, and Command of Officers according to Rank	16
Salutes—Funeral Escorts	17
Badges of Rank	18
Allowance of Rooms, Fuel, and Camp and Garrison Equipage	20
Transportation—the Ration	21
Allowance of Clothing	22
Forts, Castles, Batteries, &c.	23
Military Posts	26
Military Terms and Number of the Army	29
Army Telegraph Lines	30
Experiments with Armor	32
Army Appropriations	33
Ordnance	34
Iron-clad Steamers for River, Harbor, and Coast Defence—Fortification Appropriations	35
Defences of Boston Harbor	37
Pay of the Navy	37
U. S. Navy, including Vessels purchased and built	46
The Stone Fleet	53
Iron-plated Vessels	54
Population of Cities, Towns and Villages in U. States	55
Population by States	60
Slave Population	61
Population of African Descent on the Continent	62
Routes and Distances by Railroad and Water	62
Governors of States and Territories, for 1862	65
English Navy	67
French Navy	72
French Army and Navy	73
Spanish Navy	77
Russian Navy	78
All other Foreign Navies	79
Rebel Forces in the Field	84
Strength of Canada and the States on the Border	84
Summary of the Military and Naval Forces of the "Great Powers"	86
Official Statement of the British Navy for 1862	87
British Fleet in American Waters	87
What England has expended in Armaments since the Commencement of the Rebellion in the U. States	87
Population of the Globe	88
Colonial Population in 1715	90
The Government of the World, 1862	91
Dimensions of Big Ships	94
Length of Steamship Routes	94
Quick Passages of Ocean Steamships	95
Rates of U. S. Postage	95
Rates of Letter Postage to Foreign Countries	96
Public Libraries in the U. S.	98
Cotton raised in the United States, and Amount purchased by Great Britain from 1820 to 1859	99
Opinions of the Press	100

CONTENTS OF PART II.

	PAGE
Generals and their Staffs	3–27
Regular Service	3
Volunteer Service	14
Burnside Expedition	28
Sherman's Port Royal Expedition	39
Manufacture of Ordnance	42
Western River Flotilla	43
Great Mortar Flotilla	44
300-Pounder Gun of England	46
Relative Value of Prisoners of War	46
Statistics of the Army	47
Rebel Generals of the South	48
Explanation of Military Terms	49
Signals and Telegraphs	56
Iron-plated Steam Batteries	57
Steel-clad Ships	58
Harbor Defences	60
Description of the Monitor	61
Engraving of the Monitor	63
The Cumberland — Statement of the Pilot	64
The Monitor after the Action	66
Capt. Ericsson's Description of the Monitor	67
Sketches of Capt. Ericsson, Lieut. Worden, and Chief Engineer Stimers	70
Description of the Merrimac	73
Sketch of the Commander of the Merrimac	74
Monitors to be built	74
Engraving of the Merrimac	75
Our new Iron-clad Navy	76
New Plan for Iron-clad Ships	78
Iron-clad Frigate	79
20-Inch Guns	80
Submarine Artillery Batteries	80
Bull Run Battle — Official Rebel Statement	80
Military Education	81
Stevens's Battery	82
Tax Bill	83
Stamp Duties	107
Penalties	109
Exemptions	109
Stability and Resources of the United States	110
Banks	110
New Congressional Apportionment	111
Population and Assessed Value of Real and Personal Property in the several States	112
Railways of the World	113
National Telegraph round the World	113
Pacific Telegraph and Table of Distances	114
Weight of Cannon Balls	115
Total of the Armies and Navies of the Great Powers	116
Population of Great Britain from the Census of 1861	117
Population of the Principal European Cities	117
Victories — Rebel and Union	118

OPINIONS OF THE PRESS.

FROM THE DAILY PAPERS.

THE BOOK FOR THE TIMES—Eminently useful for reference. *Boston Journal.*

Neat, cheap and useful.—*Transcript.*

A real Miniature Encyclopedia of facts and figures and very useful for reference.—*Traveller.*

A convenient and valuable work for frequent reference. It includes just the facts and figures which every body has occasion to look up.—*Springfield Republican.*

Full of valuable information, just now of especial interest, and which has been gathered together in this little volume with great care. Every one should have a copy.—*New Bedford Mercury.*

It contains a great deal of important information in a very compact form.—*New Bedford Standard.*

FROM THE WEEKLIES.

None but those who have had experience in it can have any adequate idea of the labor and care requisite in the preparation of a Manual of this kind. The compiler of the one before us has accomplished his work most creditably. He has brought together a mass of practical information of great importance, yet which the masses could never have gained without such a Manual.—*Christian Era*

STATISTICAL POCKET MANUAL.

An exceedingly valuable little work.—*Congregationalist.*

We have examined the work and find that it is just what a man wants for reference at the present time.—*Vineyard Gazette.*

Most useful book.—*Pilot.*

This is a very convenient embodiment of *facts*, answering hundreds of questions which are constantly arising in these times. All information with reference to the power of the nation is given.—*Zion's Herald.*

This little work contains many facts and figures of general interest, and which it is oftentimes difficult to find when needed for reference.—*New England Farmer.*

D. P. Butler, the distinguished phrenologist, has issued this valuable text-book.—*Banner of Light.*

It is a valuable little book,—the best of the kind that has been published, and contains a large amount of useful information. It ought to be in every family,—*Trumpet and Magazine.*

It is eminently *multum in parvo*. The various information which it contains is what every family has frequent occasion to refer to in fire-side conversation.—*Christian Freeman.*

This convenient little reference book contains a variety of interesting and useful statistics.—*Herald of Progress.*

It contains, in a brief compass, a vast amount of information upon subjects now interesting the public mind. It is in a cheap and convenient form, and will be found a very useful and reliable Manual for reference.—*Witness and Advocate.*

Proportion of "fat" is prodigious.—*Independent.*

www.ingramcontent.com/pod-product-compliance
Lightning Source LLC
Chambersburg PA
CBHW021304240426
43669CB00042B/1199